Acclaim for William Dalrymple's
nine lives

"Informed, compassionate, and careful to place the emphasis where it belongs: on the extraordinary people whose stories [Dalrymple] conveys." —*Harper's*

"Strikingly colorful. . . . [Dalrymple's] point—which he makes elegantly by quoting many voices—is that, as India hurtles toward modernity, it may be losing some of its soul." —*The Washington Post*

"Luminous. . . . Consists of nine riveting and thickly reported tales of individual devotion, which together summon up a whole world and sometimes end with devastating twists. . . . *Nine Lives* will only enhance [Dalrymple's] reputation." —*The New Republic*

"Fulfills the premise that a master artist can make something very difficult look easy. . . . You don't have to know a thing about India to enjoy this book, but when you're done you will know and appreciate much more about its people and their various lives—of the body, of the spirit and of the heart." —*The Seattle Times*

"Fascinating. . . . These might seem like exotic characters, but Dalrymple allows them to tell their own stories, and they emerge as deeply sympathetic and human." —*Newsday*

"Triumphant. . . . Not only illuminates India's relationship with religion but casts the genre itself in a new light. . . . A wise and rewarding book fizzing with Dalrymple's signature erudition and lightness of touch. . . . The travel book of the year."
—*The Guardian* (London)

WILLIAM DALRYMPLE
nine lives

William Dalrymple is the author of six previous acclaimed
works of history and travel, including *City of Djinns*, which
won the Sunday Times Young British Writer of the Year
Award and the Thomas Cook Travel Book Award; the best-
selling *From the Holy Mountain*; *White Mughals*, which won
Britain's most prestigious history prize, the Wolfson; and
The Last Mughal, which won the Duff Cooper Prize for History and Biography. He divides his time between New Delhi
and London, and is a contributor to *The New York Review of
Books*, *The New Yorker*, and *The Guardian*.

www.williamdalrymple.com

nine lives

nine lives

IN SEARCH OF THE SACRED
IN MODERN INDIA

WILLIAM DALRYMPLE

VINTAGE DEPARTURES
Vintage Books
A Division of Random House, Inc.
New York

FIRST VINTAGE DEPARTURES EDITION, JUNE 2011

Copyright © 2009 by William Dalrymple
Map and illustrations copyright © 2009 by Olivia Fraser

Portions of this work previously appeared in slightly different form in *The Guardian*,
The Times (London), and *The New Yorker*.

Grateful acknowledgment is made to the following for permission to reprint previously
published material:

Cambridge University Press: Excerpt from *The Epic of Pabuji* by John D. Smith, copyright © 1991
by The Faculty of Oriental Studies. Reprinted by permission of Cambridge University Press.
Hohm Press: Excerpt from *Grace and Mercy in Her Wild Hair* by Ramprasad Sen, copyright © 1999
by Ramprasad Sen. Reprinted by permission of Hohm Press. Oxford University Press India:
Excerpt from *The Interior Landscape* by A. K. Ramanujan, copyright © 1994. Reprinted by permis-
sion of Oxford University Press India, New Delhi. University of California Press: Excerpts from
When God Is a Customer by A. K. Ramanujan, copyright © 1994 by University of California Press.
Reprinted by permission of University of California Press.

The Library of Congress has cataloged the Knopf edition as follows:
Dalrymple, William.
Includes bibliographical references and index.
Nine lives: in search of the sacred in modern India / by William Dalrymple.—1st U.S. ed.
p. cm.
1. India—Religion. 2. Religious biography—India. I. Title.
BL2001.3.D35 2010
294.092 254—dc22
2010006362

Vintage ISBN: 978-0-307-47446-9

Author photograph © Karoki Lewis
Book design by Maggie Hinders

www.vintagebooks.com

Printed in the United States of America

To Sammy

CONTENTS

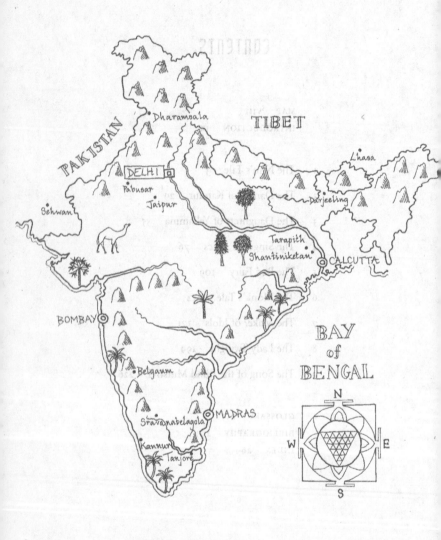

INTRODUCTION

The idea for this book was born sixteen years ago, on a high, clear, Himalayan morning in the summer of 1993. I was corkscrewing my way up from the banks of the river Bhagirathi, along the steep sides of a thickly wooded valley. The track was soft and mossy, and it led though ferns and brackens, thickets of brambles and groves of tall Himalayan cedar trees. Small waterfalls tumbled through the deodars. It was May, and after a ten-day trek I was one day's walk from my destination: the great Himalayan temple of Kedarnath, believed by Hindus to be one of the principal homes of Lord Shiva and so, along with Mount Kailash in Tibet, one of the two candidates for the Hindu Mount Olympus.

I was not alone on the road. The previous night I had seen groups of pilgrims—mainly villagers from Rajasthan—camping beside the temples and bazaars at the bottom of the mountain, warming their hands over small driftwood fires. Now, in the light of morning, their numbers seemed to have miraculously multiplied, and the narrow mountain track appeared like a great sea of Indian humanity. Every social class from every corner of the country was there. There were groups of farmers, illiterate labourers and urban sophisticates from north and south all rubbing shoulders like something out of a modern Indian *Canterbury Tales*. The rich rode horses or were carried up in *doolies*, a strange cross between a wicker deckchair and a rucksack; but the vast majority of poor pilgrims had no option but to walk.

Every half mile or so I would come across groups of twenty or thirty villagers straining up the steep mountain path. Barefoot, bent-backed old men with grey moustaches would be leading their veiled wives up the slopes; others, more pious, would be bowed in prayer before small shrines—often no more than piles of pebbles and a calendar poster.

Sadhus, India's wandering holy men, also filled the road in dazzling profusion. As I wandered through the knee-high columbines, buttercups and hollyhocks of the high-altitude pastures, I passed a constant stream of lean, fit, hardy men with matted, dreadlocked hair and thick beards leaping up the track. Some travelled in groups; other travelled alone and many of these appeared to be locked in deep meditation as they walked, weighed down by heavy metal tridents, in an effort to find *moksha* in the clear air and crystal silence of the mountains.

As I clambered up the track, I fell into conversation with an ash-smeared and completely naked sadhu of about my own age. I had always assumed that most of the Holy Men I had seen in India were from traditional village backgrounds and were motivated by a blind and simple faith. But as soon as we began talking it became apparent that Ajay Kumar Jha was in fact a far more cosmopolitan figure than I had expected. Ajay and I walked together along the steep ridge of a mountain, with the great birds of prey circling the thermals below us. I asked him to tell me his story and after some initial hesitation, he agreed.

"I have been a *sanyasi* [wanderer] only for four and a half years," he said. "Before that I was the sales manager with Kelvinator, a Bombay consumer electricals company. I had done my MBA at Patna University and was considered a high flyer by my employers. But one day I just decided I could not spend the rest of my life marketing fans and fridges. So I just left. I wrote a letter to my boss and to my parents, gave away my belongings to the poor, and took a train to Benares. There I threw away my old suit, rubbed ash on my body and found a monastery."

"Have you never regretted what you did?" I asked.

"It was a very sudden decision," replied Ajay. "But no, I have never regretted it for a minute, even when I have not eaten for several days and am at my most hungry."

"But how did you adjust to such a change in your life?" I asked.

"Of course at first it was very difficult," he said. "But then everything worthwhile in life takes time. I was used to all the comforts: my father was a politician and a very rich man by the standards of our country. But I never wanted to live a worldly life like him."

We had now arrived at the top of the ridge and the land fell steeply on every side. Ajay gestured out over the forests and pastures laid out at our feet, a hundred shades of green framed by the blinding white of the distant snow peaks straight ahead.

"When you walk in the hills your mind becomes clear," he said. "All your worries disappear. Look! I carry only a blanket and a water bottle. I have no possessions, so I have no worries."

He smiled: "Once you learn to restrain your desires," he said, "anything becomes possible."

The sort of world where a committed, naked naga sadhu could also be an MBA was something I was to become used to in the course of my travels for this book. Last November, for example, I managed to track down a celebrated tantric at a cremation ground near Birbhum in West Bengal. Tapan Goswami was a feeder of skulls. Twenty years ago he had been interviewed by an American professor of comparative religion, who went on to write a scholarly essay on Tapan's practice of spirit-summoning and spell-casting, using the cured skulls of dead virgins and restless suicides. It sounded rich material, albeit of a rather sinister nature, so I spent the best part of a day touring the various cremation grounds of Birbhum before finally finding Tapan sitting outside his small Kali temple on the edge of the town, preparing a sacrifice for the goddess.

The sun was sinking now, and the light was beginning to fade; a funeral pyre was still smoking eerily in front of the temple. Everywhere, flies snarled in the hot, still air. Tapan and I talked of Tantra, as the light faded, and he confirmed that in his youth, when the professor had interviewed him, he had indeed been an enthusiastic skull-feeder. Yes, he said, all that had been written about him was true, and yes, he did occasionally still cure skulls and summon their dead owners so as to use their power. But sadly, he said, he could not talk to me about the details. Why was that? I asked. Because, he said, his two sons were now successful opthamologists in New Jersey. They had firmly forbidden him from giving any more interviews about what he did in case rumours of the family dabbling in Black Magic damaged their profitable East Coast practice. Now he thought he might even give away his skulls, and go and join them in the States.

Living in India over the last few years, I have seen the country change at a rate that was impossible to imagine when I first moved there in the late eighties. On returning to live again in Delhi after nearly a decade away, I took a lease on a farmhouse five kilometres from the boom town of Gurgaon, on the south western edge of Delhi. From the end of the road you could just see in the distance the rings of new housing estates springing up, full of call centres, software companies and fancy apartment blocks, all rapidly rising on land that only two years earlier had been virgin farmland. Six years later, Gurgaon has galloped towards us at such a speed that it now almost abuts the edge of our farm, and what is proudly touted as the largest mall in Asia is coming up a quarter of a mile from the house.

The speed of the development is breathtaking to anyone used to the plodding growth rates of Western Europe: the sort of construction that would take twenty-five years in Britain comes up here in five months. As is now well known, India is already on the verge of overtaking Japan to become the third largest economy in the world, and according to CIA estimates, the Indian economy is expected to overtake that of the U.S. by roughly 2050.

So extraordinary is all this that it is easy to overlook the fragility and unevenness of the boom. As you leave Gurgaon and drive down the Jaipur Highway, it is like heading back in time to an older, slower, pre-modern world. Within twenty minutes of leaving the Gurgaon headquarters of Microsoft or Google Asia, cars and trucks are beginning to give way to camel and bullock carts, suits, denim and baseball hats to dusty cotton *dhotis* and turbans. This is a very different India indeed, and it is here, in the places suspended between modernity and tradition, that most of the stories in this book are set. For here, outside the great burgeoning megacities of India and Pakistan, in the small towns and villages, South Asian religion is in a state of fascinating and unpredictable flux.

Much has now been written about the way that India is moving forward to return the subcontinent to its traditional place at the heart of global trade, but so far little has been said about the way these huge earthquakes have affected the diverse religious traditions of South Asia, or how the people who live out these rich traditions have coped with living in the eye of the storm. For while the West often likes to imagine the religions of the East as deep wells of ancient, unchanging wisdom, in reality much of India's religious identity is closely tied to specific social groups, caste practices and father-to-son lineages, all of which are changing very rapidly as Indian society transforms itself at speed.

All this raises many interesting questions: What does it actually mean to be a holy man or a Jain nun, a mystic or a tantric seeking salvation on the roads of modern India, as the Tata trucks thunder past? Why does one individual embrace armed resistance as a sacred calling, while another devoutly practices *ahimsa,* or non-violence? Why does one think he can create a god, while another thinks that god can inhabit him? How is each specific religious path surviving the changes India is currently undergoing? What changes and what remains the same? Does India still offer any sort of real spiritual alternative to materialism, or is it now just another fast developing satrap of the wider capitalist world?

Certainly on my travels around India for this book I found many worlds strangely colliding as the velocity of this process accelerates. Outside Jodhpur, I visited a shrine and pilgrimage centre that has formed around an Enfield Bullet motorbike. Initially erected as a memorial to its owner, after the latter suffered a fatal crash, the bike has now become a centre of pilgrimage, attracting pilgrims—especially devout truck drivers—from across Rajasthan in search of the miracles of fertility it was said to effect. In Swamimalai, near Tanjore in Tamil Nadu, I met Srikanda Stpathy, an idol maker, the thirty-fifth of a long line of sculptors going back to the legendary Chola bronze makers. Srikanda regarded creating gods as one of the holiest callings in India—but now has to reconcile himself to a son who only wants to study computer engineering in Bangalore. In Kannur in northern Kerala, I met Hari Das, a well-builder and part-time prison warden for ten months of the year, who polices the violent running war between the convicts and imprisoned gangsters of the two region's rival political parties, the far-right RSS and the hard-left Communist Party of India. But during the *theyyam* dancing season, between January and March, Hari has a rather different job. Though he comes from an untouchable Dalit background, he nevertheless is transformed into an omnipotent deity for three months a year, and as such is worshipped as a god. Then, at the end of March, he goes back to the prison.

In Jaipur, I spent time with Mohan Bhopa, an illiterate goatherd from Rajasthan, who keeps alive a 4,000-line sacred epic that he, now virtually alone, still knows by heart. Living as a wandering bard and storyteller, he remembers the *slokas* of one of the great oral epics of Rajasthan, praising the hero-God Pabuji. Mohan told me, however, that his ancient recitative art is now threatened by the lure of Bollywood and the televised Hindu epics shown on Indian TV, and he has had to adapt the old bardic tradition in order for it to survive. The epic which Mohan recites contains a regional variant on the "national" *Ramayana* myth. In the mainstream Ramayana tradition, the hero Lord Ram goes to Lanka to rescue his wife Sita who has been captured by the demon king Ravana. In the Rajasthani version of the myth, the hero is Papuji, and he goes to Lanka not to rescue a kidnapped spouse, but to rustle Ravana's camels. It is exactly these sort of regional variants and self-contained local cults which are being lost and menaced in the slow homogenisation of what the eminent Indian historian Romila Thapar calls the new "syndicated Hinduism" of middle-class urban India.

Other people I met on my journey had had their worlds impacted by modernity in a more brutal manner: by invasions, by massacres, and by the rise of often violent political fundamentalist movements. A great many of the lives of the searchers and renouncers I talked to were marked by suffering, exile and frequently, great pain; a large number turned out to be escaping personal, familial or political tragedies. Tashi Passang, for example, was a Buddhist monk in Tibet until the Chinese invaded in 1959. When his monastery came under pressure from the Chinese, he decided to take up arms to defend the Buddhist faith. "Once you have been a monk, it is very difficult to kill a man," he told me. "But sometimes it can be your duty to do so." Now living in exile in the Indian Himalayas he prints prayer flags in an attempt to atone for the violence he committed after he joined the Tibetan resistance. Others, banished from their families and castes, or destroyed by interreligious or political violence, had found love and community in a band of religious ecstatics, sheltered, accepted and even revered where elsewhere they might be shunned.

With stories like these slowly filling my notebooks, I set out to write an Indian equivalent of my book on the monks and monasteries of the Middle East, *From the Holy Mountain*. But the people I met were so extraordinary, and their own stories and voices so strong, that in the end I decided to write *Nine Lives* in a quite different form. Twenty years ago, when my first book, *In Xanadu*, was published at the height of the eighties, travel writing tended to highlight the narrator: his adventures were the subject; the people he met were sometimes reduced to objects in the background. With *Nine Lives* I have tried to invert this, and keep the narrator firmly in the shadows, so bringing the lives of the people I have met to the fore and placing their stories firmly centre stage. In some cases, to protect their identities, I have changed the names and muddied the details of some of my characters, at their own request.

As each of these characters live in the self-contained moral universes of their own religious and ethical systems, I have tried not to judge, and though my choices and arrangement no doubt reveal something of my views and preferences, I have tried to show rather than tell, and to let the characters speak for themselves. This may leave the book less analytical than some would wish, but by rooting many of the stories in the darker side of modern Indian life, with each of the characters telling his or her own story, and with only the frame created by the narrator, I have made a conscious effort to try to avoid imposing myself on the stories told by my nine characters, and so hope to have escaped many of the clichés about "Mystic India" that blight so much Western writing on Indian religion. For this is not the story of my religious journey, but of that of the nine subjects of this book. And though some of the stories deal with those on the wildest and most exotic fringes of Indian religious life, I have always attempted to humanise rather than exoticise.

Nine Lives is conceived as a collection of linked non-fiction short stories, with each life representing a different form of devotion, or a different religious path. Each life is intended to act as a keyhole into the way that each specific religious vocation has been caught and transformed in the vortex of India's metamorphosis during this rapid period of transition, while revealing the extraordinary persistence of faith and ritual in a fast-changing landscape.

It is, of course, a personal and entirely subjective selection: these are simply the stories of nine people from nine traditions that happen to interest or appeal to me. The book makes no claims to be comprehensive, and there are many traditions which I have completely left out: there are, for example no Sikhs, Christians, Parsis or Jews in this book, though all have long and interesting histories in the soil of South Asia.

Nor do I deal at any length with the politics or economics of modern Indian religious life, or the mobilization of religion by elements within the Indian state and its political parties. Although as a young foreign correspondent newly arrived in India in the late eighties I covered in detail the rise of Hindu fundamentalism in India, and reported from the ground on L.K. Advani's Rath Yatra, the destruction of the Babri Masjid in Ayodhya and the massacres of thousands of Muslims in Gujarat, these are not subjects I discuss here. Equally, I do not investigate the world of gurus and ashrams and TV godmen, though these are all fascinating subjects, as is the whole story of the slow erosion of Nehruvian secularism in the face of massive revival of middle class religiosity; to give just one very telling statistic, more than 50 percent of package tours organized in modern India are to pilgrimage destinations.

Instead *Nine Lives* focuses beyond the political sphere and behind the headlines, on the diverse traditional religious systems of South Asia, and particularly the deeply embedded heterodox, syncretic and pluralist religious and philosophical folk traditions which continue to defy the artificial boundaries of modern political identities. It is these which are being eroded as Hinduism's disparate, overlapping multiplicity of religious practices, cults, myths, festivals and rival deities are slowly being systemised into a relatively centralised nationalist ideology that now increasingly resembles the very different structures of the three Abrahamic religions.

As I found on my travels, increasingly it is the small gods and goddesses that are falling away and out of favour as faith becomes more centralized, and as local gods and goddesses give way to the national hyper-masculine hero deities, especially Lord Krishna and

Lord Rama, a process scholars call the "Rama-fication" of Hinduism. Ironically, there are strong parallels in the way this new Hinduism is standardising faith to what is happening in South Asian Islam—a religion Hindu nationalists routinely demonise. There too, the local is tending to give way to the national as the cults of local Sufi saints—the warp and woof of popular Islam in India for centuries—loses ground to a more standardised, middle-class and textual form of Islam, imported from the Gulf and propagated by the Wahhabis, Deobandis and Tablighis in their madrassas.

Yet to my surprise, for all the changes and development that have taken place, an older India endures, and many of the issues that I found my holy men discussing and agonising about remained the same eternal quandaries that absorbed the holy men of classical India or the Sufis of the Middle Ages, hundreds of years ago: the quest for material success and comfort against the claims of the life of the spirit; the call of the life of action against the life of contemplation; the way of stability against the lure of the open road; personal devotion against conventional or public religion; textual orthodoxy against the emotional appeal of mysticism; the age-old war of duty and desire.

The water moves on, a little faster than before, yet still the great river flows. It is as fluid and unpredictable in its moods as it has ever been, but it meanders within familiar banks.

The interviews of this book took place in eight different languages, and in each case I owe a huge debt to those who accompanied me on the trips and helped me talk to my subjects: Mimlu Sen, Santanu Mitra, Jonty Rajagopalan, Prakash Dan Detha, Susheela Raman, H. Padmanabaiah Nagarajaiah, Prathibha Nandakumar, Tenzin Norkyi, Lhakpa Kyizom, Tenzin Tsundue, Choki Tsomo, Masood Lohar, and my old friend Subramaniam Gautham, who accompanied me on trips to both Tamil Nadu and Kerala. Toby Sinclair, Gita Mehta, Ram Guha, Faith and John Singh, Ameena Saiyid, Wasfia Nazreen, Sam Mills, Michael Wood, Susan Visvanathan, Pankaj Mishra, Dilip Menon and the late Bhaskar Bhattacharyya all gave helpful advice, while Varsha Hoon of Connexions Inc. organised all the logistics of travel, and tolerated my frequent last minute changes of plan with patience and ingenuity. Geoffrey Dobbs kindly lent me his beautiful island, Taprobane, to begin this book and it was there that I wrote the first of these stories, "The Nun's Tale."

For help with translations of devotional poetry, I am indebted to A.K. Ramanujan's two wonderful collections of ancient verse, *When God Is a Customer* (University of California Press, 1994) and *The Interior Landscape* (OUP India, 1994); to Ramprasad Sen's *Grace and Mercy in Her Wild Hair* (Hohm Press, 1999); to Deben Bhattacharya's *The Mirror of the Sky* (Allen & Unwin, 1969); to Anju Makhija and Hari Dilgir for their translation of *Seeking the Beloved* by Shah Abdul Latif (Katha, New Delhi, 2005); to John D. Smith for his translations of Pabuji verse in *The Epic of Pabuji: A Study, Transcription and Translation* (Cambridge University Press, 1991); and lastly to Vidya Dehejia for translations from classical Tamil hymns and inscriptions.

As before, many people were kind enough to read through drafts of the book and offer suggestions: Rana Dasgupta, Wendy Doniger, Paul Courtwright, Daniyal Mueenuddin, Ananya Vajpayi, Isabella Tree, Gurcharan Das, Jonathan Bond, Rajni George, Alice Albinia, Chiki Sarkar, Salma Merchant, Basharat Peer, and especially Sam Miller, who was a much more useful reader to me than I, to my shame, was to him with the manuscript of his wonderful Delhi book. My heroic agent, the legendary David Godwin, has been a rock throughout. I have also been blessed with inspirational publishers: Sonny Mehta at Knopf, Ravi Singh of Penguin India, Marc Parent of Buchet Chastel and especially Michael Fishwick of Bloomsbury, who has been the editor of all seven of my books—this is our twentieth anniversary together.

My lovely family, Olivia and my children, Ibby, Sam and Adam, have been as generous and delightfully distracting as ever. This book is dedicated to my gorgeous Sammy, whose own book of stories, co-written with his little brother, has been growing rather quicker, and contains even more magic, than that of his Daddy.

WILLIAM DALRYMPLE
Mira Singh Farm, New Delhi, July 1, 2009

nine lives

The Nun's Tale

Two hills of blackly gleaming granite, smooth as glass, rise from a thickly wooded landscape of banana plantations and jagged palmyra palms. It is dawn. Below lies the ancient pilgrimage town of Sravanabelagola, where the crumbling walls of monasteries, temples and *dharamsalas* cluster around a grid of dusty, red earth roads. The roads converge on a great rectangular tank. The tank is dotted with the spreading leaves and still-closed buds of floating lotus flowers. Already, despite the early hour, the first pilgrims are gathering.

For more than 2,000 years, this Karnatakan town has been sacred to the Jains. It was here, in the third century BC, that the first Emperor of India, Chandragupta Maurya, embraced the Jain religion and died through a self-imposed fast to the death, the emperor's chosen atonement for the killings for which he had been responsible in his life of conquest. Twelve hundred years later, in AD 981, a Jain general commissioned the largest monolithic statue in India, sixty feet high, on the top of the larger of the two hills, Vindhyagiri.

This was an image of another royal Jain hero, Prince Bahubali.

The prince had fought a duel with his brother Bharata for control of his father's kingdom. But in the very hour of his victory, Bahubali realised the folly of greed and the transience of worldly glory. He renounced his kingdom and embraced instead the path of the ascetic. Retreating to the jungle, he stood in meditation for a year, so that the vines of the forest curled around his legs and tied him to the spot. In this state he conquered what he believed to be the real enemies—his passions, ambitions, pride and desires—and so became, according to the Jains, the first human being to achieve *moksha,* or spiritual liberation.

The sun has only just risen above the palm trees, and an early morning haze still cloaks the ground. Yet already the line of pilgrims—from a distance, tiny ant-like creatures against the dawn-glistening fused-mercury of the rock face—are climbing the steps that lead up to the monumental hilltop figure of the stone prince. For the past thousand years this massive broad-shouldered statue, enclosed in its lattice of stone vines, has been the focus of pilgrimage in this Vatican of the Digambara, or Sky Clad Jains.

Digambara monks are probably the most severe of all India's ascetics. They show their total renunciation of the world by travelling through it completely naked, as light as the air, as they conceive it, and as clear as the Indian sky. Sure enough, among the many ordinary lay people in lungis and saris slowly mounting the rock-cut steps are several completely naked men—Digambara monks on their way to do homage to Bahubali. There are also a number of white-clad Digambara nuns, or *matajis,* and it was in a temple just short of the summit that I first laid eyes on Prasannamati Mataji.

I had seen the tiny, slender, barefoot figure of the nun in her white sari bounding up the steps above me as I began my ascent. She climbed quickly, with a pot of water made from a coconut shell in one hand, and a peacock fan in the other. As she climbed, she gently wiped each step with the fan in order to make sure she didn't stand on, hurt or kill a single living creature on her ascent of the hill: one of the set rules of pilgrimage for a Jain *muni,* or ascetic.

It was only when I got to the Vadegall Basadi, the temple which lies just below the summit, that I caught up with her—and saw that despite her bald head Mataji was in fact a surprisingly young and striking woman. She had large, wide-apart eyes, olive skin and an air of self-contained confidence that expressed itself in a vigour and ease in the way she held her body. But there was also something sad and wistful about her expression as she went about her devotions; and this, combined with her unexpected youth and beauty, left one wanting to know more.

Mataji was busy with her prayers when I first entered the temple. After the glimmering half-light outside, the interior was almost completely black, and it took several minutes for my eyes fully to adjust to the gloom. At the cardinal points within the temple, at first almost invisible, were three smooth, black marble images of the Jain *Tirthankaras*, or Liberators. Each was sculpted sitting Buddha-like in the *virasana samadhi*, with shaved head and elongated ear-lobes. The hands of each *Tirthankara* was cupped, and they sat cross-legged in a lotus position, impassive and focused inwards, locked in the deepest introspection and meditation. *Tirthankara* means literally "ford-maker," and the Jains believe these heroic ascetic figures have shown the way to Nirvana, making a spiritual ford through the rivers of suffering, and across the wild oceans of existence and rebirth, so as to create a crossing place between *samsara* and liberation.

To each of these figures in turn, Mataji bowed. She then took some water from the attendant priest and poured it over the hands of the statues. This water she collected in a pot, and then used it to anoint the top of her own head. According to Jain belief, it is good and meritorious for pilgrims to express their devotion to the *Tirthankaras*, but they can expect no earthly rewards for such prayers: as perfected beings, the ford-makers have liberated themselves from the world of men, and so are not present in the statues in the way that, say, Hindus believe their deities are incarnate in temple images. The pilgrim can venerate, praise, adore and learn from the example of the *Tirthankaras*, and they can use them as a focus for their meditations. But as the ford-makers are removed from the world they are unable to answer prayers; the relationship between the devotee and the object of his devotion is entirely one way. At its purest, Jainism is almost an atheistic religion, and the much venerated images of the *Tirthankaras* in temples represent not so much a divine presence as a profound divine absence.

I was intrigued by Mataji's intense dedication to the images, but as she was deep in her prayers, it was clear that now was not the moment to interrupt her, still less to try to talk to her. From the temple, she headed up the hill to wash the feet of Bahubali. There she silently mouthed her morning prayers at the feet of the statue, her rosary circling in her hand. Then she made five rounds of the *parikrama* pilgrim circuit around the sanctuary, and as quickly as she had leapt up the steps, she headed down them again, peacock fan flicking and sweeping each step before her.

It was only the following day that I applied for, and was given, a formal audience—or as the monks called it, *darshan*—with Mataji at the monastery guest house; and it was only the day after that, as we continued our conversations, that I began to learn what had brought about her air of unmistakable melancholy.

"We believe that all attachments bring suffering," said Prasannamati Mataji, after we had been talking for some time. "This is why we are supposed to give them up. It is one of the main principles of Jainism—we call it *aparigraha*. This was why I left my family, and why I gave away my wealth."

We were talking in the annex of a monastery prayer hall, and Mataji was sitting cross-legged on a bamboo mat, raised slightly above me on a low dais. The top of her white sari was now modestly covering her plucked head. "For many years, I fasted, or ate at most only once a day," she continued. "Like other nuns, I often experienced hunger and thirst. I tried to show compassion to all living creatures, and to avoid all forms of violence, passion or delusion. I wandered the roads of India barefoot." As she said this, the nun ran a hand up the hard and callused sole of her unshod foot. "Every day I suffered the pain of thorns and blisters. All this was part of my effort to shed my last attachments in this illusory world.

"But," she said, "I still had one attachment—though of course I didn't think of it in that way."

"What was that?" I asked.

"My friend Prayogamati," she replied. "For twenty years we were inseparable companions, sharing everything. For our safety, we Jain nuns are meant to travel together, in groups or in pairs. It never occurred to me that I was breaking any of our rules. But because of my close friendship with her, I formed not just an attachment, but a strong attachment—and that left an opening for suffering. But I only realised this after she died."

There was a pause, and I had to encourage Mataji to continue. "In this stage of life we need company," she said. "You know, a companion with whom we can share ideas and feelings. After Prayogamati left her body, I felt this terrible loneliness. In truth, I feel it to this day. But her time was fixed. When she fell ill—first with TB and then malaria—her pain was so great she decided to take *sallekhana*, even though she was aged only thirty-six."

"*Sallekhana*?"

"It's the ritual fast to the death. We Jains regard it as the culmination of our life as ascetics. It is what we all aim for, and work towards as the best route to Nirvana. Not just nuns—even my grandmother, a lay person, took *sallekhana*."

"You are saying she committed suicide?"

"No, no: *sallekhana* is not suicide," she said emphatically. "It is quite different. Suicide is a great sin, the result of despair. But *sallekhana* is as a triumph over death, an expression of hope."

"I don't understand," I said. "If you starve yourself to death, then surely you are committing suicide?"

"Not at all. We believe that death is not the end, and that life and death are complementary. So when you embrace *sallekhana* you are embracing a whole new life—it's no more than going through from one room to another."

"But you are still choosing to end your life."

"With suicide, death is full of pain and suffering. But *sallekhana* is a beautiful thing. There is no distress or cruelty. As nuns our lives are peaceful, and giving up the body should also be peaceful. You have the *Tirthankaras'* names on your lips, and if you do it slowly and gradually, in the prescribed way, there is no pain; instead there is a gentle purity in all the privations.

"At all stages you are guided by an experienced *mataji* or guru. Everything is planned long in advance—when, and how, you give up your food. Someone is appointed to sit with you and look after you at all times, and a message is sent out to all members of the community that you have decided to take this path. First you fast one day a week, then you eat only on alternate days: one day you take food, the next you fast. One by one, you give up different types of food. You give up rice, then fruits, then vegetables, then juice, then buttermilk. Finally you take only water, and then you have that only on alternate days. Eventually, when you are ready, you give up that too. If you do it very gradually, there is no suffering at all. The body is cooled down, so that you can concentrate inside on the soul, and on erasing all your bad karma.

"At every stage you are asked: are you prepared to go on, are you sure you are ready for this, are you sure you don't want to turn back? It is very difficult to describe, but really it can be so beautiful: the ultimate rejection of all desires, the sacrificing of everything. You are surrounded, cradled, by your fellow monks. Your mind is fixed on the example of the *Jinas*."

She smiled. "You have to understand that for us death is full of excitement. You embrace *sallekhana* not out of despair with your old life, but to gain and attain something new. It's just as exciting as visiting a new landscape or a new country: we feel excited at a new life, full of possibilities."

I must have looked surprised, or unconvinced, because she stopped and explained what she meant using the simplest images. "When your clothes get old and torn," she said, "you get new ones. So it is with the body. After the age of thirty, every year it becomes weaker. When the body withers completely, the soul will take a new one, like a hermit crab finding a new shell. For the soul will not wither, and in rebirth you simply exchange your torn and damaged old clothes for a smart new suit."

"But you could hardly have felt excited when your friend left you like this."

"No," she said, her face falling. "It is hard for those who are left." She stopped. For a moment Mataji lost her composure; but she checked herself.

"After Prayogamati died, I could not bear it. I wept, even though we are not supposed to. Any sort of emotion is considered a hindrance to the attainment of Enlightenment. We are meant to cultivate indifference—but still I remember her."

Again her voice faltered. She slowly shook her head. "The attachment is there even now," she said. "I can't help it. We lived together for twenty years. How can I forget?"

Jainism is one of the most ancient religions of the world, similar to Buddhism in many respects, and emerging from the same hetero-dox classical Indian world of the Ganges basin in the early centuries BC. Like Buddhism, it was a partly a reaction to Brahminical caste consciousness and the readiness of the Brahmins to slaughter huge quantities of animals for temple sacrifices—but the faith of the Jains is slightly more ancient, and much more demanding than Buddhist practice. Buddhist ascetics shave their heads; Jains pluck their hair out by the roots. Buddhist monks beg for food; Jains have to have their food given to them without asking. All they can do is to go out on *gowkari*—the word used to describe the grazing of a cow—and sig-nal their hunger by curving their right arm over their shoulder. If no food comes before the onset of the night, they go to bed hungry. They are forbidden to accept or in any way handle money.

In ancient India, the Jain monks were also celebrated for their refusal to wash, and like the Coptic monks of Egypt, equated a lack of concern for outward appearance with inner purity. One early inscription at Sravanabelagola admiringly refers to a monk so begrimed with filth that "he looked as if he wore a closely fitting suit of black armour." Today the monks are allowed to wipe them-selves with a wet towel and to wash their robes every few weeks; but bathing in ponds or running water or the sea is still strictly forbid-den, as is the use of soap.

Unlike Buddhism, the Jain religion never spread beyond India, and while it was once a popular and powerful faith across the sub-continent, patronised by the princes of a succession of Deccani dynasties, today there are only four million Jains left, and these are largely limited to the states of Rajasthan, Gujarat, Madhya Pradesh and Karnataka. Outside India, the religion barely exists, and in con-trast to Buddhism, is almost unknown in the West.

The word Jain derives from *Jina*, meaning liberator or spiritual conqueror. The *Jinas* or *Tirthankaras*—ford-makers—were a series of twenty-four human teachers who each discovered how to escape the eternal cycle of death and rebirth. Through their heroic *tapasya*—bodily austerities—they gained omniscient and transcendent knowledge which revealed to them the nature of the reality of the great theatre of the universe, in every dimension. The most recent of those, according to the Jains, was the historical figure of Mahavira (599–529 BC)—the Great Hero—a prince of Magadha, in modern Bihar, who renounced the world at the age of thirty to become a wandering thinker and ascetic.

Mahavira elaborated to his followers a complex cosmological system that the Jains still expound 2,600 years later. Like followers of other Indian faiths they believe in an immortal and indestructible soul, or *jivan*, and that the sum of one's actions determines the nature of one's future rebirth. However, the Jains diverge from Hindus and Buddhists in many ways. They reject the Hindu idea that the world was created or destroyed by omnipotent gods, and they mock the pretensions of the Brahmins, who believe that ritual purity and temple sacrifices can bring salvation. As a Jain monk explains to a group of hostile Brahmins in one of the most ancient Jain scriptures, the most important sacrifice for Jains is not some *puja*, or ritual, but the sacrifice of one's own body: "Austerity is my sacrifical fire," says the monk, "and my life is the place where the fire is kindled. Mental and physical effort are my ladle for the oblation, and my body is the dung fuel for the fire, my actions my firewood. I offer up an oblation praised by the wise seers consisting of my restraint, effort and calm."

Crucially, the Jains differ from both Hindus and Buddhists in their understanding of karma, which for other faiths means simply the fruit of your actions. Jains, however, conceive of karma as a fine material substance that physically attaches itself to the soul, polluting and obscuring its potential for bliss by weighing it down with pride, anger, delusion and greed, and so preventing it from reaching its ultimate destination at the summit of the universe. To gain final liberation, you must live life in a way that stops you accumulating more karma, while wiping clean the karma you have accumulated in previous lives. The only way to do this is to embrace an ascetic life and to follow the path of meditation and rigorous self-denial taught by the *Tirthankaras*. You must embrace a life of world renunciation, non-attachment and an extreme form of non-violence.

The soul's journey takes place in a universe conceived in a way that is different from that of any other faith. For Jains, the universe is shaped like a gigantic cosmic human body. Above the body is a canopy containing the liberated and perfected souls–*siddhas*–who, like the *Tirthankaras*, have escaped the cycle of rebirths. At the top of the body, level with the chest, is the celestial upper world, the blissful home of the gods.

At waist level is the middle world, where human beings live in a series of concentric rings of land and ocean. The central landmass of this world–the continent of the Rose Apple Tree–is bounded by the mighty Himalayas, and set within ramparts of diamonds. At its very centre, the *axis mundi*, lies the divine sanctuary of the *Jinas*, Mount Meru, with its two suns and two moons, its parks and woods and its groves of wish-granting trees. Adjacent to this, but slightly to the south, lies the continent of Bharata or India. Here can be found the great princely capitals, surrounded by ornamental lakes blooming with lotus flowers.

Below this disc lies the hell world of the Jains. Here souls who have committed great sins live as hell beings in a state of terrible heat, unquenchable thirst and endless pain, under the watch of a group of malignant and semi-divine jailers, the *asuras*, who are strongly opposed to the dharma of the *Tirthankaras*.

In this world, there are no creator gods: depending on its actions and karma, a soul can be reincarnated as a god, but eventually, when its store of merit is used up, the god must undergo the agonies of death and fall from heaven, to be reborn as a mortal in the middle world. The same is true of hell beings. Once they have paid through suffering for their bad actions, they can rise to be reborn in the middle world and again begin the cycle of death and rebirth–depending on their karma, as human beings, animals, plants or tiny unseen creatures of the air. Like the fallen gods, former hell beings can also aspire to achieving *moksha*, the final liberation of the soul from earthly existence and suffering. Even the *Tirthankara* Mahavira, the Great Hero himself, spent time as a hell being, and then as a lion, before rising to be a human and so finding the path to Enlightenment. It is only human beings–not the hedonistic gods–who can gain liberation, and the way to do this is completely to renounce the world and its passions, its desires and attachments, and to become a Jain ascetic. As such, the monk or nun must embrace the Three Jewels, namely right knowledge, right faith and right conduct, and to take five vows: no violence, no untruth, no stealing, no sex, no attachments. They wander the roads of India, avoiding any acts of violence, however small, and meditating on the great questions, thinking about the order and purpose of the universe, and attempting to ford the crossing places that lead through suffering to salvation. For the Jains, then, to be an ascetic is a higher calling than to be a god.

It is a strange, austere and in some ways very harsh religion; but that, explained Prasannamati Mataji, is exactly the point.

At ten o'clock each day, Prasannamati Mataji eats her one daily meal. On my third day in Sravanabelagola, I went to the *math*, or monastery, to watch what turned out to be as much a ritual as a breakfast.

Mataji, wrapped as ever in her unstitched white cotton sari, was sitting cross-legged on a low wooden stool which itself was raised on a wooden pallet in the middle of an empty ground-floor room. Behind her, her fan and coconut water pot rested against the wall. In front, five or six middle-class Jain laywomen in saris were fussing around with small buckets of rice, dal and masala chickpeas, eagerly attending on Mataji, whom they treated with extreme deference and respect. Mataji, however, sat with eyes lowered, not looking at them except glancingly, accepting without comment whatever she was offered. There was complete silence: no one spoke; any communication took place by hand signals, nods and pointed fingers.

As I approached the door, Mataji signalled with a single raised palm that I should remain where I was. One of the women explained that as I had not had a ritual bath, and had probably eaten meat, I must stay outside. Notebook in hand, I observed from the open door.

For an hour, Mataji ate slowly, and in total silence. The woman waited for her to nod, and then with a long spoon put a titbit of food into her cupped and waiting hands. Each morsel she then turned over carefully with the thumb of her right hand, looking for a stray hair, or winged insect, or ant, or any living creature which might have fallen into the strictly vegetarian food, so rendering it impure. If she were to find anything, explained one of the laywomen, the rules were clear: she must drop the food on the floor, reject the entire meal and fast until ten o'clock the following morning.

After she had finished her vegetables, one of Mataji's attendants poured a small teaspoonful of ghee onto her rice. When a woman offered a further spoonful of dal, the slightest shake of Mataji's head indicated that she was done. Boiled water was then poured, still warm, from a metal cup into the waiting bowl of Mataji's hands. She drank some, then swirled a further cupful of it around in her mouth. She picked her teeth with her finger, and washed water around her gums, before spitting it out into a waiting spittoon. After that, she was finished. Mataji rose and formally blessed the women with her peacock fan.

When the full ritual of the silent meal was finished, Mataji led me to the reception room of the monastery guest house. There she sat herself down cross-legged on a wicker mat in front of a low writing desk. On this were placed the two volumes of the scriptures she was currently studying, and about which she was writing a commentary. At a similar desk at the far end of the room sat a completely naked man—the maharaj of the *math,* silently absorbed in his writing. We nodded to each other, and he returned to his work. He was there, I presumed, to chaperone Mataji during our conversation: it would have been forbidden for her to stay alone in a room with a male who was not her guru.

When she had settled herself, Mataji began to tell me the story of how she had renounced the world, and why she had decided to take the ritual of initiation, or *diksha,* as a Jain nun.

"I was born in Raipur, Chattisgarh, in 1972," said Mataji. "In those days my name was Rekha. My family were wealthy merchants. They hailed from Rajasthan but moved to Chattisgarh for business reasons. My father had six brothers and we lived as a joint family, all together in the same house. My parents had had two boys before I was born, and for three generations there had been no girls in the family. I was the first one, and they all loved me, not least because I was considered a pretty and lively little girl, and had unusually fair skin and thick black hair, which I grew very long.

"I was pampered by all of them, and my uncles would compete to spoil me. I was very fond of *rasgulla* and *pedha* [milky sweetmeats] and each one of my uncles would bring boxes for me. If I had gone to sleep by the time they returned from their warehouse they would wake me to give me the sweets, or sometimes a big pot of sweet, syrupy *gulab jamun*. Every desire of mine was fulfilled, and I was everyone's favourite. Nobody ever beat or disciplined me, even in jest. In fact I do not remember even once my parents raising their voice, still less hitting me.

"It was a very happy childhood. I had two best friends, one was a Jain from the rival Svetambara sect, the other a Brahmin girl, and their parents were also textile merchants. So we would all play with our dolls, and our families would get their tailors to design elaborate saris and *salwars* for them. When we were a little older, my uncles would take us to the movies. I loved Rekha, because she had the same name as me, and Amitabh Bachchan because he was the number-one hero in those days. My favourite movie was *Coolie*.

"Then, when I was about thirteen, I was taken to meet a monk called Dayasagar Maharaj—his name means the Lord of the Ocean of Compassion. He was a former cowherd who had taken *diksha* when he was a boy of only ten years old, and now had a deep knowledge of the scriptures. He had come to Raipur to do his *chaturmasa*—the monsoon break when we Jains are forbidden to walk in case we accidentally kill the unseen life that inhabits the puddles. So for three months the maharaj was in our town, and every day he used to preach and read for all the young children. He told us how to live a peaceful life and how to avoid hurting other living creatures: what we should eat, and how we should strain water to avoid drinking creatures too small to be seen. I was very impressed and started thinking. It didn't take long before I decided I wanted to be like him. His words and his teachings totally changed my life.

"Within a few weeks I decided to give up eating after the hours of darkness, and also gave up eating any plant that grows beneath the earth: onions, potatoes, carrots, garlic and all root vegetables. Jain monks are forbidden these as you kill the plant when you uproot it—we are allowed to eat only plants such as rice which can survive the harvest of their grain.

"When I also gave up milk and jaggery—two things I loved—as a way of controlling my desires, everyone tried to dissuade me, especially my father, who once even tried to force-feed me. They thought I was too young to embark on this path, and everyone wanted me to be their little doll at home. This was not what I wanted.

"When I was fourteen, I announced that I wanted to join the Sangha—the Jain community of which my maharaj was part. Again my family opposed me, saying I was just a young girl, and should not worry about such things. But eventually, when I insisted, they agreed to let me go for a couple of weeks in the school holidays to study the dharma, hoping that I would be put off by the harshness of the Sangha life. They also insisted that some of the family servants should accompany me. But the life of the Sangha and the teachings I heard there were a revelation to me. Once I was settled in, I simply refused to come back. The servants did their best to persuade me, but I was completely adamant, and the servants had to go back on their own.

"Eventually, after two months, my father came to take me home. He told me that one of my uncles had had a son, and that I was to come home as there was to be a big family function. I agreed to come, but only if he promised to bring me back to the Sangha afterwards. My father promised to do so, but at the function all my relations insisted that I was too young, and that I should not be allowed to go back. I stayed with my family for one month, and then insisted that they return me. They refused. So for three days I did not eat—not even a drop of water. The atmosphere at home was very bad. There was a lot of pressure and everyone was very angry, and they called me stubborn and uncaring. But eventually, on the third day, they gave in, and did return me to the Sangha.

"They stayed in close touch, sending money and clothes, and paying for me to go on pilgrimages. They knew my guru would take good care of me, and I think in some ways they were pleased I had taken a pious path; but in their hearts they still didn't want me to take full *diksha*. I, on the other hand, was happy in the Sangha, and knew I had taken the right path. When you eat a mango, you have to throw away the stone. The same is true of our life as *munis*. No matter how attached you are to your family and to the things of this world, whatever efforts you make, ultimately you have to leave them behind. You simply cannot take them with you. However powerful you are, however knowledgeable, however much you love your mother and father, you still have to go. Worldly pleasures and the happiness of family life are both equally temporary. There is no escape. Birth and death are both inevitable; both are beyond our control.

"Like a small child who goes to school and then grows up to become an adult; or like a small mango that gets bigger and bigger, changes its colour and becomes ripe; so ageing and death are innate in our nature. We have no choice. Each of us is born, goes through childhood, becomes an adult, ages and dies. It's a natural process and you can't go back, at least until your next life. The only thing is to accept this, and to embrace the Jain path of knowledge, meditation and penance as the sole way to free yourself from this cycle. It's the only way to attain the absolute.

"After spending some time with the Sangha I felt I had understood this, and that I was living in the best way I could. The more you lead a good life, the clearer and sharper your thoughts on such things become—you begin to be able to cut through the illusions of the world, and to see things as they really are. Suddenly it seemed to me that, though I loved my family, they were only really interested in making money and displaying their wealth—many lay Jains are like this, I fear.

"If you close the door, you cannot see; open it a little and all becomes clear. Just as a burned seed does not sprout, so once you renounce the world you will not be sucked into the whirlpool of *samsara*. I was quite clear now that what I was doing was right. I also found that following this spiritual path brought happiness in this life—something I had not really expected.

"For me, the Sangha was itself like a rebirth, a second life. I felt no real homesickness, nor any wish to return to my old life. The gurus taught me how to live in a new way: how to sit as a Jain nun, how to stand, how to talk, how to sleep. Everything was taught anew, as if from the beginning. I felt happy in this new life; I felt sure I was on the path to salvation, and was no longer being distracted by the outside world. I knew I had done the right thing, and even though I didn't want to hurt my family, I was only sad that I had already wasted so much of my life.

"I really had no time for worrying, anyway. Our guruji made sure we were totally occupied with lectures, study, classes and travel. All the time, in between days of walking, our lessons in Sanskrit and Prakrit were continuing. I found I loved Sanskrit—I loved its complexity and perfection—and after a while I was good enough to read some of our Jain literature and scriptures in the languages in which they were written. We are encouraged to carry on studying and gaining in knowledge until we can get rid of the last delusions of *samsara*. Twenty-four years I have been studying now, and I still have a lot to learn.

"In those early days, we also began to learn how to meditate. Our guru trained us to get up at 3 a.m., and on the days we were not travelling, we would spend the early morning—the most peaceful time of the day—in meditation, striving for self-knowledge. We were trained to think of the twenty-four *Tirthankaras*, to visualise them, and to contemplate within our hearts their attributes, their lives and the decisions they had made. We were shown how to sit in a full lotus—the *padmasana*—with our eyes closed. My ability grew with my studies: first I studied the Sanskrit scriptures, then during the meditation I would recollect what I had read, and attempt to visualise what I had studied. Like a spider making a cobweb, with meditation you need patience to keep building. Once you know all about the *Tirthankaras* it is not difficult to picture them. It is like a child learning to cycle: as you cycle, you master the art, until eventually you hardly notice that you are cycling at all. But as with the bicycle, the first steps can be very hard, and very disheartening.

"Learning the scriptures, learning Prakrit and Sanskrit, learning to meditate, learning to accept *tapasya*—it is all a very slow process. When you sow a seed, you have to wait for it to grow and become a tree and bear fruit—a coconut palm will not fruit for many years. It is the same with us. There is a lot of time between sowing the seed and reaping the produce. You do not sow the seed and expect to get the fruits the next day. With our *tapasya*, with the deprivations we experience, you do not expect to get immediate rewards, or even necessarily to get the rewards at all in this life. You may only get the rewards many lives into the future.

"Like the *Tirthankaras*, you should have faith in the Jain path: faith is everything. For without the spiritual knowledge that the Jain faith contains you can never attain liberation. Spiritual knowledge is like ghee in the milk: you can't see it, so initially you just have to trust that it is there. Only if you learn the proper techniques can you reap the full benefits of the milk's potential: you must learn the way of splitting the milk into curds, then how to churn the curds and finally how to heat the butter to get ghee. The sun is always there, even if the clouds are covering it. In the same way, the soul is trying to reach for liberation, even if it is encumbered by sin and desire and attachments. By following the Jain path you can clear the cloud, and learn the method to get the ghee from the milk. Without the Jain dharma you are a soul tormented and you cannot know any lasting happiness. But with a guru to show you the right path, and to teach you the true nature of the soul, all this can be changed.

"By following the Jain dharma, by living a life full of good deeds, you can gradually erase your bad karma. And, if you are lucky, and steadfast in your pursuit of this goal, you can finally achieve *moksha*."

"At the end of two years with the Sangha," continued Prasannamati Mataji, "I finally made up my mind that I would take *diksha*. That November they plucked my hair for the first time: it's the first step, like a test of your commitment, because if you can't take the pain of having your hair plucked out you are not going to be ready to take the next step. That day, I performed a fast, and that evening one of the senior *matajis* of the Sangha applied the ash of dried cow dung.

This acts as a sort of natural antiseptic if you bleed, as well as stopping the hand from slipping during the plucking.

"I had very beautiful long thick hair, and as I was still very young my guru wanted to cut it with scissors then shave my head with a razor, so as not to inflict such pain on me. But I insisted, and said there was no going back now. I was a very obstinate girl: whatever I wanted to do I did. So they agreed to do what I wished. I think everyone was rather amazed at my stubbornness, and my determination.

"The whole ritual took nearly four hours, and was very painful. I tried not to, but I couldn't help crying. I didn't tell my parents about my decision, as I knew they would try to stop me, but somehow they heard, and came rushing. By the time they arrived, the ceremony was almost over. When they saw me with a bald head, and scars and blood all over my scalp where my hair had once been, my mother screamed, and my father burst into tears. They knew then that I would never turn back from this path. After that, whenever the Sangha would arrive at a village, the maharaj would show me off: 'Look, he would say. This one is so young, yet so determined, doing what even the old would hesitate to do.'

"It was about this time that I met my friend Prayogamati. One day, our Sangha happened to walk into her village, and as her father was a rich merchant, who lived in a very large house, they invited us to stay with them. Prayogamati was the same age as me, fifteen, a beautiful, fragile, sensitive girl, and she came down every day to our room to talk to us. We quickly became very close, talking late into the night. She was fascinated by my life in the Sangha, and I had never met anyone who seemed to understand me the way she did, someone who shared all my beliefs and ideals. She was about to be engaged to the son of a rich diamond merchant, and the match had been arranged for her, but she told me that she was really much more interested in taking *diksha*. She also knew that her family would not allow her to do this.

"After a week, we left the village, setting off to the next town on foot before dawn. That evening, Prayogamati borrowed some money from her mother, saying she wanted to go to a circus. Instead, she took two outfits from her room, and jumped on a bus.

Late that night she found us and asked the maharaj to accept her. Her family realised what had happened, and her father and brothers came and begged her to return, but she refused and our guruji said it was up to her to decide. From that point we were together for twenty years. We took *diksha* together, and travelled together, and ate together, and spent our monsoon *chaturmasa* together. Soon we became very close.

"Except for the *chaturmasa*, it is forbidden for us to stay long in one place, in case we become attached to it. So most nights we would sleep in a different place and our life together was full of variety. Some nights we would stay in the house of a rich man, sometimes in a school, sometimes a *dharamsala*, sometimes in a cave or in the jungle. Jains regard it as a great honour to have us, and Hindus also come to do *darshan*. So if no Jain house is available, Hindus would always be happy to take us in. We cannot eat food cooked by Hindus, but we can take raw materials from them and cook it ourselves.

"People think of our life as harsh, and of course in many ways it is. But going into the unknown world and confronting it without a single rupee in our pockets means that differences between rich and poor, educated and illiterate, all vanish, and a common humanity emerges. As wanderers, we monks and nuns are free of shadows from the past. This wandering life, with no material possessions, unlocks our souls. There is a wonderful sense of lightness, living each day as it comes, with no sense of ownership, no weight, no burden. Journey and destination became one, thought and action became one, until it is as if we are moving like a river into complete detachment."

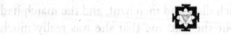

"We lived in this manner for a full four years before the time came for Prayogamati and me to take formal *diksha*—much longer than we had hoped, or expected. But both our families said, 'Let our other children get married first.' We both agreed to this, as we didn't want to upset our parents any more than we had already. But we came

here to Sravanabelagola and took a vow in front of Bahubali, promising that as soon as the family weddings were over we would take
diksha. The wedding of my brother was in January of the fourth year,
and finally, in March, the day of our *diksha* arrived.

"Our maharaj and the *matajis* dressed up my friend and me as
brides. We wore identical clothes, jewellery and *mehndi* [henna decorations on the hands]. We even looked alike, so often people con-
fused us. All my childhood, I never wore any jewellery, just a watch
and a single gold chain around my neck. But for the *diksha*, we were
dressed in jewels and diamonds then taken together in a chariot
around thirteen villages near our family *haveli* at Karavali in
Udaipur district. Before us went drummers and trumpeters and men
clashing cymbals, and as we passed, we would throw rice and
money to the crowds. Every day we would give food to the people—
sometimes we would feed a whole village, sometimes we would just
distribute sweets or dates and jaggery. For a whole month this continued until we were thoroughly sick of all this display. This surprised both of us, because this was a day we had longed for: for four
years now we had delayed the ceremony, and now it was upon us,
all we wanted was to get through it, and head off back on the road.

"But the day of *diksha* itself made it all worthwhile. I really think
it was the happiest day of my life. Both our parents came, and all
our relatives. It was a huge public event—20,000 people gathered,
and it became impossible to control the crowd.

"On the final day, the day of the *diksha* ceremony, Prayogamati
and I both fasted: no food and not a drop of water passed our lips.
We rose very early and offered food instead to our maharaj, and
then we left the house and walked to the stage where the ceremony
was to be held. For the previous fortnight we had gone everywhere
in chariots or on the back of elephants; but now it was back to our
own two feet. When we got to the stage we said prayers in praise of
the *Tirthankaras*, and then we formally asked permission from the
maharaj to take *diksha*. He gave his assent, and amid lots of trumpeting we were led off the stage.

"Then came the time for saying farewell to our families. We both
tied *rakhis* around our brothers' wrists—a final expression of sisterly
love—before saying goodbye to them. After that our relationship of

brother and sister was supposed to end—they were to be like strangers to us. Then we said goodbye to our parents; we embraced and wished each other farewell. After this, they were no longer our parents—they were to be just like any other member of society. We all wept, but I think our parents were also proud of us: to have a monk or a nun in the family is considered a great blessing in our community. And after all, we had left our families for several years by this stage, so it wasn't a great change for them. In their minds, we had taken *diksha* many years before.

"After the farewell, we were led off for the hair-plucking ceremony. This time we had to do it ourselves, which was much harder. After it was finished—it only took half an hour as our hair was already short—we were given a holy bath in a *shamiana* tent. We were both stripped and washed by other *matajis* in a mixture of milk, ghee, turmeric and *atta,* and then in a final bath of water. For us it was like a baptism. When we both came out, we were given robes of white cloth. Our ornaments were taken off, one by one, a symbol of our sacrifice.

"Then we were led back onto the stage, and told our new names. I was no longer Rekha; for the first time in my life I was addressed as Prasannamati Mataji. For the first time my friend became Prayogamati. Then we were both lectured by our guruji. He told us clearly what was expected of us: never again to use a vehicle, to take food only once a day, not to use Western medicine, to abstain from emotion, never to hurt any living creature. He told us we must not react to attacks, must not beg, must not cry, must not complain, must not demand, must not feel superiority, must learn not to be disturbed by illusory things. He told us that we must be the lions that kill the elephant of sexual desire. He told us we must cultivate a revulsion for the world, and a deep desire for release and salvation. And he told us all the different kinds of difficulties we should be prepared to bear: hunger, thirst, cold, heat, mosquitoes. He warned us that none of this would be easy.

"Then he gave us our water pot and peacock fan, the symbol of our commitment to non-violence, and we were led off the stage for the last time. In our new position as *munis,* we were led through crowds of people, all of whom were now asking for our blessing.

"That night we spent on the roof of the house where we were

staying. The following morning, we got up before dawn and ate—we had fasted all the previous day. Then without telling anyone, we slipped away. We looked for the signs that led towards Gujarat, and began to walk.

"Only then did we really begin our wandering life as fully ordained nuns."

"Everyone had warned us about the difficulty of this life," said Prasannamati Mataji. "But in reality, we had left everything willingly, so did not miss the world we had left behind. Not at all. It is the same as when a girl gets married and she has to give up her childhood and her parents' home: if she does it in exchange for something she really wants, it is not a sad time, but instead a very joyful one. Certainly, for both Prayogamati and me, it was a very happy period in our lives, perhaps the happiest. Every day we would walk and discover somewhere new.

"Walking is very important to us Jains. The Buddha was enlightened while sitting under a tree, but our great *Tirthankara,* Mahavira, was enlightened while walking. We believe that walking is an important part of our *tapasya.* We don't use cars or any vehicles, partly because travelling so fast can kill so many living creatures, but partly also because we have two legs and travelling on foot is the right speed for human beings. Walking sorts out your problems and anxieties, and calms your worries. Living from day to day, from inspiration to inspiration, much of what I have learned as a Jain has come from wandering. Sometimes, even my dreams are of walking.

"Our guru had taught us how to walk as Jains. While walking, as well as meditating on the earth and the scriptures, and thinking of the purpose of our lives, we were taught to concentrate on not touching or crushing any living creature. You have to be aware of every single step, and learn to look four steps ahead. If a single ant is in your path you should be ready to jump or step aside. For the same reason, we must avoid standing on green plants, dew, mud, clay or cobwebs—who knows what life forms may be there?

"Not hurting any sentient being and protecting the dharma is really the heart and soul of the dharma. We believe there is a little of *paramatma*—the spirit of God—in all living creatures, even those which are too small to see. So much of our discipline is about this: only drinking filtered water, only eating in daylight so we can really see what we are eating. At the end of each walk we do a special ritual to apologise for any creatures we have inadvertently hurt.

"But it was while walking that Prayogamati began to realise that her health was failing. Because she had difficulty in keeping up with me, we noticed that there was something wrong with her joints. She began to have real difficulty in walking, and even more so in sitting or squatting.

"For ten years her condition got worse: by the end, it pained her to move at all, and she had difficulty moving or sitting. Then one afternoon she was studying the scriptures in a monastery in southern Karnataka when she began coughing. Her cough had become worse and worse, and she had begun to make this deep retching noise. But this time when she took her hand away from her mouth she found it was covered in blood. After that, there was nothing more for a week, but then she began coughing up blood very regularly. Sometimes, it was a small amount—just enough to make her mouth red—at other times she would cough up enough to fill a small teacup or even a bowl.

"I guessed immediately that it was TB, and got special permission from our guruji to let her see a doctor. Western medicine is forbidden to us, as so much of it is made by using dead animals, or by torturing animals during the testing process. But given the seriousness of the situation, our guruji agreed to let a Western doctor look at her, though he insisted that only herbal medicine could be given to her and only at the time of her daily meal.

"Prayogamati remained very calm, and for a long time she hoped that she might still recover her health. Even when it became clear that this was something quite serious, she remained composed and peaceful. I think it was always me that was more worried. She kept assuring me that she was feeling better already and that it was nothing serious; but in reality you didn't have to be a doctor to see that her health was rapidly deteriorating.

"Her digestive system became affected, the bloody coughing continued, and after a while she started showing blood when she went for her ablutions too. Eventually I got permission to take her to a hospital where she had an MRI scan and a full blood test. They diagnosed her problem as Cox's Syndrome—advanced TB of the digestive system. They said that her haemoglobin was very reduced, and her chances were not good. One doctor said that if we had come earlier they could have helped, but we had left it much too late.

"That same day Prayogamati decided to embrace *sallekhana*. She said she would prefer to give up her body rather than have it taken from her. She said she wanted to die voluntarily, facing it squarely and embracing it, rather than have death ambush her and take her away by force. She was determined to be the victor, not the victim. I tried to argue with her, but like me, once she took a decision it was almost impossible to get her to change her mind. Despite her pain and her illness, she set out that day to walk a hundred kilometres to see our guru, who was then in Indore, staying at the Shantinath Jain temple.

"We got there after a terrible week in which Prayogamati suffered very badly: it was winter—late December—and bitterly cold. But she refused to give up and when she got to Indore she asked our guruji's permission to begin the process of embracing *sallekhana*. He asked Prayogamati if she was sure, and she said yes. When he learned that she would anyway probably not have very long to live, he gave his assent.

"Throughout 2004, Prayogamati began gradually reducing her food. One by one, she gave up all the vegetables she used to eat. She began eating nothing at all on several days of the week. For eighteen months she ate less and less. Normally *sallekhana* is very peaceful but for Prayogamati, because of her illness, her end was full of pain.

"My job was to feed her, and look after her and read the pre-scribed texts and mantras. I was also there to talk to her and give her courage and companionship. I stayed with her twenty-fours hours a day, and took the leadership of her *samadhi*. Throughout she toler-ated everything, all the pain and discomfort, and stayed completely calm—such calmness you can hardly imagine! I always enjoyed her company, and always learned from her, but never more than towards the end. She showed how it is possible to keep quiet and smilingly show acceptance no matter how much you are suffering. Such a person will not be born again.

"By September 2005 she was bedridden, and I remained continually by her side for three months, until the beginning of December. By this stage she was eating only five things: pomegranate juice, milk, rice, mung dal and sugar. Every day she would eat a little less. In the last weeks she was given protein injections by a Jain doctor, but she was very weak. She had to summon all her strength to perform the observations that have to be followed during *sallekhana*. Despite not eating, and hardly drinking, her body had somehow swelled up because of the disease, and she continued to lose a lot of blood every time she performed her ablutions. At the end, she was also running a terrible fever of 105 degrees, and was covered in sweat. In the afternoon she would feel cold; in the evening she would burn. I asked the doctors, what is the reason for this? They did some tests and said that she had caught malaria as well. They gave her some injections, but it didn't really help.

"During these last days our guruji was not there—he had gone away for a function. So for the last days I was the only person she knew in that temple, though many *munis* were there to sing and chant and support her.

"The next day the fever was still there. Again the doctor came, and she asked for some food, but she could not stand—in fact she could not even open her mouth. He advised her to drink half a glass of milk, and this she took. For some reason she wanted to clean her teeth, but she didn't have the strength, and the doctor advised her to rest. She was very frustrated by this.

"Just after 1:30 p.m. I went to take my food, and was just about to start eating when Prayogamati cried out loudly. I rushed to look after her—it was clear her condition was not good at all. There was no one around except a boy at the gate, so I sent him off for the doctor. When I came back, I held her hand and she whispered that she wanted to stop all remaining food. Her suffering was too much for her now. She said that for her death was as welcome as life, that there was a time to live and a time to die. 'Now,' she said, 'the time has come for me to be liberated from this body.'

"By that time, our guruji had returned, and he gathered the community. By early afternoon all the gurus and *matajis* were there guiding her and sitting together around the bed. Others came to touch her feet. The room was full of people, and so was the veranda outside. Everyone was chanting the *namokara* mantra, singing *bhajans* and *kirtans* and reading the Jain texts which explain the nature of the soul. Everyone was there to support Prayogamati, to give her courage as she began to slip away.

"Around 4 p.m., the doctor said he thought she was about to die, but she held on until 9 p.m. It was very peaceful in the end. It was dark by then, and the lamps were all lit around the room. Her breathing had been very difficult that day, but towards the end it became easier. I held her hand, the monks chanted and her eyes closed. For a while, even I didn't know she had gone. She just slipped away.

"When I realised she had left, I wept bitterly. We are not supposed to do this, and our guruji frowned at me. But I couldn't help myself. I had followed all the steps correctly until she passed away, but then everything I had bottled up came pouring out. Her body was still there, but she wasn't in it. It was no longer her.

"The next day, 15 December, she was cremated. They burned her at 4 p.m. All the devotees in Indore came: over 2,000 people. It was a Sunday. The following morning, at dawn, I got up and headed off. There was no reason to stay.

"It was the first time as a nun that I had ever walked anywhere alone."

The following day, after she had finished her breakfast, I went to say goodbye to Prasannamati Mataji.

"Her time was fixed," she said quickly reverting to the subject of Prayogamati, like a pigeon returning to its coop. "She passed on. She's no longer here. I have to accept that reality. All things decay and disappear in time."

Mataji fell silent, apparently lost in thought. There was a long pause. "Now my friend has gone," she said eventually, "it is easier for me to go too."

"What do you mean?"

"I have seen over forty *sallekhanas*," she said. "But after Prayoga-mati's, I realised it was time I should set out to that end as well."

"You mean you are thinking of following . . . ?"

"I am on the path already," said Mataji. "I have started cutting down the food I eat. I have given up milk or curds, salt and sugar, guava and papaya, leafy vegetables and ladies' fingers. Each month I give up something new. All I want to do now is to visit a few more holy places before I go."

"But why?" I asked. "You are not ill like she was. Isn't it an absurd waste of a life? You're only thirty-eight."

"I told you before," she said. "*Sallekhana* is the aim of all Jain *munis*. It is the last renouncement. First you give up your home, then your possessions. Finally you give up your body."

"You make it sound very simple."

"When you begin to understand the nature of reality, it is very simple. It is a good way—the very best way—to breathe your last, and leave the body. It is no more than leaving one house to enter another."

"Do you think you will meet her in another life?" I said. "Is that it?"

"It is uncertain," said Mataji. "Our scriptures are full of people who meet old friends and husbands and wives and teachers from previous lives. But no one can control these things."

Again Mataji paused, and looked out of the window. "Though we both may have many lives ahead of us, in many worlds," she said, "who knows whether we will meet again? And if we do meet, in our new bodies, who is to say that we will recognise each other?"

She looked at me sadly as I got up to go and said simply, "These things are not in our hands."

2

The Dancer of Kannur

In the midnight shadows of a forest clearing bounded on one side by a small stream and a moonlit paddy field, and on the other by the darkness of a rubber plantation and a green canopy of coconut palms, lit only by a bonfire and a carpet of flickering camphor lights, a large crowd has gathered, silhouetted against the flames. Most have walked many miles through the darkness to get here. They are waiting and watching for the moment when, once a year, the gods come down to earth, and dance.

For twenty minutes now a troupe of six sweat-glistening half-naked, dark-skinned Dalit drummers have been raising their tempo: the insistent beats they are rapping out on the goat-hide *cenda* drums with their small, hard tamarind-wood drumsticks are getting gradually yet distinctly louder and faster and more frenzied. The song telling the myth of the god about to be incarnated has been sung, and in front of the shrine, at the centre of the clearing, the first of the dancers has just been possessed—seized by the gods, as they put it. Now he is frenetically pirouetting around the clearing, strutting and jabbing, unsheathed sword in one hand, bow and a quiver of arrows in the other. Instinctively, the crowd draws back, towards the shadows.

Behind the shrine, on the edge of the clearing, there is a palm-thatch hut, and this has been commandeered by the *theyyam* troupe as their green room. Inside, the next dancer to go on, a fanged female figure representing the goddess Bhagavati, with a red-painted face, supporting a huge red-gilt, mirrored headdress, is getting ready to summon the deity. The young male dancer who is about to take in the goddess is putting the final touches to his breastplate and adjusting the headdress, so that the facets flash in the flames.

Prostrate on a palm mat amid the discarded clothes, the unused costumes and the half-made headdresses, immobile at the rear of the hut, lies the dark and muscular figure of the man I have come to see. Hari Das, one of the most celebrated and articulate *theyyam* dancers in the area, is naked but for a white lungi, and he is lying on his back as a young boy applies makeup to his face and body. His torso and upper arms are covered with yellow paint, and his cheeks are smeared with orange turmeric, which gives off a strongly pungent smell. Two black paisleys are painted around his eyes and a pair of mango-shaped patches on his cheeks are daubed with bright, white rice paste. On these, using a slim strip of coconut leaf, the makeup boy is skilfully drawing loops and whorls and scorpion-tail trumpet spirals, then finishing the effects with a thin red stripe across his cheek bones.

I sit down on the mud floor beside him, and we chat as the makeup boy begins the slow transformation of Hari Das into the god Vishnu. I ask whether he is nervous, and how the possession comes about: what does it feel like to be taken over by a god?

"It's difficult to describe," says Hari Das. "Before it happens I always get very tense, even though I have been doing this for twenty-six years now. It's not that I am nervous of the god coming. It's more the fear that he might refuse to come. It's the intensity of your devotion that determines the intensity of the possession. If you lose your feeling of devotion, if it even once becomes routine or unthinking, the gods may stop coming."

He pauses as the makeup boy continues applying face paint from the pigment he is mixing on the strip of banana leaf in his left hand.

Hari Das opens his mouth, and the makeup boy carefully applies some rouge to his lips.

"It's like a blinding light," he says eventually. "When the drums are playing and your makeup is finished, they hand you a mirror and you look at your face, transformed into that of a god. Then it comes. It's as if there is a sudden explosion of light. A vista of complete brilliance opens up—it blinds the senses."

"Are you aware of what is happening?"

"No," he replies. "That light stays with you all the way through the performance. You become the deity. You lose all fear. Even your voice changes. The god comes alive and takes over. You are just the vehicle, the medium. In the trance it is God who speaks, and all the acts are the acts of the god—feeling, thinking, speaking. The dancer is an ordinary man, but this being is divine. Only when the head-dress is removed does it end."

"What is it like when you come to from the trance?" I ask.

"It's like the incision of a surgeon," he says, making a cutting gesture with one hand. "Suddenly it's all over, it's gone. You don't have any access to what happened during the possession or the performance. You can't remember anything that happened in the trance. There is only a sensation of relief, as if you've off-loaded something."

The second dancer is now gazing intently in a small hand mirror at the entrance of the hut, identifying himself with the goddess. As I watch, the dancer stamps his feet, ringing the bells and cowrie shells on his anklets. He stamps again, loudly and more abruptly. Then he jerks his body suddenly to one side, as if hit by a current of electricity, before stretching out his hands and sinking into a strange crouching position. His body is quivering, his hands shaking, and his eyes are flicking from side to side. The figure who had been still, silently staring, only seconds earlier is now transformed, twisting his head in an eerie series of movements that is part tropical fish, part stinging insect, part reptile, part bird of paradise. Then he is gone, bounding out into the clearing, under the stars, closely followed by two attendants holding burning splints.

Hari Das is now getting to his feet and preparing to put on his own costume. I ask: "Is this a full-time job, becoming a god?"

"No," he replies, a little sadly. "For nine months a year I work as a manual labourer. I build wells during the week, then at the week-end I work in Tellicherry Central Jail. As a warder."

"You're a prison warder?"

"I need to make a living. I am poor enough to be ready to do virtually anything if someone pays me a daily wage. It's not for pleasure—it's very dangerous work."

"In what sense?"

"The inmates rule the jail. Many have got political backing. No one dares to mess with them. The jail authorities are totally under their control." He shrugs. "Every day the local newspaper has some new horror story. They are always cutting off the noses and hands of their political rivals on the parade ground, or in the cells at night.

"In fact, there are two jails around here: one for the RSS [a far right-wing Hindu organisation] in Tellicherry, and the other in Kannur for their political rivals, the Communist Party [CPM]. The two parties are at war: only yesterday the RSS attacked a CPM village near Mahe, killing three people with home-made bombs. In Kannur it is said that the mouth doesn't speak, the sword does. If you abuse someone's father he may forgive you. But if you abuse his party, then he will instantly cut you into pieces. Both jails contain those the police catch for such crimes and they're notorious for housing all the worst political goons [thugs]. If a Communist ever ends up in Tellicherry or an RSS *kar sevak* [activist] is put in Kannur you can guarantee he won't last twenty-four hours—or at least will have lost several body parts by the time he comes to eat his next breakfast."

"Can't this be stopped?" I ask.

"Occasionally someone tries," says Hari Das. "One day a new superintendent came here from Bihar and severely punished one of the big gang leaders. Before he got home that night, the superinten-dent's home had been burned to the ground."

Hari Das laughs. "All the prisoners have mobile phones and can order any sort of act from inside the prison. The head warden once brought in a jammer to try to stop them, but within the week some-one had got to it and poured seawater into it so that it jammed itself. That was the end of that."

He smiles. "I keep my head down. I never beat a prisoner, and just try to avoid being beaten up myself. I know that if I tried to do the job properly I would soon be beheaded—I would no longer have a body. Even the superintendent has the same worry. We all just try to get through the day alive, and intact."

"And all the *theyyam* dancers lead double lives like this?"

"Of course," says Hari Das. "Chamundi over there makes wedding decorations and Narasimha is a waiter at a hotel. That boy playing Bhagavati is a bus conductor and Guligan the Destroyer"—he nodded at another dancer still putting on makeup in the back of the hut—"is a toddy tapper. It's his job to pluck coconuts from the top of the palm trees and collect the fermented coconut juice."

"So you are only part-time gods?"

"Only during the *theyyam* season, from December to February. We give up our jobs and become *theyyam* artists. For those months we become gods. Everything changes. We don't eat meat or fish and are forbidden to sleep with our wives. We bring blessings to the village and the villagers, and exorcise evil spirits. We are the vehicle through which people can thank the gods for fulfilling their prayers and granting their wishes. Though we are all Dalits even the most bigoted and casteist Namboodiri Brahmins worship us, and queue up to touch our feet."

His costume is now on and he picks up the mirror, preparing to summon the deity. "For three months of the year we are gods," he says. "Then in March, when the season ends, we pack away our costumes. And after that, at least in my case, it's back to jail."

Separated from the rest of India by the towering laterite mountain walls of the Western Ghats, the wet, green and tropical slither of coastline stretching along the south-west flank of the Indian subcontinent is perhaps the most fecund and bucolic landscape in India—"God's own country," as the Malayalis call their state.

For many centuries Kerala was the Indian terminus of the Spice Route, and the most important trading post in the great medieval trading network which stretched from Venice through Egypt down to the Red Sea and across the Gulf to India. The ancient trade in the spices and pepper that for centuries grew—and still grow—so abundantly here brought generations of incomers to this part of India, all of whom in turn slowly became absorbed into its richly composite civilisation.

Kerala was probably the biblical Ophir, from where King Solomon received apes, ivory and peacocks. It was at this period that pioneering Jewish traders seem to have first crossed the Red and Arabian seas to bring the pungent flavours of India to the Middle East and the Mediterranean world. The now-vanished Keralan port of Muziris, described by Pliny the Elder as *primum emporium Indiae*, was the spice entrepôt to which the Roman Red Sea merchant fleet headed each year to buy pepper, pearls, spices and Indian slave girls for the Mediterranean market.

The Arabs followed the Jews and the Romans. Then on 18 May 1498, the Portuguese mariner Vasco da Gama reached the Malabar coast from Europe, intent on wresting the spice trade from the Moors. The beach where da Gama landed, a little to the north of Calicut, is today marked by an obelisk. Two hours' drive farther north is the coastal town of Tellicherry, site not only of Hari Das's notorious jail, but also of one of the earliest East India Company trading posts.

Behind the grim black stone walls with pepper-pot sentry posts, and beyond the gatehouse with its Elizabethan belfry decorated with unexpected statues of two Jacobean gentlemen in cavalier breaches and wide-brimmed hats, lie a succession of spice warehouses, arsenals and dungeons. Here the very first Britons in India stocked their merchandise and made plans to expand out from their warehouses to seize control of the wider hinterland. Some of them lie here still, resting in their domed classical tombs on the headland above the breakers where once were loaded the cargoes that went to spice the stews of Shakespeare's London.

The fertility of the soil, which attracted centuries of merchants, still defines this land. Everything, it seems, is teeming with life here, and the life spills out from the backyards onto the backwaters and waterways, the wide lagoons and overgrown canals. From the steps of the canals comes the slap of wet cloth on stone where the women in smocks stand ankle deep in water, busy with their washing, or peeling their vegetables, or cleaning the day's rice amid a scattering of blue water hyacinths. Nearby, their menfolk are repairing their boats or weaving coir ropes under the Chinese fishing nets, while naked little boys stand soaping themselves, up to their ankles in river mud. The houses are covered with trellises for the climbing roses, and washing is hung up to dry between palms. Flotillas of ducks quack and stretch their wings. An egret suddenly swoops low over the water, a flash of white against the green.

All this seems the most gentle, benign and benevolent landscape imaginable; yet in reality Kerala has always been one of the most conservative, socially oppressive and rigidly hierarchical societies in India. When the British traveller and doctor Francis Buchanan passed through the area at the beginning of the nineteenth century he found caste inequalities and restrictions so severe that a warrior-caste Nair was considered within his rights instantly to behead and kill a lower-caste man if the latter dared to appear on the same road at the same time. The exact distances that the different castes had to keep from each other were laid down in arcane legal codes, as was the specific way that different castes should tie their lungis or even dress their hair.

As late as the early years of the twentieth century, lower-caste tenants were still regularly being murdered by their Nair landlords for failing to present sweets as tokens of their submission. Today people are rarely murdered for violations of caste restrictions—except sometimes in the case of unauthorised cross-caste love affairs—but in the presence of persons of the upper castes, Dalits are still expected to bow their heads and stand at a respectful distance.

These inequalities are the fertile soil from which *theyyam* grew, and the dance form has always been a conscious and ritualised inversion of the usual structures of Keralan life: for it is not the pure and sanctified Brahmins into whom the gods choose to incarnate, but the shunned and insulted Dalits. The entire system is free from Brahmin control. The *theyyams* take place not in Brahminical temples but in small shrines in the holy places and sacred groves of the countryside, and the priests are not Brahmin but Dalit. The only role for the upper caste is that, as land owners, they sometimes have the right to appoint a particular family as hereditary *theyyam* dancers for a particular shrine, rather like a village squire in England having the right to choose the parish priest.

The word *theyyam* derives from *daivam,* the Sanskrit word for "god." Some scholars maintain that the *theyyams* of northern Malabar are a rare survival of some pre-Aryan, non-Brahminical Dravidian religious system that was later absorbed into Hinduism's capacious embrace. Others argue that the *theyyams* were tolerated as an acceptable safety valve to allow complaints against the misdeeds of the upper castes to be expressed in a ritualised and non-violent manner. Either way, there is no doubt that today they are a stage on which the social norms of everyday life are inverted, and where for a short period of the year, position and power are almost miraculously transferred to the insignificant and powerless.

The stories around which the *theyyam* performances are built range from tales of vampire-like blood-drinking *yakshis, devis* and witches, and the myths of serpent and animal deities, to the deeds of local heroes and ancestors. Many, however, concentrate on issues of caste, and of the social and moral injustices that caste tensions have provoked. Frequently they question the limits of acceptable behaviour, especially the abuse of power, as the upper castes struggle to keep their place at the top of the caste pyramid and oppress the lower castes in order to do so. In many of the *theyyam* stories, a member of the lower castes infringes or transgresses accepted caste restrictions and is unjustly punished with rape (in the case of women) or death (in the case of men, and sometimes women too), and then is deified by the gods aghast at the injustices perpetrated by the Brahmins and the other ruling castes.

In one *theyyam* story, for example, a Dalit boy of the Tiyya caste is driven by hunger to steal a mango while grazing the cattle of a high-caste farmer. As he is up the tree and in the act of gorging himself on the farmer's fruit, the farmer's niece happens to pass by and sits beneath the tree. While she is there a mango that the boy has been holding falls on her, so polluting her and revealing his theft. The boy runs away but, returning many years later, is caught bathing in the village pond by the farmer, and is immediately beheaded. In atonement, the dead Dalit is deified and becomes immortal in a local form of one of the great Hindu gods; and it is in this form that he is still reincarnated in the body of *theyyam* dancers today. With the establishment of a cult, a shrine and a *theyyam*, the angry spirit is propitiated and calmed, the dead are redeemed and morality is seen to triumph over immorality, justice over injustice.

This obsession with caste infringements and the abuse of upper-caste or courtly authority, with divinity, protest and the reordering of relations of power, is something that Hari Das believes lies at the heart of this ritual art form, and he sees *theyyam* as a tool and a weapon to resist and fight back against an unjust social system as much as a religious revelation. Two months after seeing him in performance, when I next met Hari Das again to ask him about all this, he was not wearing a *theyyam* costume; indeed he was wearing nothing but a grimy loincloth, and his torso was smeared with wet mud.

"I didn't think you'd recognise me," he said, wiping sweat and mud from his forehead. He pointed to the well from which he had just emerged, pickaxe in hand. "There was one Brahmin last month who worshipped me during a *theyyam*, reverently touching my feet, with tears in his eyes, kneeling before me for a blessing. Then the following week I went to his house to dig a well as an ordinary labourer. He certainly didn't recognise me."

"How do you know?"

"There were five of us in the team, and he gave us lunch. But we had to take it outside on the veranda and there was no question of being allowed into his house. He used an extra-long ladle so that he could serve us from a safe distance. And he used plantain leaves so that he could throw them away when we had finished: he didn't want to eat from anything we had touched, and he told us he didn't want us to come inside the house and wash the dishes ourselves. Even the water was left for us in a separate bucket, and he did not even allow us to draw water from the well we had dug for him. This happens even now, in this age! I can dig a well in a Namboodiri [Brahmin] house and still be banned from drawing water from it."

Hari Das shrugged his shoulders. "Many of the upper castes have changed the way they behave to us Dalits, but others are still resolute in their caste bigotry, and refuse to mix with us or eat with us. They may pay respect to a *theyyam* artist like me during the *theyyam* itself, but outside it they are still as casteist as ever."

We sat down by the edge of the well, and Hari Das cleaned his hands in a bucket of water that one of his team brought over. "*Theyyam* turns the world upside down," he explained. "If the Brahmins advise you to be pure and teetotal and vegetarian, a *theyyam* god like Mutappan will tell you to eat meat, to drink and be jolly."

"You think the *theyyam* can help the lower castes fight back against the Brahmins?"

"There is no question—that is the case," said Hari Das. "Over the past twenty or thirty years it has completely altered the power structure in these parts. The brighter of the *theyyam* artists have used *theyyam* to inspire self-confidence in the rest of our community. Our people see the upper castes and the Namboodiris bowing down to the deities that have entered us. That self-confidence has encouraged the next generation, so that even those who are not *theyyam* players have now educated themselves, gone to school and sometimes college. They may still be poor, but their education and self-esteem have improved—and it's *theyyam* that has helped them."

I asked: "Is it that the *theyyam* stories provide inspiration?"

"Certainly," replied Hari Das. "Many of the *theyyam* stories mock the Brahmins and the Nairs. They criticise them for the way they treat their fellow human beings, especially us Dalits. Let me tell you one story of the deity known as Pottan Devam. Our ancestors turned it into one of the most popular of all *theyyams*, the *Pottan Theyyam,* and used it to show the Brahmins that they couldn't just treat us like dirt."

By this stage, the entire well-building team had emerged from the hole in the ground, many carrying baskets of stone and mud, and were sitting around on the ground, axes and buckets to one side, listening to what Hari Das had to say.

"One day," he continued, "according to the story of the *Pottan Theyyam,* the great god Shiva wanted to teach the Brahmins a lesson. He wanted them to stop being so proud and chose a very clever way to achieve this. He decided to humiliate the highest and cleverest of all the Brahmins of Kerala, the great saint and teacher Adi Shankacharya. This was a man who was very near to Enlightenment, a great saint, but who was held back from achieving Nirvana by his own arrogant pride, and his refusal to see the common humanity he shared with all men, whether high or low in rank.

"So one day, to teach him a lesson, to clear his mind of these notions and unseat him from his pedestal of pride, Lord Shiva and his wife Parvati played a joke on him and took the form of a poor landless Pullaya [Dalit] couple, and their son Nandikesan accompanied them. They were dressed like day labourers—rather like I am now—covered in dirt and mud from the fields. Worse still, Lord Shiva made himself smell of meat and drink, and swayed around as if he had spent the whole night drinking toddy. To complete the effect, he placed a great pitcher of toddy under his arm, and in his right hand he held a half coconut shell which he used to drink the spirit.

"In this state, they came across Adi Shankacharya just as the saint was crossing the narrow causeway that led across a paddy field. In Keralan society, it was always the rule that Pullaya and other low-caste persons should jump in the mud of the paddy rather than obstruct the path of a Brahmin, but in this case Lord Shiva and his family kept heading straight for Shankacharya, lurching drunkenly from side to side as he did so, and asking the old man who was coming towards them to move aside.

"Shankacharya of course was furious, and berated the three of them. How dare a family of polluted, stinking, drunken, meat-eating untouchables cross the path of a pure and unpolluted Brahmin? 'You smell as if you have never taken a bath in your entire life,' he shouted. Such a thing had never happened before. If they didn't all step down off the causeway, immediately, Shankacharya said he would make sure that all three Pullayas were beheaded—this crime, he said, not even a god could forgive.

"Lord Shiva swayed around, and said, 'All right, I admit I have had a drink or two. And it's certainly been a while since I last had a bath. But your Honour, please: if I am to get down from this causeway maybe you could first explain to me what is the real difference between you—a fine, high Brahmin, as you say—and my family here, who you tell me are so unclean and filthy? You have asked me a question, now answer some questions of mine. Answer these questions satisfactorily and I promise you I will happily get down into the mud, and tell my wife and son to do likewise.

" 'This is my first question: if I cut my hand and you cut yours, we both have red blood. Maybe you would like to tell me what the difference is, if any? Secondly, we eat the same rice, do we not, and from the same fields? Thirdly, do you not use the bananas my caste grows to offer to your gods? Fourthly, do you not use the flower garlands our women make to dress your deities? And fifthly, does not the water you drink and use in your temple rituals come from the wells that we Pullayas toil to build?'

"Shankacharya could not reply to these questions, and seeing his stupefied silence, Lord Shiva asked him more questions, and continued to berate him. 'Just because you use beautiful metal dishes to eat your food upon, and we use plantain leaves and cups of betel leaf, does this mean we are not the same species? You Namboodiris may ride on elephants while we ride on the backs of bullocks, but does that make us bullocks too?'

"This relentless questioning not only confounded Shankacharya, it also made him wonder how it could be that an illiterate, ill-educated Dalit could ask such sophisticated and penetrating philosophical questions. So Shankacharya began to meditate, even as he stood there on the causeway of the rice field. Then his sixth sense opened and instead of the Pullaya and his family, he dimly began to perceive Lord Shiva, the Devi Parvati and their son Nandikesan. Shankacharya was horrified at what he had done, and there and then he jumped into the mud of the rice paddy and prostrated himself before his lord, reciting a series of *slokas* in his praise:

> Salutations, O Lord of the mountains!
> Salutations, O Crescent-crested Lord!
> Salutations, O Ash-smeared Divine!
> Salutations, O Rider on the eternal bull!
> Salutations, O Lord of Lords!

"After Lord Shiva had forgiven him, Shankacharya asked a question in turn: 'Tell me, O Lord, why did you take this strange form to present yourself to me, your most devoted devotee?' To this Lord Shiva answered: 'Truly, you are a wise man and well on the path to salvation! But you will never get there unless you understand that all men are deserving of respect and compassion. It was to teach you this that I took this form, for I realised that only then would you understand. You have to fight against prejudice and ignorance, and use your great knowledge to help people of every caste, not just your Brahmins. Only then will you attain true Enlightenment.'

"Shankacharya bowed his head and replied: 'Thank you, my Lord. Now I understand. But in order to make the generations to come also understand, I am going to initiate a *theyyam* which will celebrate you in your current form. Before I do that, however, I will consecrate some temples where I will install your idol in this form of the Pottan Devam so that we humans may worship you.' So Shankacharya made the shrine, and it is this form of Shiva as a Pullaya that is today one of the chief deities of this part of Malabar, and this *theyyam* which is now among the most popular of all *theyyams*. It is also one of the longest," added Hari Das. "I have seen *Pottan Theyyam* rituals which have gone on for twenty-four hours.

"This happened thousands of years ago," added Hari Das. "It was a form of true Enlightenment. The great modern reformers such as Karl Marx or [the Dalit political leader] Ambedkar are really only reinforcing the lessons taught to us by the great god Shiva."

A couple of hours later, after he had washed and changed, Hari Das came to the house I was staying in outside Kannur, on a bluff above the sea. We sat drinking chai on the veranda as the sun set, and he began to tell his story.

"I grew up in extreme poverty," said Hari Das. "Like me, my father was a day labourer, who also did *theyyam* during the season. Today *theyyam* can bring in much more than labouring—in a good season, after expenses, maybe Rs 10,000 a month—but in those days earnings were very meagre; maybe only Rs 10 and bag of rice for a single night.

"I lost my mother when I was three years old. She had some small injury—a piece of metal pierced her foot—but it went septic, and because she couldn't afford a real doctor she saw a man in the village instead. He must have made it worse. Certainly he failed to cure her. She died quite unnecessarily; at least that is what I feel.

"To be honest, I can hardly remember her. All I remember is her kindness, and her kissing me and encouraging me to be good. But I am no longer sure whether the face I see when I try to think of her is actually her. There is no photograph. In those days no one in our community had access to cameras, or anything like that.

"Within a year, when I was four, my father married again. I never lived with my stepmother. I am not quite sure what happened—presumably my father thought he could not cope—but I was given to my *peri-amma*, my mother's elder sister, to look after. She lived in a different village, six miles away. The house had two rooms. It was unplastered, but it had a pukka tile roof. As my father had no money to give, my *peri-amma* had to pay for everything. I was lucky: although she was also very poor, she loved me, and was very good to me. So were my three stepsisters and my stepbrother. They were all ten years older than me, and they showered me with love.

"My father would visit every so often, and I was fond of him, though in those days fathers were fathers and sons were sons. We would never play together—he was very formal with me, more like my guru—and sometimes when he came to visit I would run away rather than face the very strict interrogation he would give me about school. He had never been himself, and was completely illiterate, so he regarded education as very serious, almost a religious affair. My real affection was soon for my *peri-amma*, who was always there for me. I'm not sure about my stepmother. She's all right, I suppose.

"Maybe *theyyam* is in my blood, because although I never lived with my father, I always wanted to be a *theyyam* artist like him. Even as a child I would play at *theyyam*, beating a piece of tin to make a noise like the *theyyam* drums. As I grew older, I became very proud of him, and the sight of him being worshipped by so many people made me swell with happiness—who would not be proud to see their father being worshipped by the whole village? I went regularly to watch him performing the *theyyam* from the age of five, and by the age of nine I was certain that this was what I too wanted to do.

"Eventually, soon after my tenth birthday, I went to my father and asked him to begin teaching me. He looked at me and said, 'Hari Das, *theyyam* is your birthright, but your body is not yet strong enough. You have to be as strong as a wrestler to be a dancer. Just

think of the weight of some of the costumes you will have to carry.'
I knew he had a point: some of the headdresses alone are forty feet
high. So he asked me to wait and develop my body, and become
stronger. This I did, practising weights with heavy stones, and
wrestling and running and training every evening after school.

"It was four years later, at the age of fourteen, that I finally began
formal lessons with my father, and it was not until I was seventeen
that I had my first performance. In between lay three years of inten-
sive training. Together we made a temporary shelter, a shack of
coconut leaves, which became my training place. First he taught me
to drum, not on a real drum, but on a slab of stone which we would
beat with sticks. This was to make me sensitive to the different beats
and tempos of the *theyyam* drummers, for each *theyyam* has a different rhythm and you need to be aware of all the ways the drummers
can subtly change the mood of a *theyyam* by altering the beat.

"After that he would narrate the *thottam* story-songs that invoke
the deity of each *theyyam*, and these I had to learn by heart, so that I
would get the words exactly right. Some are short, but a few of the
thottams are very long: there is one Vishnu *thottam* that takes two
hours to sing in full. Then, in turn, we learned the mudra [gestures],
nadana [steps] and facial expressions for each of the different
deities, as well as how to apply the makeup: it is critical that this is
exactly correct for each of the different *theyyams*, for unless the
dancer has the skills, and knows all the moves, the gods cannot
incarnate fully in the dancer—it is like not having the right equipment to make a machine work. My father was a good teacher, formal and strict, but also very patient. Sometimes that was necessary,
for I was a slow learner.

"Finally, he borrowed money from the village money lender and
bought me my first costume. Some of these are very expensive: the
headgear—*thallapaali*—for some of the *theyyams* can cost as much as
Rs 5,000, while one silver anklet can cost Rs 2,500.

"Before my first peformance I was very nervous. I was ambitious
to become a great *theyyamkkaran*, to have good improvisation and
to add lots of colour to the traditional way of doing a *theyyam*. As a
performer you can't ever be boring, people lose interest, and I was
constantly looking for ways to improve my performance; but I also

feared failure. Unlike other Keralan dance forms such as *Kathakali,* *theyyam* is not a fixed composition—it depends on the artist and his skills and his physical strength. Also in a *theyyam* there is no screen between the performer and the devotees, so before you go out for your first performance you have to be as near to perfection as you can. You can train for the makeup and the steps and the story and the costume, but you cannot train for a trance—that comes only with a real *theyyam* performance.

"For my first performance I was to be Guligan the Destroyer, and wear an eighteen-foot-high headdress. I don't think I have ever been so frightened in my life. I was worried about silly little things: what happened if I needed to pee in the middle of a performance? What would happen if I fouled myself? But in the event, my first performance went very well.

"All I can remember is going to the green room, getting made up and putting on the costume. Then I went to the Guligan shrine, and bowed my head before the deity, praying with folded hands. Usually the deity comes when you look in the mirror and see your face as the face of the god; but on that first occasion it happened even before I had looked, when I made the gesture of lifting my hands above my head. This is a formal invitation for the god to enter you. This act of worship, this call, directed at the heavens, brings the god down. If you pray to God with a sincere heart and focus on one deity with all your mind—like Arjun focussing the aim of his arrow on the eye of the fish in the *Mahabharata,* so that you can see nothing but that which you are aiming at, and the rest of the world does not exist—then that is the moment when you cease to be the dancer and become instead that deity. From that moment it is not the dancer who dances, but the god.

"Things are unclear after that. I remember ceasing to feel like a man. Everything, body and soul, is completely subsumed by the divine. An unknown *shakti* [sacred energy] overpowers all normal life. You have no recollection of your family, your parents, your brothers and sisters—nothing.

"My first sensation on coming back that first time was nervousness: about whether my god and the audience and especially my father had liked the performance. I felt a contrast between my body, which was tired from the exertions and having to carry this weight for several hours, and my heart, which felt very light, despite all my worries and concerns. There was a sensation of relief, a bit like the end of a headache. Then my father came to the changing room and congratulated me, telling me it was well done, and I remember feeling as if some great thirst had been quenched.

"After that I lost all my fear of performance, and I knew for sure that this was the sacred path I was meant to follow."

The following evening, after he had finished work, Hari Das joined me again. We went to a street restaurant in the main bazaar of Kannur, and ordered *appam* and stew. He looked exhausted, and I asked which was more tiring: building wells, policing Tellicherry jail or performing *theyyam* all night?

"*Theyyam* is the most exhausting," he replied. "No question. During the season a dancer cannot eat properly or sleep after dark—you are dancing all night, almost every night. The god blesses you and you find the strength somehow. All you can do is rest between performances, and sleep all day to recoup your strength. If you do not do this, your body will give way. *Theyyam* dancers have a very low life expectancy; most die before they hit fifty. It's very demanding: the costumes are very heavy and we use strings to tie the costumes on and these rub and inhibit the blood circulation. Many of my colleagues turn to drink, because toddy gives you strength and helps you to make the facial expressions.

"That said, all these different jobs are tough. The jail work is the most frightening, but the least demanding physically. All you have to do is wander around all day with a *lathi* [cane] and avoid getting knifed. There is no satisfaction at all in that job—the only point of doing it is the cheque for Rs 6,000 that arrives on the first day of every month. Nothing else.

"My second job, as a well builder, is different again. As a labourer you live by the sweat of your brow." Hari Das opened the palms of his hands to show the calluses and blisters. "There is some little satisfaction in that job, getting a well built properly, with all the stonework nicely done. You've met my team. Every day we shovel and dig and line the walls of wells for the houses of farmers, usually Namboodiris or Nairs. When the well gets deep–fifty, sixty, seventy, eighty feet–we have to suspend ourselves on coir ropes and pulleys and dangle ourselves down the well shaft, sometimes resting on wooden slats or discarded car tyres. It's difficult and can be very arduous. We keep going down, lowering the platform as we go, and when we hit water we have to remove the slush in baskets. Sometimes we slip, and some of my friends have had quite serious injuries that way. Very occasionally the well collapses and when that happens we can get really badly hurt. This is always a fear, but we still have no option but to carry on and to finish the job. It's dirty work, in every sense. My wife won't let me near the house until I've had a proper bath.

"As a labourer you sweat blood on the roads or inside the well shaft. But in *theyyam* you have to invest body, heart, mind and soul. If you do not feel for the story your eyes will be soulless and without expression. The blood has to come to your face from your heart. The hardest technically is the Vishnumurti *theyyam*, especially the opening scene where the demon king Hiranyakashipu doubts the existence of the god Narasimha, and to punish him, Narasimha, who is half-man and half-lion, breaks out of one of the pillars in his palace, smashes open the wall with his mace and devours him, tearing out his heart and drinking his blood.

"It is demanding mentally too. When the *theyyam* artist is setting out for a performance, however sad and despondent he is inside, he cannot show it on his face. He has to appear happy, and he should spread goodness and good cheer when he arrives in a village. But being a *theyyam* artist is also the most satisfying, and the only job of the three that really brings in both money and satisfaction.

"My wife certainly prefers it, as *theyyam* makes me famous in the villages. Before I was married, all the girls were interested in me for this reason, too. To be honest, there is a lot of unrequited love in a performer's life. They are meant to respect us as vehicles of the gods, but actually many of the girls who are watching the performance are thinking of quite different things. It's natural, I suppose.

Many of my friends say I shouldn't complain, but I don't like it. Things can get very complicated. It is difficult to lead a happy domestic life and have admirers. In this job it is important to have a good reputation—one scandal could destroy you. So I keep these women at arm's length.

"Brahmins are another problem. Twenty or thirty years ago they were very uppity. Now they are better, but they still have all the power. When they watch *theyyam* they have this sense of discomfort, as they know that the stories often criticise their caste, and seek to reform their behaviour. There are many *thottam* songs, for example, that tell stories showing the importance of doing good acts to your fellow men, reminding the Brahmins that their bad acts to those of lesser birth than themselves cannot escape the scrutiny of the sun and the moon which watch over everything. Their bad acts will not go unnoticed, and the songs advise them instead to adopt good and kind ways. Sometimes they tell this in a very angry manner. At other times these lessons are told very gently and poetically.

"One of my favourites tells the story of two disciples of a guru, called Chaitra and Maitra. One day the guru gave them one rupee each and took them to two empty rooms. He asked them to use that one rupee to fill the room. Maitra rushed out to the bazaar and tried to find something for one rupee with which he could fill his room. Of course there was nothing for that price. And then he thought: 'I will go to the garbage seller,' and from him he bought a mountain of stinking rubbish and proudly piled it high in his room. But Chaitra meditated in his room and then calmly went out and bought a matchbox, an incense stick and an oil lamp. He lit the flame, filling the room not just with light but also a beautiful fragrance.

"When the guru came to inspect the two rooms, he turned away in disgust from the room with the garbage, but happily walked into the illuminated room which smelt of jasmine and sandalwood. The song tells the listeners to ponder the beauty of the story, and the lesson it contains: that good acts and good karma will bring people to you and cause them to love you, but bad acts will disgust them and send them away.

"Despite the criticisms they contain, many Brahmins still believe and have reverence for the *theyyams,* and when their priests and temples and astrologers are unable to solve their problems, they come to us and ask the deities for advice. In fact people everywhere in this part of Kerala are still very devoted to *theyyam;* all the different Hindu castes, and even some of the Muslims and Christians too, though they can be more secretive in their devotions. I think people like it because in a temple or a church you see only an inanimate image. Here you see the god in the flesh and you can speak to him and ask him about your worries. People believe very strongly that in a *theyyam* the god speaks to them directly. That is why people will travel a long way to see a performance, and once there will patiently queue to have a word with the god.

"As for the future, it's true that many of the small shrines to village deities have gone, and many of the small local gods and their stories have been lost and forgotten. But of late I sense that there has been a revival. Some villages who neglected their *theyyams* found that their crops failed and they experienced *dosham—* misfortunes of some kind or another. So they consulted astrologers, who advised calling us back to begin celebrating the different village *theyyams* again.

"In other places, some of the more famous village shrines are now transforming themselves into big temples and people are coming all the way from Cochin and even Trivandrum to see the performances. People have even begun to sell posters and DVDs of the more celebrated *theyyams.* And the different political parties have all started supporting different deities—the RSS has adopted one *theyyam* deity, even though they are really a party of the upper castes, and the CPM support another, even though they are supposed to be atheists. So there is new patronage coming in, and it is possible to make a much better living than my father could ever have imagined.

"Certainly this generation seem much more interested than in my father's time. Back then, many of the people in the towns dismissed what we did as superstition, saying that there is nothing in the *Vedas* about *theyyam* and that it is all a load of Dalit nonsense. For all the development and technology we now have, people still have not forgotten the power of the *theyyam.* They still know, for example, that a *Pottan Theyyam* can stop even the worst epidemics, and that other *theyyams* have the power to give jobs or help women conceive healthy children. One Brahmin came to my house last week saying he had been out of work for six months, despite going to the temple and praying every day. Yet after attending one of my *theyyams* he found a job in the Collectors' Office the following day. He said the *theyyam* did what his own family temple had failed to do.

"I hope my two boys will take on my mantle when they are older. Already they are showing some skills. One is three, and the other is five. I feel good when I see them playing at *theyyam* and when they ask me to beat a drum for them. The only worry is money. Both my boys are at school, and if in future they can earn more money by learning some other skill, who knows whether they will carry on the family tradition? Some of my friends who are *theyyam* artists have educated their children and they have risen to be police officers and even military personnel. Sometimes these children take a leave of absence and come home in the winter to perform the *theyyams*, but with many professions that is impossible. As our people rise up and become more educated, I fear for the future. Who in the villages will still be able to take off three months to do this work? We will see."

Nine months later, I was back in Kerala for Christmas, and went up to Kannur to see Hari Das. It was again the *theyyam* season, and I timed my visit to coincide with the day on which Hari Das was performing in the same forest *kavu* shrine where I had met him the previous year.

I arrived early one morning, between the end of a night *theyyam* and the beginning of the day performance. People were milling about the clearing in the teak forest, plumping themselves down where they thought they could have the best view or, in the case of some of the ladies, moving white plastic chairs under a tarpaulin which had been erected to one side. The performers were sitting on a bench outside their makeup hut, yawning; one of the dancers was curled up on a palm mat snoozing in the shade nearby. Hari Das was again being made up to play the Vishnumurti *theyyam,* and while I waited for him to appear, I chatted to some of the devotees who had come for the performance.

Prashant, a large, dark-skinned man of around thirty, newly returned from the Gulf, had sponsored the performance, and was directing matters from his seat on a log at the side of the clearing. He had been away for two years in Saudi Arabia doing construction work and had liked it: "I made lots of money," he said. "Those Saudis are tough fellows, but they know how to reward their workers." He was sponsoring this performance to say thank you to his village *theyyams* for his safe return with all his savings intact. There was a nice irony, I thought, in the money of the most puritanical and intolerant of Wahhabis being used to fund such a fabulously and unrepentantly pagan ceremony.

Beside Prashant was his childhood friend Shiju, who had come all the way from his job working in the railways in Chennai for the performance. "In 1995, when I was thirteen years old, I was diagnosed with cancer," he told me. "It was non-Hodgkins lymphoma and I underwent chemotherapy in Chennai. After a while the doctors said there is only so much we can do for you—now you just have to turn to God. My grandparents, who live in a village not far from here, came and told the goddess Bhagavati about me. She told them that within a month I would be completely well. Her power strengthened the hands of the doctor who took care of me, and I made an immediate, miraculous recovery. As no one—least of all the doctors—could explain it, we all believe that it was the goddess who cured me. Since then my family have never missed a single *theyyam* at this shrine. Each year we come all the way from Chennai to seek blessings and give thanks."

We were still talking when the drumming began. Within a few minutes it was loud enough to hurt the ears, thumping into the body with an almost physical impact. I withdrew some distance from the shrine and the makeup hut, and took my seat in the front row of the crowd, as the *thottam* song of invocation was sung.

This time, Chamundi was the first deity out, a much more sinister *theyyam* than any I had witnessed the previous year. Red-faced, black-eyed and white-armed, with rouged lips, large red metal breasts and a halo of palm spines that looked like the blade of a giant circular saw, the deity emerged into the clearing rattling her bracelets and hissing like a snake. She circled the shrine, her face distorted and twitching from side to side, like a huge lizard. Her mouth opened and closed silently, her ruff of palm spikes swivelled and every so often she let out a loud cockatoo-like shriek. There was something agitated, disturbed and unpredictable about this eerie figure strutting malevolently around the edge of the crowd, glaring every so often at some individual who met her gaze; yet there was also something unmistakably regal about her, demanding attention and deference. Two priests, stripped to the waist, approached her, heads bowed, with a bowl of toddy, which she drank in a single gulp.

As she was drinking, the drums reached a new climax and suddenly a second deity appeared, leaping into the clearing with a crown of seven red cobra heads, to which were attached two huge round earrings. A silver-appliqué chakra disc was stuck in the middle of his forehead, and round his waist was a wide grass farthingale, as if an Elizabethan couturier had somehow been marooned on a forgotten jungle island and been forced to reproduce the fashions of the Virgin Queen's court from local materials. His wrists were encircled with bracelets of palm spines and exora flowers. It was only after a minute that I realised it was Hari Das. He was unrecognisable. His eyes were wide, charged and staring, and his whole personality seemed to have been transformed. The calm, slightly earnest and thoughtful man I knew from my previous meetings was now changed into a frenzied divine athlete. He made a series of spectacular leaps in the air as he circled the *kavu*, twirling and dancing, spraying the crowd with showers of rice offerings.

After several rounds in this manner, the tempo of the drums slowly lowered. As Chamundi took her seat on a throne at one side of the main entrance to the shrine, still twitching uneasily, the Vishnumurti *theyyam* approached the ranks of devotees, in a choreographed walk, part strut, part dance. All of the devotees and pilgrims had now respectfully risen from their seats or from the ground, and stood with heads bowed before the deity.

In one hand the Vishnumurti held a bow and a quiver of arrows;

in the other a sword. These he used to bless the devotees, who bowed their heads as he approached. With the blade of the sword he touched the outstretched hands of some of the crowd. "All will be well!" he intoned in a deep voice in Malayalam. "All the darkness will go! The gods will look after you. They will protect you and be your friend! Do not worry! God is everywhere!" Between these encouraging phrases in the local dialect he muttered a series of Sanskrit mantras and incantations. The personality of the deity was quite distinct from that of Chamundi—as benign and reassuring as the latter was disturbing and potentially dangerous, even psychotic.

The deity now returned to the shrine, and taking a throne, looked on as the various priests and attendants prostrated themselves before him, each offering a drink of toddy. Like Chamundi, Vishnumurti drank the offering in a single gulp. This was the signal for the spiritual surgery to begin and the devotees to queue up and approach the deities for individual advice and blessing. Vishnumurti's queue was noticeably longer than that of the goddess; only the brave—mostly elderly women—approached Chamundi.

One by one the petitions were presented. Old women asked for grandchildren, unemployed men for jobs, young women for husbands and farmers for good harvests. To each, Vishnumurti offered reassuring advice: "Your family will be showered with blessings," he said to one woman. "The evil times are over. Peace and calm will return to your family home. You will be like Saraswati, illuminating the darkness." "I will look after you," he said to an old man, "and I will take care of your sons. Both your kids are going to be fine. Don't take the path towards evil and you will always be able to lift your head in public! Never worry." To a little boy: "Listen to your parents and you will do well in your exams and have a bright future."

After an hour or so of this, the queues began to dwindle, and the drums struck up again. Such was the reassuring calm of the gods' surgery that nothing prepared me for what followed. As the tempo rose, the attendants handed both deities coconuts, which they took over to a sacrificial altar and threw down with such force that they exploded.

Then the gods were handed huge cleavers. From one side a pair of squawking chickens was produced, each held by the feet and flapping and crowing frantically. Another attendant appeared, holding an offering of rice on a palm leaf plate. Seconds later, the cleaver descended and the chickens were beheaded. The head of each was thrown away and blood gushed out in a great jet on to the rice. Then, as the drums reached a climax, both deities lifted the flapping carcasses up to their faces, blood haemorrhaging over their costumes and headdresses. Together Chamundi and Vishnumurti placed the severed neck of a chicken in their mouths, each drinking deeply of the blood for a full minute. Only then did they put the carcass down, on to its feet, so that the headless chicken ran off, scrabbling and flapping as if still alive. Only after another full minute had passed did the chickens finally pitch over and come to rest at the edge of the crowd.

One last triumphal lap of the shrine followed before the deities bowed to their devotees and headed back to the green room. There, as they stood with their hands raised in *namaskar*, their headdresses were removed by the attendants. By the time I had made it through the surging crowd, Vishnumurti had gone and Hari Das was back again. The makeup boy removed his busk and breastplate and he lay down on his back on a palm mat. He was spent, breathing heavily with his eyes closed. Finally he opened his eyes, and seeing me, smiled. I asked if he felt any of the spirit of the deity remaining in him.

"Nothing," he said. "It's all over—gone. Now there is no relationship with that state of being. All you feel is exhaustion, and lightness, and sometimes hunger too. But mostly, just deep exhaustion."

"When is your next *theyyam*?" I asked.

"Tonight. The *kavu* is about three hours away by bus."

"It's another all-nighter?"

"Of course." Hari Das shrugged. "I'm not complaining," he said. "The season may be hard work, but it's what I live for, what I look forward to for the rest of the year."

The boy who had played Chamundi had his costume off now, and was heading down to the stream below the clearing to bathe. He looked at Hari Das to see if he was going to come too, but the latter indicated that he should go ahead.

"These two months are very happy," he said. "I am very satisfied. I love coming out to remote places like this to perform. *Theyyam* has made me what I am. All my self-esteem comes from this. I am here in a village far from mine because of my fame as a *theyyam* artist. The rest of the year, no one here would even greet me or invite me to share a cup of tea with them. But during the season no one knows me as Hari Das. To them I am like a temple, if not a god. Suddenly I have status and respect."

The makeup boy was now cleaning the pigment, the sweat and the congealed chicken blood off his face.

"Is it hard going back to normal life?" I asked.

"Yes," he said. "Of course. All of us find it so." He smiled. "At the end of the season we just pack up our things and prepare to go back to our jobs—to being a bus conductor, or a well builder, or life in prison. There is a total disconnect with this life. We are all sad. But at least we all know it will come back the next season."

Hari Das got up and together we walked down towards the steps of the makeshift ghat where Chamundi was already neck deep in water, washing himself clean.

"The other ten months are very hard," said Hari Das. "But there is no way around it. That's reality, isn't it? That's life. Life is hard."

3

The Daughters of Yellamma

Of course, there are times when there is pleasure," said Rani Bai. "Who does not like to make love? A handsome young man, one who is gentle . . ."

She paused for a moment, looking out over the lake, smiling to herself. Then her face clouded over. "But mostly it is horrible. The farmers here, they are not like the boys of Bombay."

"And eight of them every day," said her friend Kaveri. "Sometimes ten. Unknown people. What kind of life is that?"

"We have a song," said Rani. " 'Everyone sleeps with us, but no one marries us. Many embrace us, but no one protects.' "

"Every day my children ask, 'Who is my father?' They do not like having a mother who is in this business."

"Once I tried to open a bank account with my son," said Rani. "We went to fill in the form, and the manager asked: 'Father's name?' After that, my son was angry. He said I should not have brought him into the world like this."

"We are sorry we have to do this work. But what is the alternative?"

"Who will give us jobs? We are all illiterate."

"And the future," said Kaveri. "What have we to look forward to?"

"When we are not beautiful, when our bodies become ugly, then we will be all alone."

"If we live long enough to be old and to be ugly," said Kaveri. "So many are dying."

"One of our community died last week. Two others last month."

"In my village, four younger girls have died," said Kaveri. "My own brother has the disease. He used to be a truck driver, and knew all the girls along the roads. Now he just lies at home drinking, saying, 'What difference does it make? I will die anyway.' "

She turned to face me. "He drinks anything he can get," she said. "If someone told him his own urine had alcohol in it, he would drink that too."

"That can't be easy to live with."

Kaveri laughed harshly. "If I were to sit under a tree and tell you the sadness we have to suffer," she said, "the leaves of that tree would fall like tears. My brother is totally bedridden now. He has fevers and diarrhoea."

She paused. "He used to be such a handsome man, with a fine face and large eyes. Now those eyes are closed, and his face is covered in boils and lesions."

"Yellamma never wanted it to be like this," said Rani.

"The goddess is sitting silently," said Kaveri. "We don't know what feelings she has about us. Who really knows what she is thinking?"

"No," said Rani, firmly shaking her head. "The goddess looks after us. When we are in distress, she comes to us. Sometimes in our dreams. Sometimes in the form of one of her children."

"It is not the goddess's doing."

"The world has made it like this."

"The world, and the disease."

"The goddess dries our tears," said Rani. "If you come to her with a pure heart, she will take away your sadness and your sorrows. What more can she do?"

It was the goddess Yellamma we had come to Saundatti to see—Rani Bai, Kaveri and me. We had driven over that morning from Belgaum, through the rolling green plains of cotton country high on the Deccan plateau in northern Karnataka. The women, who had been dedicated to the goddess as children, normally took the old slow bus to visit their mother's temple, so they had jumped at the chance to make the journey to see her in the comfort of a taxi.

It was hot and muggy, not long after the end of the rains, and the sky was bright and cloudless. The road led through long avenues of ancient banyan trees, each with an intricate lattice of aerial roots. These were cut into an arch over the tarmac so that at times the road seemed to pass through a long dark wooden tunnel, with the roots rising above and to either side of the road, like flying buttresses flanking the long nave of a Gothic cathedral.

As we neared Saundatti, however, the green tunnel came to an end, and the fields on either side gave way to drier, dustier, poorer country. The trees, the cane breaks and the cotton fields were replaced by dry strips of sunflowers. Goats picked wearily through dusty stubble. Women in ragged clothing sold onions laid out on palm-weave mats placed along the side of the road. Existence here felt more marginal, more tenacious.

After some time, a long red stone ridge appeared out of the heat haze. The ridge resolved itself into the great hogback of Saundatti, and at the top, rising up from near-vertical cliffs, was the silhouette of the temple of Yellamma. Below, and to one side, stretched a lake of an almost unearthly blue. It was here, according to the legend, that the story had begun.

Yellamma was the wife of the powerful *rishi* Jamadagni, who was himself an incarnation of the god Shiva—he had arisen out of the ritual fire while his father, the King of Kashmir, was performing a *mahayagna,* or great sacrifice. The couple and their four sons lived in a simple wooden hermitage by the lake. Here, the sage punished his body and performed great feats of austerity. After the birth of his fourth child, these included a vow of complete chastity.

Every day Yellamma served her husband, and fetched water from the river for his rituals. For this, she used a pot made of sand, and carried it home in the coils of a live snake. One day, as Yellamma was fetching water, she saw a heavenly being, a *gandharva*, making love to his consort by the banks of the river. It was many years since Yellamma had enjoyed the pleasures of love, and the sight attracted her. Watching from behind a rock, hearing the lovers' cries of pleasure, she found herself longing to take the place of the beloved.

The sudden rush of desire destroyed her composure. When she crept away to get water for her husband as usual, she found to her horror she could no longer create a pot from sand, and that her yogic powers of concentration had vanished. When she returned home without the water, Jamadagni immediately guessed what had happened. In his rage, he cursed his wife. In seconds, Yellamma became sickly and ugly, covered in boils and festering sores. She was turned out of her home, cursed to wander the roads of the Deccan, begging for alms. No one recognised her as the once-beautiful wife of Jamadagni.

Later, when she returned home and asked for forgiveness, Jamadagni was angrier still. Disturbed from completing his great sacrifice, he ordered each of his four sons to behead their outcaste mother. The first three refused to do so, but the youngest and most powerful, Parashurama, finally agreed; he cut off his mother's head with a single stroke. Pleased with such obedience, Jamadagni gave Parashurama a boon: whatever he asked would be done. Parashurama, however, was not just an obedient son; he was also a loving one, and without hesitation he asked for Jamadagni to revive his mother. The sage had no choice but to fulfil his promise, and he did as Parashurama had asked. But still Jamadagni would not be appeased. He vowed never to look at Yellamma's face again, and went off to continue his feats of asceticism in a cave high in the Himalayas. There, he was later joined by Parusharama, whose story is told in the *Mahabharata*, where he appears as the teacher of powerful mantras and secret weapons to another wandering outcaste, Karna.

The story is a harsh and violent one, and Jamadagni belongs to that class of irascible holy men who fill Sanskrit literature with their fiery and unforgiving anger. In contrast, the goddess Yellamma, like Sita in the *Ramayana*, is a victim, wrongly suspected of infidelities she never actually committed. Though she had been a good wife, her husband threw her out, disfigured her beauty and cursed her to beg for a living. She was rejected by all.

Though the story is full of sadness and injustice, *devadasis*—as those who have been dedicated, or "married," to a god or goddess are known—like Rani Bai, tell the tale as they believe that it shows how their goddess is uniquely sympathetic to their fate. After all, their lives are little better than hers: cursed for crimes of love outside the bonds of marriage, rejected by their children, condemned like Yellamma to live on the roads, begging for favours, disfigured by sadness and without the protection of a husband.

I got a little glimpse of the tensions in the life of a *devadasi* on arrival in Saundatti. We had gone to a tea shop near the lake, at my suggestion. It was a bad idea. *Devadasis* are a common sight in Saundatti, where they often beg in the bazaars on Yellamma's holy days of Tuesday and Friday, and during her month-long festival, holding small statues of the goddess on their heads. But they don't usually brave the tea shops on the main street, at least not if they are as striking as Rani Bai. Long before the glasses of hot, sweet chai had arrived, the farmers at the other tables had started pointing at Rani Bai, and gossiping.

They had come from their villages to sell their cotton at the market, and having got a good price, were now in a boisterous mood. Although both Kaveri and Rani Bai had the red tikka of the married woman on their forehead, Rani Bai's *muttu*—her *devadasi* necklace of red and white beads—and her jewellery, her painted face and her overly dressy silk sari had given her away. Kaveri was almost an old woman now, or at least looked like one; in fact she was only a few years older than me, in her late forties. Though you could see that she had once been beautiful, the harshness of her life, and the many sadnesses she had suffered, had turned her prematurely halfway to a matron, and she no longer attracted attention.

But Rani Bai was different. She was at least ten years younger than Kaveri, in her late thirties, and was tall, long-limbed and still undeniably lovely. She had a big, painted mouth, full lips, a firm brown body and an attractively bawdy and lively manner. She did not keep her gaze down, as Hindu women are supposed to in the villages; instead, she spoke with a loud voice and every time she gesticulated about something—and her hands were constantly dancing about as she talked—her bracelets rattled. She wore a bright lavender silk sari, and had rings sparkling on each of her toes and up the curve of each ear. So the farmers in their cotton *dhotis* with walrus moustaches sat there as we sipped our tea together, looking greedily at her and undressing her with their eyes.

Before long, they were loudly speculating at the relationship she might have with me, the *firangi;* her cost; what she would and would not do; the pros and cons of her figure, wondering where she worked and whether she gave discounts. Rani had been telling me in the car about the privileges of being a *devadasi*, about the way people respected her, how she was regarded as auspicious and was called even to upper-caste weddings to give her blessings. So the incident, and the open disrespect she had been shown, had particularly upset her.

When we finally fled the chai shop, to a chorus of laughter and bawdy remarks from the farmers, her mood changed. No longer was she in feisty holiday spirits, and as she sat under a banyan tree beside the lake at the edge of the town, she became melancholy. It was then that she told me how she had come to this life.

"I was only six when my parents dedicated me," she said. "I had no feelings at the time, except wondering: why have they done this? We were very poor and had many debts. My father was desperate for money as he had drunk and gambled away all that he had earned and more, and he said, 'This thing will make us rich, it will make us live decently.'

"At that age, I had no devotional feelings for the goddess, and dreamed only of having more money and living a luxurious life in a pukka house with a tile roof and concrete walls. So I was happy with this idea, though I still didn't understand where the money would come from, or what I would have to do to get it.

"Soon after I had had my first period, my father sold me to a shepherd in a neighbouring village for Rs 500, a silk sari and a bag of millet. By that stage, I knew a little of what might lie ahead, for I had seen other neighbours who had done this to their daughters, and saw people coming and going from their houses. I had asked my parents all these questions, and repeated over and over again that I did not want to do sex work. They had nodded, and I thought they had agreed.

"But, one day, they took me to another village on the pretext of looking after my sister's newborn baby, and there I was forcibly offered to the shepherd. I was only fourteen years old.

"It happened like this. The night we arrived with my sister, they killed a chicken and we had a great feast with *rotis* and rice—all the luxuries even the rich could dream of. Then my mother went home to our village, and I went to sleep with my aunt. I was asleep when the man came, around nine. It was all planned.

"I realised something was going to happen and started crying. But my aunt, who was also a *devadasi*, said, 'You should not cry. This is your dharma, your duty, your work. It is inauspicious to cry.' The man was about twenty-two, and very strong. My aunt left the house, and I tried to kick him and scratch him, but he took me by force. After that, he cheated me and never gave the full Rs 500 he had promised my father. Though I had given my body to him, he used me, and then cheated me.

"The next morning, I shouted at my aunt. I said, 'You are a whore and you have made me into a whore.' She just laughed at me. Often, I still curse my mother. Because of that woman, my life has been wrecked. For two years, I was very upset, and we did not talk. During that time, I refused to do any sex work. Instead, I worked in the onion fields here, earning 50 paise a day.

"Eventually, I went to Bombay with my *devadasi* aunt, who had promised to show me the city. We went by train and I was very excited as it was my first visit. I did not know that I would be tricked again. But when we arrived, she took me straight in a rickshaw to a brothel. There she handed me over to the *gharwalli*—the madam—who was a friend of hers.

"The *gharwalli* was very sly. She did not force me, and she was very nice to me. She gave me lots of sweets and chocolates, and introduced me to the other girls. They were all dressed up in fine clothes and good saris with amazing jewellery on their wrists. I had never seen so much gold or so much silk! In fact, I had never seen anything like this on any woman in Belgaum. I thought this was the good life. The *gharwalli* offered my aunt Rs 2,000 for me, as I was very good-looking; but she did not ask me to do any *dhanda* [sex work] at first, and let me take my time. That first month, all I had to do was to help cook and clean the house, and I was happy with that. I liked Bombay. I ate fabulous biryani at the Sagar Hotel and once when I was in the streets I saw Amitabh Bachchan pass by in his car.

"Before long, a rich man came and saw me at my duties, cleaning the house. He refused all the other girls and demanded to have me. I was scared as he was very hefty, very fat. Much fatter even than you. So, instead, the *gharwalli*, who was very clever, sent some younger boys to me. They were lean and good-looking, and a nice match for me. Eventually, I agreed to sleep with one of them. They were very sensitive with me, not like the men here. We didn't use a condom—I didn't know about them in those days.

"Finally I agreed to take the big man. He offered Rs 5,000 for me, and the *gharwalli* gave me half—Rs 2,500! It would have taken me twenty years to earn that picking onions in my village, and I wasn't even a virgin; I was already used goods. So I stayed, and even though I got some diseases that first year, I remained in that house for four years.

"By that time, I had had my first two children—a daughter and a son—and it was partly for them that I went back to my village. I lived with my mother, and for the past eighteen years I have done *dhanda* in our house in the village. After some time, I got a lover—a big man locally. He has a family—a wife, two sons and two daughters—and used to give me money. With him, I had a second daughter. He wanted more children by me, and I didn't. That was how we eventually parted, even though we had been happy together.

"Because I am still good-looking, I have been lucky and I've made good money. I can still earn Rs 200 to 300 from a single client. It's true that I sometimes feel this is not dignified work. There is a lot of insecurity. But I have looked after and married off my sister, I feed my mother and my son, and I now have eight acres of land with the money I have earned. On it, we keep four buffaloes and four bullocks. Thanks to the generosity of the goddess, I will escape this work when I have saved some more, and live by selling the milk and curd from the animals."

It was only when I specifically asked about her daughters that Rani told me what had happened to them.

"One was a singer. She eloped when she was fourteen. She came back a year later, but no one would marry her. So she became a *devadasi*."

"And the other?"

"The other had a skin disease and had white patches on her thighs. We went to many doctors but they could not cure it. Like her sister, she found it hard to get married, so I had to dedicate her too."

"But how could you do that when you were so angry with your own mother for dedicating you? You just said yourself this is undignified work."

"My daughters scolded me," admitted Rani Bai, "just as I scolded my mother."

"Didn't you feel guilty?"

"I didn't like it," said Rani. "But there was no alternative."

"So where are they now?" I asked. "Here? Or in Bombay?"

There was a long pause when I asked this. Then Rani said, simply, "I have lost them."

"What do you mean?" I asked.

"Both have passed away. Maybe it was because of some sins in a past life that the goddess cursed me in this way. One lost weight and died of a stomach disease. The other had fevers."

Rani didn't say so explicitly at the time, but I later learned that both her daughters had died of AIDS. One had died less than a year earlier, aged only fifteen. The other had died six months later, aged seventeen.

The *devadasis* stand in the direct line of one of the oldest professions in India. The word comes from Sanskrit: *"deva"* means god and *"dasi"* means "a female servant." At the heart of the institution lies the idea of a woman entering for life the service of the god or goddess. The nature of that service and the name given to it have wide regional variations and have changed through time; only recently have most *devadasis* come to be working exclusively in the sex trade.

Some experts trace the institution to the ninth century. Others maintain it is far older and claim that what is arguably the most ancient extant piece of Indian art, the famous small bronze of a naked dancing girl from Mohenjo-daro, dating to around 2500 BC, is believed by some archaeologists to depict an ancient *devadasi*. By the time of Ashoka in 300 BC, a piece of graffiti in a cave in the Vindhya hills of central India recalls the love of Devadinna, a painter, who had fallen for "Sutanuka, the slave girl of the god." There are large numbers of images of temple dancing girls from the first centuries AD onwards, and detailed inscriptions and literary references from the sixth century. The poetry of the ninth-century Shaivite saint Manikkavacakar, for example, describes adolescent temple girls "with auspicious eyes," "rows of bracelets," "heaving bosoms adorned with pearls and shoulders shining with ashes" as they decorate the temple in preparation for a festival.

Several of these early inscriptions are from the area immediately around Saundatti: one from AD 1113 can be found at Alanahalli, only a few miles from Yellamma's temple, which is one of the very earliest to use the word *devadasi*. Another, at Virupaksha near Bijapur, records a *devadasi* gifting her temple a horse, an elephant and a chariot. The largest collection of inscriptions, however, come from the Chola temples around Tanjore in Tamil Nadu, where the great Chola kings of the eleventh, twelfth and thirteenth centuries boast of gifting thousands of *devadasis*, or *tevaratiyars*, to the temples they founded. These royal temples were conceived as palaces of the gods, and just as the Chola king was attended on by 10,000 dancing girls— they worked in rotation, according to the Chinese traveller Chau Ju-kua, so that 3,000 attended him at any given time—so the gods also had their due share of devoted attendants. The vast entourages added to the status of rulers, whether heavenly or terrestrial, and were believed to surround both with a luminous and auspicious female presence.

Not all the "temple women" referred to in such inscriptions were necessarily dancing girls, courtesans or concubines, as has sometimes been assumed: some of them seem to have been more like nuns, busy with their devotions and temple cleaning duties. Others appear to have been domestic and personal servants of the temple Brahmins. A few had honoured and important roles in the temple rituals, keeping the images of the deities free of flies, fanning the idols, honouring them with sandalwood paste and jasmine garlands, "carrying pots of water in the divine presence," delivering prayers and food for the deity, singing and playing music in the sanctuary and replenishing the temple lamps.

By the sixteenth century, however, when Portuguese traders from Goa began to visit the great Hindu capital of Vijayanagara in southern India, there are fuller and more explicitly sensual descriptions of temple women:

> who feed the idol every day, for they say that he eats; and when he eats women dance before him who belong to that pagoda, and they give him food and all that is necessary, and all girls born to these women belong to the temple.
>
> These women are of loose character, and they live in the best streets that there are in the city; it is the same in all cities, their streets have the best rows of houses. They are very much esteemed, and are classed amongst those honoured ones who are the mistresses of the captains; any respectable man may go to their houses without any blame attracting thereto.

If the partially sexualised nature of the temple women is described by the early Portuguese sources, the same is evident in the great profusion of images of the voluptuous temple dancing girls that cover the pillars of so many temples in the south—Tiruvannamalai alone has several hundred. These highly suggestive images seem to hint that the modern confusion and embarrassment at the idea of troupes of young girls being kept to entertain the gods, and the priests who attended upon them, was clearly not shared by the kings and merchants who built and patronised the great temples of medieval southern India.

There is, moreover, a whole body of explicitly sexual poetry from sixteenth-century southern India in which the love of a devotee for the deity is envisaged as being akin to the love of a temple dancing girl for her client. Some of the most famous of these were discovered carved in an early form of Telugu on copper plates and kept in a locked room in the temple of Tirupathi. Although the copper plates were first brought to the attention of scholars in the early 1920s, it wasn't until the end of the twentieth century that they were translated into English, by the poet A.K. Ramanujan (1929–1993). In most, the god, usually a form of Krishna, has the upper hand: he is a good-looking and desirable but thoroughly unreliable lover who plays games that drive his devotees to despair. In some cases, the courtesans clearly don't fully realise who their client is:

> You are handsome, aren't you,
> Adivaraha,
> And quite skilled at it, too.

> Stop these foolish games.
> You think there are no other men in these parts?
> Asking for me on credit,
> Adivaraha?
> I told you even then
> I won't stand for your lies.

> *Handsome, aren't you?*

> Prince of playboys, you may be,
> But is it fair
> To ask me to forget the money?
> I earned it, after all,
> By spending time with you.
> Stop this trickery at once.
> Put up the gold you owe me
> And then you can talk,
> Adivaraha.

Handsome, aren't you?

Young man:
Why are you trying to talk big,
As if you were Muvva Gopala [Krishna]?
You can make love like no one else,
But just don't make promises
You can't keep.
Pay up,
It's wrong to break your word.

Handsome, aren't you?

In other, later poems, however, it is sometimes the *devadasi* who has the upper hand:

I am not like the others.
You may enter my house,
but only if you have the money.
If you don't have as much as I ask,
A little less would do.
But I will not accept very little,
Lord Konkanesvara.
To step across the threshold
Of my main door,
It'll cost you a hundred in gold.

For two hundred you can see my bedroom,
My bed of silk,
And climb into it.

Only if you have the money.

To sit by my side
And to put your hand
Boldly into my sari:
That will cost ten thousand.

And seventy thousand
Will get you a touch
Of my full round breasts.

Only if you have the money.

Three crores to bring
Your mouth close to mine,
Touch my lips and kiss.
To hug me tight,
To touch my place of love,
And get to total union,

Listen well,
You must bathe me
In a shower of gold.

But only if you have the money.

These poems of union and separation have sometimes been read as metaphors for the longing of the soul for the divine, and of the devotee for god. Yet they are also clearly an expression of unembarrassed joy at sexuality, part of a complex cultural tradition in pre-colonial India where the devotional, metaphysical and the sexual are not regarded as being in any way opposed; on the contrary, they were seen to be closely linked. Because of their fertility, the temple girls were auspicious.

The *devadasis* still retain this auspiciousness in Karnataka today, and for exactly the same reason: they are seen as symbols of fertility. There is, however, an almost unimaginable gulf separating the *devadasis* of ancient poems and inscriptions and the lives lived by women like Rani Bai today. In the Middle Ages, the *devadasis* were drawn from the grandest families in the realm, among them princesses of the Chola royal family—as well as from slaves captured in war. Many were literate and some were highly accomplished poets; indeed at the time they seem to have been almost the only literate women in the region. Their confidence and self-possession is evident in much of the poetry, while their wealth is displayed in the inscriptions recording their generous gifts to their temples.

Today, however, the *devadasis* are drawn exclusively from the lowest castes—usually from the Dalit Madar caste—and are almost entirely illiterate. Around a quarter come from families where there are already *devadasis* among their immediate relations, and in some of these families there is a tradition that one girl in every generation should be dedicated to the goddess.

While many medieval temple women had honoured positions within the temple hierarchy, the overwhelming majority of modern *devadasis* are straightforward sex workers; the *devadasis* I talked to estimated that only about one out of twenty of those dedicated as children manage to escape into other careers, not least because almost all of them begin work soon after puberty, and so leave school long before they can get the qualifications that might open up other opportunities. They usually work from home rather than brothels or on the streets, and tend to start younger, and to take more clients, than commercial sex workers. Maybe partly because of this larger number, the infection rate of *devadasis* is also slightly higher than that of other sex workers.

The main outlines of the working lives of the daughters of Yellamma are in reality little different from those of other workers in the sex trade. This does not, however, stop the *devadasis* from drawing elaborate distinctions between their sacred vocation and the work of their commercial sisters, which they take great pleasure in looking down upon.

Ironically, it was partly well-meaning social reform which contributed to this marked drop in status. In the nineteenth century, Hindu reformers, reacting to the taunts of Victorian missionaries, began to attack the institution of temple dancers and sacred prostitution. Successive waves of colonial and post-colonial legislation slowly broke the ancient links that existed between the *devadasis* and the temples, driving them out of the temple precincts and eroding their social, economic and spiritual position. Most recently, the 1982 Karnataka Devadasi (Prohibition of Dedication) Act drove the practice completely underground, outlawing the dedication of young girls and threatening any priest who assisted in such ceremonies with years of harsh imprisonment. All around the lake, and on the road up to the temple, the government has now put up huge warning signs:

DO NOT DEDICATE YOUR DAUGHTER.
THERE ARE OTHER WAYS OF SHOWING YOUR DEVOTION.

and

DEDICATING YOUR DAUGHTER
IS UNCIVILISED BEHAVIOUR.

For all their efforts, however, the reformers have not succeeded in ending the institution, only demeaning and criminalising it. There are currently estimated to be around a quarter of a million *devadasis* in the states of Maharashtra and Karnataka, about half of them living around Belgaum. Every year, several thousand are added to their number—estimates range widely from 1,000 to 10,000 dedications annually—and they still make up around a quarter of the total sex workers in Karnataka. For the very poor, and the very pious, the *devadasi* system is still seen as providing a way out of poverty while gaining access to the blessings of the gods, the two things the poor most desperately crave.

This is why several thousand girls, usually aged between about six and nine years old, continue to be dedicated to the goddess annually. Today, the dedication ceremony tends to happen at night, in small village temples, and sometimes without the presence of Brahmins. When Brahmins do consent to attend, they charge as much as Rs 5,000 to the parents of the girl, because of the risk they now have to take in doing so. A feast is thrown, prayers said, then the young *devadasi* is presented with her *muttu*, which represents her badge of office as a sacred prostitute. Her duties and privileges are explained to her. If the girls are dedicated when they are very young, as is usually the case, they then return to a normal childhood. Only when they hit puberty are they wrenched from the lives they have led, and offered out for their first night to be deflowered by the highest bidder in the village, usually for sums ranging from Rs 50,000 to 100,000.

Later that day, I visited the Yellamma temple with Rani Bai and Kaveri. It was a fine ninth-century building, packed with pilgrims from across the state, and we had to queue for some time to get *darshan* of the goddess. Ahead of us were a party of excitable eunuchs from Bijapur. The girls had recovered their spirits and now chatted away with the eunuchs as they waited. They were clearly happy to be in the home of their protectress.

"I feel very devotional whenever I am here," said Rani.

"You feel her presence so strongly in her temple," said Kaveri.

"She is very near," said Rani.

"How do you know?" I asked.

"It's like electricity," she replied. "You can't see it, but you know it's there, and you can see its effects."

When we arrived before the idol, the priests blessed us with a camphor lamp and Kaveri explained that the image of the goddess had emerged from the hillside. "No one made it," she whispered.

Having bowed before the deity and made an offering, I asked one of the Brahmins whether they still performed *devadasi* dedications. The priest looked cagey.

"What do we know of these women?" he said, looking around to his fellow pundits for support.

"We used to bless their necklaces," said one of the older priests.

"Then give them back to them. But now that is illegal."

"That was our only role."

"What they do is their own business," said the first. "This is nothing to do with us."

That evening, after we had dropped off Kaveri in Belgaum, I drove Rani Bai back to the house where she lived and worked, in a nearby town. This was located in Mudhol, in a back alley of the town where many *devadasis* have settled. More than a hundred worked here in a small warren of streets off the main highway heading to Bangalore.

It was a dark lane, lit by a single, dim street light. Dogs sat next to open gutters, while half-naked children played in the side alleys. It was perhaps the depressing nature of her surroundings that led Rani—always the optimist, always the survivor—to talk up the positive side of her career.

"We still have many privileges," she said as we approached her house on foot, since the lanes were too narrow here for the car. "If a buffalo has a calf, the first milk after the birth is brought to the *devadasis* to say thank you to the goddess. During the festival of Yellamma, the people bring five new saris to us as gifts. Each full moon we are called to the houses of Brahmins and they feed us. They touch our feet and pray to us because they believe we are the incarnation of the goddess."

"Still this goes on?" I asked, thinking of the attitude of the Brahmins at the temple.

"Still," said Rani. "When we are called for *pujas* like this, we feel very proud.

"There are so many things like this," she continued. "When a child is born, they make a cap for the baby from one of our old saris. They hope then that the love of Yellamma will be on that child. If a girl is getting married, they take a piece of coral from us *devadasis* and they put it in the girl's *mangalsutra* [wedding necklace]. If they do this, they believe the woman will experience long life and never suffer widowhood.

"Also," she continued, "unlike other women, we can inherit our father's property. No one ever dares curse us. And when we die, the Brahmins give us a special cremation ceremony."

We stepped over a dog, sleeping, half in, half out of an open sewer.

"You see, we are not like the ordinary whores," said Rani, as we finally approached her house. "We have some dignity. We don't pick people up from the side of roads. We don't go behind bushes or anything like that. We spend time with our clients and talk to them. We are always decently dressed—always wear good silk saris. Never t-shirts or those miniskirts the women wear in Bombay."

We had arrived at her door now. Outside, suspended on the wall of the house, was a small cubby-hole stall selling cigarettes and *paan*. Here sat Rani Bai's younger sister, squatting down and handing out individual *beedis* and cigarettes to passers-by. The sisters greeted each other, and I was formally introduced. As Rani led the way in, she continued:

"You see, we live together as a community and this gives us some protection. If any client tries to burn us with a cigarette, or tries to force himself on us without wearing a condom, we can shout and everyone comes running."

Inside, in contrast to the street, everything was immaculately clean. The space inside was divided in two by a large cupboard which almost touched the shack's roof. The front half of the room was dominated by the large bed where Rani plied her trade. To one side, on a shelf, were several calendar pictures of the goddess. At the back half of the room was a second bed—the one Rani slept in. Here were all her beautifully clean pots and pans, stacked neatly in racks, and below was her kerosene burner for cooking. Above all these, on a cupboard, were a large mirror and Rani's family photos: pictures of her son and her old boyfriend—a handsome man with a Bollywood-film-star moustache and dark glasses. Beside that were small, passport-sized shots of her two dead daughters. Both were pretty girls, shot smiling when they were around twelve or thirteen, full of youth and hope.

Rani took the photos from my hand and replaced them on the cupboard. Then she led me back to the front half of the room and indicated that I should sit on the bed. Perhaps prompted by the association, I asked her whether her auspicious status made any difference to her clients when they came to be entertained here.

"No," she said. "There is no devotional feeling in bed. Fucking is fucking. There I am just another woman. Just another whore."

"And do you feel safe from the disease here?" I asked. "Are you confident that the condoms can protect you?"

"No," she said. "There is always fear. We know that even if you persuade all your clients to wear a condom, one broken one can infect us. And once we are infected there is no cure. We will die—if not today, then tomorrow."

She paused. "You see, I know what it's like. I watched both my daughters die, as well as at least six of my friends. I nursed many of them. Some lost their hair. Some had skin diseases. Some just became very, very thin and wasted away. One or two of the most beautiful girls became so repulsive that even I did not want to touch them."

She shivered, almost imperceptibly. "Of course we feel very scared," she said. "But we must continue this work if we are to eat. We have a lot of misery to bear. But that is our tradition. That is our karma. We try to show our happy side to the clients to keep attracting them, and put all our efforts into doing a good job."

"So do you have any hopes for the future?"

"I am saving," she said. "As I told you, I have bought a little land, and one day I hope if I can get some more buffaloes and a few goats, maybe I can save enough to retire there and live by selling the milk and curds. Yellamma will look after me."

"You know that?"

"Of course. If it wasn't for her, how could an illiterate woman like me earn Rs 2,000 in a day? Yellamma is a very practical goddess. I feel she is very near. She is with us in good times and bad."

We parted soon after, and I drove back to Belgaum. Later, I asked one of the project managers of the NGO working with the *devadasis* about AIDS and how their families reacted to infection.

"It's terrible," she said. "The families are happy to live off them and use the money they earn. But as soon as they become infected, or at least become bedridden and sick, they are just dumped in a ditch—sometimes literally. Just abandoned. We had a case before Christmas with one girl. She was taken to a private hospital in Bijapur after she had complained of severe headaches. The hospital ran some tests and found she was HIV-positive and on top of that had a brain tumour. She began treatment, but her family checked her out because of the expense and took her home. When we tried to find her, the family gave several conflicting accounts of where she was—different family members said she was in different hospitals. In fact, she had been taken home, thrown in a corner and left to starve to death. We found her in a semi-comatose state, completely untended by the same family members she had been supporting for years. She wasn't even being given water. We took her straight back to the hospital ourselves, but it was too late. She died two weeks later."

"Then it's a good job Rani will be retiring before too long," I said.

"That is what she told you?"

"She said she would get some land and some buffaloes and try to make a living from that."

"Rani Bai?"

"Yes."

"I shouldn't really be telling you this," she said. "But Rani is infected—she's been HIV-positive for eighteen months now. I've seen the tests."

"Does she know this?"

"Of course," she said. "It's not full-blown AIDS, at least not yet. The medicines can delay the onset of the worst symptoms. But they can't cure her."

She shrugged her shoulders. "Either way, it's highly unlikely she'll ever retire to that farm," she said. "It's the same as her daughters. It's too late to save her."

4

The Singer of Epics

The landscape, as we neared Pabusar, was a white, sun-leached expanse of dry desert plains, spiky acacia bushes and wind-blown camel thorn. The emptiness was broken only by the odd cowherd in a yellow turban, patiently leading his beasts through the dust, and by a long, slow convoy of nomads in camel carts, pursued by a rear-guard of barking dogs.

Once, as we turned off the main Jaipur–Bikaner highway, we passed a group of Rabari women, in saris of bright primary colours, resting in the narrow shade of a single, gnarled desert tree; abandoned road-building equipment lay scattered all around them. A little later, we saw a group of three Jain nuns in white robes, with masks over their faces, pushing a fourth in a white wheelchair through the open desert as the heatwaves shimmered and slurred around them. Though it was winter, it was still very hot, and a hot, dry wind blew in from the scrub and through the open car window, furring our mouths and setting our teeth on edge, and gritting the seats of the car.

With me as we drove through this bleak land was my friend

Mohan Bhopa, and his wife, Batasi (which means "Sugar Ball"). Mohan Bhopa was a tall, wiry, dark-skinned man of about sixty, with a bristling grey handlebar moustache and a mischievous, skull-like grin. He wore a long red robe and a tightly tied red turban. Batasi was somewhat younger than he, a silent, rugged desert woman of fifty who had lived all her life in the wilderness. As we drove, she kept almost all her face shrouded in a high-peaked red veil.

Mohan was a bard and a village shaman; but rarer and more intriguing still, he and Batasi, though both completely illiterate, were two of the last hereditary singers of a great Rajasthani medieval poem, *The Epic of Pabuji*. This 600-year-old poem is a fabulous tale of heroism and honour, struggle and loss, and finally, martyrdom and vengeance. Over time, it seems to have grown from a local saga about the heroic doings of a reiver-chieftain protecting his cattle to the epic story of a semi-divine warrior and incarnate god, Pabu, who died protecting a goddess's magnificent herds against demonic rustlers. The cow kidnappers are led by the wicked Jindrav Khinchi, whom Pabuji defeats and kills. Pabuji also protects the honour of his women from another villain, a barbaric, cow-murdering Muslim plunderer named Mirza Khan Patan, and wins a great victory over Ravana, the ten-headed Demon King of Lanka, from whom he steals a herd of camels as a wedding gift for his favourite niece.

When this 4,000-line courtly poem is recited from beginning to end—which rarely happens these days—it takes a full five nights of eight-hour, dusk-till-dawn performances to unfold. Depending on the number of chai breaks, *bhajans* (devotional hymns), Hindi film songs and other diversions added into the programme, it can on occasion take much longer. But the performance is not looked upon as just a form of entertainment. It is also a religious ritual invoking Pabuji as a living deity and asking for his protection against ill-fortune.

The epic is always performed in front of a *phad*, a long narrative painting made on a strip of cloth, which serves as both an illustration of the highlights of the story and a portable temple of Pabuji the god. India has many other traditions of legends, stories and epics being told by wandering picture-showmen; but in none of the other traditions have the pictures been elevated to the status of an incarnate *murti*, equivalent in holiness to an image in a temple. The audience is primarily made up of the traditionally nomadic and camel-herding Rabari caste, for whom Pabuji is the principal deity; but other castes also attend the performances, especially the Rajputs of Pabu's own warrior caste.

As we drove through the seemingly empty desert landscape, Mohan pointed out features invisible to the untutored eye of an outsider: here, he said, on this side, where now there were just a few stumps, stood until recently an ancient *oran*, or sacred grove. It was holy to Pabu's ally and friend, the Rajasthani snake deity Gogaji, who also has an oral poem and a living cult in his memory. For centuries no one had dared to touch the *oran*, said Mohan, believing that anyone who stole the wood would be struck down by the snakes guarding it. But three or four years ago, loggers had come, chopped down all the trees and carted away the wood to Jaipur: "If people are no longer bothered by the threats of Goga's snake bites," he said, "how will they fear the anger of Pabu?"

I asked if there were still any *orans* left sacred to Pabu.

"Yes," he said. "There is one close to our village. So far we've been able to guard the trees. People only pick the fallen wood for cremations. But who knows for how long it will be safe in times like these?"

Mohan went on to tell a story of how the Bishnoi caste, who believe in a very strict ethic of non-violence to all forms of nature, had managed to preserve their khejri trees from loggers sent by the Maharaja of Jodhpur. They had hugged the trees, he said, even as the maharaja's axe men were felling them. Three hundred had died before the order was finally cancelled, and people still gathered every year to commemorate their sacrifice. I asked how long ago this had taken place.

"Oh, not so long ago," he said, shrugging his shoulders. "About 320 years back."

I had known Mohan and Batasi for about five years when I set off with them that morning from Jaipur. We had just done an event about the Pabuji epic to a conference, and were now heading in the direction of their village of Pabusar, which lay deep in the desert towards Bikaner.

Soon after I had first met the couple, in 2004, I wrote a long *New Yorker* article on Mohan, and after the piece was published, Mohan and I performed together at various festivals; but in all the time I had known and worked with him, I had never yet visited his home. Pabusar, he told me, was a small oasis of green in the dry desert, and was named after the hero of his epic; indeed the village supply of sweet water was believed to have appeared thanks to Pabuji's miraculous intervention. Now it was the tenth day of the full moon, the day of Pabu, when his power was at its height and he was unable to refuse any devotee. This time the epic was to be recited not in part but in full, at my request, and I was looking forward to seeing Mohan perform it.

On the lonely, potholed single-track road to Pabusar, the last leg of the journey, we began to meet other pilgrims who were coming to celebrate the modest village festivities which marked the day of Pabu. Some of the pilgrims were on foot: lonely figures trudging through the immensity of the desert in the white midnight. Other villagers rode together in tractors, pulling trailers full of women in deep-blue saris. Occasionally, we would pass through a village sheltering in the lee of a crumbling high-walled fortress, where we would see other pilgrims taking their rest in the shade of the wells that lay beside the temples. As we drove on, the settlements grew poorer and the road increasingly overrun with drifting sand. The fields of dew-watered millet grew rarer and more arid, and the camel thorn closed in. Dry weeds heeled and twisted in the desert wind.

In the end, although the drive from Jaipur was less than 120 miles, it took nearly the entire day. The roads grew almost impassable with sand, and without four-wheel drive we slipped and slalomed our way, two or three times having to push the car up modest hillocks, using sackcloth to give the wheels traction.

When we finally reached Pabusar, it was nearly sunset. The goats were being led home for the night, and the shadows of the milkweed bushes around the village were lengthening. It was the pruning season, and a few goatherds had climbed up the khejri trees to chop fodder for their goats, camels and cows. On the edge of the village I saw a lone woman in a yellow sari beating a kikkur tree with a long stick—not some Rajasthani folk ritual, as I had instantly assumed, but, Mohan assured me, merely an elderly goatherd trying to get the seed pods to drop for her hungry, bleating kids.

The village of Pabusar—Pabu's Well—was, like the roads around it, half-buried by drifting sand, and fenced around on all sides by dry-thorn bushes. We abandoned the car in a final sand-drift only a few hundred yards from Mohan's house, and walked the last stretch. Around the white shrine-temple to Pabu, beside a small water tank, a large crowd was already beginning to gather for Mohan's night performance of the epic. A brightly coloured *shamiana* tent had been erected next to it, and to one side a generator was chugging away like an old tractor. The farmers were in a relaxed mood, squatting in turbaned groups, sipping chai and smoking *beedis* and playing cards. Their cows had been given their fodder, and, crucially for herders in a desert land, they had also been given water—the key episode and the climactic moment in the Pabuji epic:

O Pabuji, the cows' little calves are weeping,
The cows' little calves are calling out to Pabuji.
O Pabuji, may your name remain immortal in the land;
O Pabuji, may your brave warriors remain immortal!

Outside Mohanji's small but newly built concrete house—a mark of some status in a poor village of conical thatched mud huts like Pabusar—Mahavir, his eldest son, was waiting for us impatiently. In his hands he held the furled *phad*. Another of Mohan's sons, Shrawan, whom I had met several times before, was also standing by, holding his *dholak* drum.

We had been expected earlier in the afternoon and the two boys, who were worried that we would miss the evening performance, spoke in an agitated manner to their father. But Mohan just smiled and led me over to his pump, where we washed. We gulped down a glass of hot masala chai, handed to us by a daughter-in-law. Then, reverently picking up the *phad*, Mohan led the way to the small Pabu shrine that he had built in his compound. There he gave thanks for his safe journey and asked the blessings of the deity for the performance. Then, without waiting for dinner, we headed off, through the sandy lanes, on the short walk to the tent where he was to perform.

The temple was a simple village affair, but newly built in marble. It had a single image chamber containing an ancient hero stone showing the mounted Pabuji in profile, sword held high. The temple, tank, well and village of Pabusar were all inexorably linked, explained Mohan. One night, during a great drought, Pabu had come in a dream to one of the poets of the Charan caste in the area. He told the man to follow the footprints from his door, through the sand, to a distant shallow valley where, said Pabu, you will find a stone. Take that stone as your marker, continued the god, and dig down thirty hands deep and there you will find an inexhaustible supply of the sweetest water in all the Shekhawati. This hero stone was the stone in the dream, said Mohan. Once it had been built into the parapet of the well, but now, since the new temple had come up, it was worshipped as a *murti*.

While he talked, Mohan placed two bamboo poles in the ground and unfurled the *phad* from right to left. It was like a wonderful Shekhawati fresco transferred to textile: a great vibrant, chaotic seventeen-foot-long panorama of medieval Rajasthan: women, horses, peacocks, carts, archers, battles, washer-men and fishermen, kings and queens, huge grey elephants and herds of white cows and buff camels, many-armed demons, fish-tailed wonder-creatures and blue-skinned gods, all arranged around the central outsized figure of Pabuji, his magnificent black mare, Kesar Kalami, and his four great companions and brothers-in-arms.

While Mohan set up, I looked closely at the *phad*. The durbar and palaces of the different players of the epic were the largest images, with Pabuji and his warriors in the centre, and the courts of his enemies, Jindrav Khinchi and Ravana, at the furthest distance from him at the two extremities. In between, all Indian life was here in this wonderfully lively, vivid textile, full of joie de vivre and folk-artistic gusto. The *phad* has a teeming energy that seems somehow to tap into the larger-than-life power of the epic's mythology to produce wonderfully bold and powerful narrative images. It is also marked by a deep love of the natural world: dark-skinned elephants charge forward, trunks and tails curling with pleasure; pairs of peacocks display their tails, white doves and red-crowned hoopoes flit between mango orchards and banana plantations. Warriors charge into battle against roaring yellow tigers, swords at the ready.

The different figures and scenes were not compartmentalised, but were clearly organised with a strict logic. Like the ancient Buddhist paintings in the caves of Ajanta, the story was arranged by geographical rather than narrative logic: more a road map to the epic geography of courtly Rajasthan than a strip cartoon of the story. If two scenes were next to each other it was because they happened in the same location, not because they happened in chronological succession, one after the other.

Seeing me peering closely at the *phad*, Mohan said that it was the work of the celebrated textile artist Shri Lal Joshi of Bhilwara. His family had been making *phads* for nearly 700 years, and their images had more power than those of any other artist.

"Even rolled up, Joshiji's *phads* keep evil at bay," said Mohan. "The way he paints it, the involvement he has with the epic, gives his *phads* more *shakti* [power] than any other. His *phads* have the power to exorcise any spirit. Just to open it is to give a blessing."

Mohan explained to me that once the *phad* was complete and the eyes of the hero were painted in, neither the artist nor the *bhopa* regarded it as a piece of art. Instead, it instantly became a mobile temple: as Pabuji's devotees were semi-nomadic herders, his temple–the *phad*–visited the worshippers rather than the other way around. It was believed that the spirit of the god was now in residence, and that henceforth the *phad* was a ford linking one world with the next, a crossing place from the human to the divine.

From this point, said Mohan, the *phad* was treated with the greatest reverence. He made daily offerings to it, and said he would pass it on to one of his children once he became too old to perform. If the *phad* got ripped or faded, he would call the original painter and take it with him to the Ganges, or the holy lake at Pushkar. There they would together decommission it, or, as he put it, *thanda karna*–make it cool, remove the *shakti* of the deity–before consigning it to the holy waters, rather like Excalibur being returned to the lake in the legends of King Arthur.

"It is always a sad moment," said Mohan. "Each *phad* gives great service, but eventually they become so threadbare you can no longer see anything. After we have laid it to rest, we throw a feast, as if it was the cremation of a family member. Then we consecrate a new *phad*. It is like an old man dying, and a child being born."

Batasi was now cleaning the space in front of the *phad*, and light-ing a clutch of incense sticks. Shrawan tightened the screws of his *dholak* drum, and began to tap out a slow beat. A small *jyot* (lamp) of cow dung was lit by Mohan, and circled in front of the image of Pabu. Then he blew a conch shell, announcing that the perform-ance was about to begin. The farmers of the village finished their card games and cups of chai, and began to gather around. It was already getting cold, the temperature dropping rapidly in the desert on winter nights, and several of the farmers pulled their shawls tightly around them, tucking the loose end under their chins.

Mohan then picked up his *ravanhatta*—a kind of desert zither, a spike fiddle with eighteen strings and no frets—and began to pluck it regularly with his thumb.

"We'd better make a start," he said. "The reading of the *phad* should begin not long after sunset. We have a long night ahead of us, and the flame of my voice only really starts to glow after mid-night."

I had first come across the *bhopas*—shamans and bards—of Rajasthan twenty years previously, when I went to live in a fort outside Jodh-pur to begin work on a book about Delhi.

Bruce Chatwin was then my hero, and his widow, Elizabeth, had told me about a remote fortress in the desert where Bruce had writ-ten his wonderful study of restlessness, *The Songlines*. Rohet Garh was built by a Rajput chieftain who had been given land by the maharaja as a reward for bravery on the battlefield. It was sur-rounded by a high, battlemented wall that faced out over a lake. In the morning, light would stream into the bedroom through cusped arches, and reflections from the lake would ripple across the ceiling beams. There were egrets nesting on an island in the lake, and pea-cocks in the trees at its side.

Though relatively close to New Delhi—only nine hours' drive to the west—Rohet existed in an utterly different world, almost in a dif-ferent century. In Delhi, the Indian middle class among whom I lived inhabited a fragile, aspirational bubble. On every side, new suburbs were springing up, full of smart apartment blocks and gyms and multiplexes. As you drove down the Jaipur Highway, however, the trappings of modernity dropped away, and the farther you went towards Jodhpur, the drier it got. Fertile fields full of yellow winter mustard were replaced by sandy melon beds and fields of drooping sunflowers. It was as if the colour was beginning to drain away from the landscape, but for the odd flash of a red sari: a woman winding her way to the village well.

Rohet Garh was the home of a *thakur*–a Rajasthani gentleman landowner. Secluded in his oasis in the Thar Desert, he had preserved the quiet, ordered way of life inherited from his feudal forebears, a way of life not wholly dissimilar to that of those reclusive tsarist landlords immortalised by Chekhov and Turgenev. To enter the gates of Rohet Garh was to walk into a world familiar from *A Month in the Country* or *Sketches from a Huntsman's Album*. Lapdogs careered over croquet lawns. Long-widowed grandmothers and great-aunts held court from far-flung dowager wings. Unmarried daughters would blush into their silks while their father loudly discussed their suitors.

Only the fortnightly expedition into "town" broke the daily routine. The entire family, along with lapdogs, Labradors and a full complement of servants, would pile into the family jeep. Then they would set off, over the scrubland, to the town house in Jodhpur. There the great-aunts would be wheeled to their rival temples, the unmarried daughters and visiting nieces would buy new *salwars* and the boys stock up on cartridges for their sand grouse shoots. Thakur Sahib would visit his bank manager, and his club. I would remain in the old fort, and I used to relish the solitude. From my desk, the desert scrub was flat and dry, and its very harshness concentrated the mind. In the following weeks, the pages of the new manuscript began to pile up.

Rajasthan was a profoundly conservative state, even by the standards of India. During the Raj, around two-fifths of India's vast landmass remained under the control of its indigenous princely rulers, and a fair proportion of this autonomous territory lay in Rajasthan, where semi-feudal rule had effectively continued up to 1971, when Indira Gandhi finally abolished the maharajas.

The absence of any form of colonial British intrusion meant that many surprising aspects of medieval Indian society had remained intact. On the one hand, this meant that the grip of the old feudal landlords—like Thakur Sahib—was stronger here than elsewhere; cases of ritual widow-burning, or suttee, were not unknown. On the other hand, castes of nomadic musicians, miniaturists and muralists, jugglers and acrobats, bards and mime artists were still practising their skills. Every prominent family of the land-holding Rajput caste, I discovered, inherited a family of oral genealogists, musicians and praise singers, who celebrated the family's lineage and deeds. It was considered a great disgrace if these minstrels were forced by neglect to formally "divorce" their patrons. Then they would break the strings of their instruments and bury them in front of their patron's house, cutting the family off from the accumulated centuries of ancestral songs, stories and traditions. It was the oral equivalent of a magnificent library being burned to cinders.

It was while I was staying at Rohet that I heard about what seemed to be the most remarkable survival of all: the existence of a number of orally transmitted epic poems, unique to the state. Those current around Rohet celebrated deified cattle heroes who died rescuing a community's cattle from rustlers. A long accumulation of hagiography had transformed the historical characters into gods: the story of a *bhomiya*, or martyr-hero, was kept alive, memorial stones were erected and in due course miracle stories began to spread, telling of how the hero had manifested himself to save his people after his death. Memorial stones became shrines, and over the centuries the legends grew into epics, and the heroes into gods, so that the different warriors at the centre of each epic became the particular deity of a different caste community.

In this form these herders acted as mediators between the members of that community and the heavens, and their epics grew into something approaching liturgies. But unlike the ancient epics of Europe—the *Iliad*, the *Odyssey*, *Beowulf* and *The Song of Roland*—which were now the province only of academics and literature classes, the oral epics of Rajasthan were still alive, preserved by a caste of wandering *bhopas* who travelled from village to village, staging performances.

"The *bhopa* is a normal villager until the god Pabuji comes to him," one of the Rohet aunts explained. "Then he has great power. People bring him the possessed, and Pabuji cures them."

"How?" I asked.

"Sometimes the *bhopa* just says a mantra over them. He tries to make the spirit speak–to reveal who he is. But," she added ominously, "sometimes he has to beat the possessed person with his rods, or cut them, and draw their blood."

One afternoon, during a long walk through the desert, I met a *bhopa* sitting outside a simple whitewashed shrine topped with a pair of saffron flags. He was very old and dressed in a tatty white *kurta-dhoti*. He had a cataract in his left eye, and he parted his great fan of beard outward at the centre of his chin. This man worked as a village exorcist, and that night I was taken to see him cast out the evil spirit that was said to have entered one of the village girls. In the light of camphor flames, drums were beaten, mantras recited, and with a dramatic shout, the spirit was ordered out.

Afterwards, I heard that there were still many other *bhopas*, out in the wild places of the desert, whose job it was to recite the great epics, some of them thousands of stanzas long. They were the men I wanted to meet: my Rajasthani Homers.

Before long, I began to read up on the different oral traditions, to try to discover why it was that they had survived in some parts of the world, such as Rajasthan, and why in other places these traditions seemed to have completely disappeared.

In the summer of 1933, a young Harvard classicist named Milman Parry caught a ship to Yugoslavia. Parry set off on his travels intending to prove in the field a brilliant idea he had dreamed up in the libraries of Cambridge, Massachusetts: that Homer's works, the foundation upon which all subsequent European literature rested, must have originally been oral poems. To study Homer properly, he believed, you had first to understand how oral poetry worked, and Yugoslavia was the place in Europe where it seemed such traditions had best survived.

On and off for the next two years, Parry toured the cafés of the Balkans. One of his assistants, Albert Lord, described the approach they adopted: "The best method of finding singers was to visit a Turkish coffee house," he wrote, "and to make enquiries there."

This is the centre for the peasant on the market day, and the scene of entertainment during the evening of the month of Ramadan. We found such a place in a side street, dropped in and ordered coffee. Lying on a bench not far from us was a Turk smoking a cigarette in an antique silver cigarette holder ... He knew of singers. The best, he said, was a certain Avdo Mede-dovich, a peasant farmer who lived an hour away. How old is he? Sixty, sixty-five. Does he know how to read and write? *Ne zna, brate!* (No, brother!) ...

Finally Avdo came and sang for us of the taking of Baghdad in the days of Sultan Selim. We listened with increasing inter-est to this homely farmer, whose throat was disfigured by a large goitre. He sat cross-legged on a bench, sawing the *gusle*, swaying in rhythm with the music ... The next few days were a revelation. Avdo's songs were longer and finer than any we had heard before. He could prolong one for days, and some of them reached 15,000 or 16,000 lines.

What Parry found in the months that followed exceeded all his hopes. By the time he returned to America in September 1935 he had made recordings of no fewer than 12,500 heroic poems, songs and epics—tales of the great Serbian defeat by the Ottomans at Kosovo, or of the deeds of long-dead Balkan heroes—and had accumulated half a ton of aluminium recording discs.

Parry, often referred to as "the Darwin of oral literature," died shortly afterwards, in a shooting accident, at the age of thirty-three; but his work revolutionised understanding of the Greek classics. Yet even while Parry was at work, the oral tradition was already begin-ning to die out in the cities of Yugoslavia. Since then, it has all but disappeared as a living institution, its end speeded by the bloody civil war that devastated the region in the 1990s.

In India, however, it seemed that an even more elaborate tradi-tion had managed to survive relatively intact. An old anthropologist friend had told me how he once met a travelling storyteller in a village in southern India at the end of the 1970s. The bard knew the *Mahabharata*—India's equivalent of the *Iliad*, the *Odyssey* and the Bible all rolled into one. The epic is the story of the rivalry of two sets of princely cousins whose enmity culminates in an Armageddon-like war on the battlefield of Kurukshetra; the *Bhagavad Gita*, for many Hinduism's most profound and holy text, lies at its heart, a dialogue, on the eve of battle, between the god Krishna and one of the princely heroes about duty, illusion and reality.

With its hundred thousand *slokas*, the *Mahabharata* is fifteen times the length of the Bible. My friend had asked the bard how he could possibly remember it all. The minstrel replied that, in his mind, each stanza was written on a pebble. The pile of pebbles lay before him always; all he had to do was remember the order in which they were arranged and to "read" from one pebble after another.

India's population may not be particularly literate—the literacy rate is officially 65 percent, compared with 77 percent in the United States—but it remains surprisingly culturally erudite. As the critic Anthony Lane noted in 2001, in the aftermath of the Islamist attacks on America, the people of New York again and again compared what had happened to them to films or TV: "It was like *Independence Day*"; "It was like *Die Hard*"; "No, *Die Hard 2*." In contrast, when the great tsunami struck at the end of 2004, Indians were able to reach for a more sustaining narrative than disaster movies: the apocalyptic calamities and world-ending floods that fill the *Mahabharata* and Indian oral literature in general. As the great American Sanskrit scholar Wendy Doniger put it, "Myths pick up the pieces where philosophy throws up its hands. The great myths may help survivors to think through this unthinkable catastrophe, to make sense by analogy."

While the *Mahabharata* is today the most famous of the Indian epics, it was originally only one of a great number. During the Mughal period, for example, the most popular was the great Muslim epic the *Dastan-i Amir Hamza*, or *Story of Hamza*. The brave and chivalrous Hamza, the father-in-law of the Prophet, journeys erratically from Iraq to Sri Lanka, via Mecca, Tangiers and Byzantium, in the service of the just Emperor Naushervan. On the way he falls in love with various beautiful Persian and Greek princesses, while avoiding the traps laid for him by his enemies: the cruel villain Bakhtak and the necromancer and arch-fiend Zumurrud Shah.

Over the centuries, as the story of Hamza was told across the Islamic world, the factual underpinning of the narrative was covered in layers of subplots and a cast of dragons, giants and sorcerers. It was in India, however, that the Hamza epic took on a life of its own. Here it grew to an unprecedented size, absorbing whole oral libraries of Indian myths and legends. In this form it began to be regularly performed in the public spaces of the great Mughal cities. At fairs and at festivals, on the steps of the Jama Masjid in Delhi or in the Qissa Khawani, the Storyteller's Street in Peshawar, the professional storytellers, or *dastan-gos*, would perform night-long recitations from memory; some of these could go on for seven or eight hours with only a short break. There was also a great tradition of the Mughal elite commissioning private performances of the Hamza epic—the greatest Urdu love poet, Ghalib, for example, was celebrated for his *dastan* parties at which the story would be expertly recited.

In its fullest form, the tale of Hamza grew to contain a massive 360 separate stories, which would take several weeks of all-night recitation to complete; the fullest printed version, the last volume of which was published in 1905, filled no fewer than forty-six volumes, each of which averaged 1,000 pages. This Urdu version shows how far the epic had been reimagined into an Indian context in the course of many years of subcontinental retelling. Though the original Mesopotamian place names survived, the world depicted is that of Mughal India, with its obsession with poetic wordplay, its love of gardens and its extreme refinement of food and dress and manners. Many of the characters have Hindu names; they make oaths "as Ram is my witness"; and they ride on elephants with jewelled howdahs. To read it is to come as close as is now possible to the world of the Mughal campfires—those night gatherings of soldiers, Sufis, musicians and camp followers that one sees illustrated in Mughal miniatures: a storyteller beginning his tale in a clearing of a forest as the embers of the blaze glow red and the eager fire-lit faces crowd around.

Today, however, while children in Persia, Pakistan and parts of

India may be acquainted with some episodes, the entire *Dastan-i Amir Hamza* no longer exists as an oral epic. In India, the last of the great *dastan-gos* who knew the epic by heart, Mir Baqar Ali, died in 1928, only a few years before sound revolutionised the nascent Indian film industry that itself had borrowed much of its style, and many of its plots, from the oral storytelling tradition. Now there are fears that the *Mahabharata* and other Hindu epics could share that fate in the twenty-first century, surviving in recorded forms only.

Given all this, it seemed extraordinary to find in modern Rajasthan performers who were still the guardians of an entire oral culture. Apart from anything else, I longed to know how the *bhopas,* who were invariably simple villagers, shepherds, cowherds and so on, often illiterate, could remember such colossal quantities of verse.

According to the Rohet aunts, while there were perhaps as many as twenty fully fledged Rajasthani epic poems that the *bhopas* still performed, two were especially popular. The most famous one told the tale of the deeds, feuds, life, death and avenging of Pabuji. Pabuji, they pointed out, was a Rajput of the Rathore clan, a member of the ruling line that would eventually produce the maharajas of Jodhpur as well as their own family; but at the time of the poem, Pabuji seemed to have been merely the chieftain of a small village named Kolu, in the desert near Jaisalmer.

The other great poem, that of Dev Narayan, was Pabuji's only real rival. Four times its size, older and now rarer than the Pabu poem, *The Epic of Dev Narayan* is much more ambitious: the tale of a humble cattle herder named Bhuj Bhagravat, who elopes with the beautiful young wife of an elderly Rajput raja, and so sparks a monumental caste war. This ultimately leads to the bloody death of Bhuj and his twenty-four brothers—deaths that are avenged, Sicilian style, by Bhuj's son, Dev Narayan, the legend's hero, and the god who has since become the special deity of the cattle-herding Gujar community.

Both folk epics were apparently based on a kernel of historical truth—Pabuji and Dev Narayan both seem to have been historical figures who flourished in the fourteenth century—before the mythological process began to elaborate their stories and turn them into gods. Significantly, the divinity of neither figure is accepted by the

Brahmins, and the gods' priests and *bhopas* are both drawn from among the lower castes.

According to the Rohet aunts, the Dev Narayan epic had been written down for the first time only some thirty years earlier. The person who did this was their distant neighbour and friend, a feisty-sounding Rajasthani rani named Laxmi Kumari Chundawat. The aunts said that Laxmi Chundawat, though frail and elderly, was still living in Jaipur, and they arranged for us to meet there, in her family's town house.

I found the old lady sitting on a cane chair on the veranda of an inner courtyard. The rani was a poised and intelligent octogenarian, whose fine bones were obscured by thick librarian's glasses, which perched heavily on her nose and gave her expression a rather owlish gleam. She told me that she had been born into the palace at Deogarh, from which her father had ruled his huge semi-desert principality. The purdah system—the seclusion of women—still operated then as much for aristocratic Hindu women as for Muslim ones, but in 1957 the rani had shocked her family by emerging from the *zenana* (women's quarters) and standing for the Rajasthan Assembly.

"The area where the story of Dev Narayan was set was in my father's principality and in my own constituency," she said. It was during her time in the assembly that she became interested in the epic, which she feared was under threat from television and the cinema. "When I realised that the epic about him was beginning to die out," she added, "I determined to do something about it."

In the early 1970s, the rani began to ask around to find out if any of the local *bhopas* still knew the entire saga by heart. Many knew the outlines, she discovered, and some knew parts in great detail, but none seemed to know the entire story. Eventually, however, she was directed to a village near Jaipur where an old grey-bearded *bhopa* named Lakshminarayan lived. She persuaded him to come to her house, along with another *bhopa* ("to encourage him"), while she went to Delhi and bought a tape recorder.

"He came to stay with me for ten or twelve weeks," she said. "He used to sing and I used to write. We did nothing else but this, six or seven hours at a time. We got the other *bhopa* to shout 'Wa! Very good! Wa Wa! Well done!' Lakshminarayan couldn't do it without someone to echo him, like drums on a battlefield. It was astonishing to me that any individual could remember such a long work. In my printed edition, it fills 626 pages.

"The *bhopa* told me he was only four years old when his father began to teach him to learn it by heart," the rani continued. "Every day, he had to learn ten or twenty lines by rote, then recite the whole poem up to that point in case he forgot what went before. Every day his father gave him buffalo milk so that his memory would improve."

When I asked the rani why she thought that the epics were beginning to die out, she was very clear. "When the stories used to be told, everyone had a horse and some cattle. Now, when a *bhopa* tells stories about the beauty of a horse, it doesn't make the same connection with the audience. And then there is the question of time: who has the time these days to spend four or five nights awake, listening to a story?"

"It's the same story with the *bhopas* themselves, and even the painters," she added. "None of them know the whole epic, or the significance of all the figures on the *phad.*"

I asked whether the *bhopas* were illiterate. Milman Parry had found in Yugoslavia that this was the one essential condition for preserving an oral epic. It was the ability of the bard to read, rather than changes in the tastes of his audience, that sounded the death knell for the oral tradition. Just as the blind can develop a heightened sense of hearing, smell and touch to compensate for their loss of vision, so it seems that the illiterate have a capacity to remember in a way that the literate simply do not. It was not lack of interest, but literacy itself, that was killing the oral epic.

This had also been the conclusion of the great Indian folklorist Komal Kothari. In the 1950s, Kothari came up with the idea of sending one of his principal sources, a singer from the Langa caste named Lakha, to adult education classes. The idea was that he would learn to read and write, thus making it easier to collect the many songs he had preserved. But soon Kothari noticed that Lakha needed to consult his diary before he began to sing, while the rest of the Langa singers were able to remember hundreds of songs—an ability that Lakha had somehow begun to lose as he slowly learned to write.

"Anyway, I've arranged a performance for you tonight," replied the rani. "Mohan Bhopa is coming here at seven. So you can ask him all about it then."

That night, when I returned to Laxmi Chundawat's mansion, the courtyard had been transformed. Lamps had been hung around the arches, amid the tangling bougainvillea. Thin white mattresses had been laid out on the ground, along with round silk bolsters to lean on, and at the end of the cloister, stretched between two poles, a *phad* had been unfurled.

"The *bhopas* have always used the *phad* as part of their performance," the rani explained. "It's a very ancient tradition. If you look at the paintings from the caves in Central Asia, such as Dunhuang"—in western China—"you'll see images of itinerant monks and storytellers with the scrolls they used then. The *phads* are the last survival of that tradition. The *bhopas* like to say that the *phad* has all nine of the essences, or *navras*, of classical Indian aesthetics—love, war, devotion and so on—in it. But in particular they say it is so full of bravery that when you tell the tale the grass gets burned around it."

At first, I didn't notice Mohan and his family squatting in the shadows. As Mohan supervised, Batasi swept the ground around the *phad* and sprinkled it with water, while Shrawan cradled his *dholak* on his knees. Mohan lit incense sticks at the base of the *phad*. Then all three of them raised their palms in the gesture of prayer to the scroll.

Before long, Laxmi Chundawat arrived with her guests, and she gave the signal for Mohan to begin. He picked up his *ravanhatta* as Batasi held up the lamp to illuminate the *phad*. Mohan played an instrumental overture, then, accompanied by his son on the *dholak*, he began to sing in a voice so filled with solemnity and sadness that even a non-Mewari speaker could tell it was some sort of elegiac invocation of the hero. Every so often, as Batasi held up the lamp, he would stop, point with his bow to an illustration on the *phad* and then recite a line of explanatory verse, the *arthav*, all the while plucking at the string with his thumb.

At the end of each *sloka*, Batasi would step forward, fully veiled, and sing the next passage, before handing the song back to her husband. As the story unfolded, and the husband and wife passed the *slokas* back and forth, the tempo increased, and Mohan began to whirl and dance, jiggling his hips and stamping his feet so as to ring the bells, and shouting out, "Aa-ha! Hai! Wa-hai!" Occasionally, as the audience clapped, he would put down his zither to dance with both hands raised, moving along the length of the *phad* with surprisingly supple and delicate and almost feminine movements.

During the performance, I asked another guest, who understood Mewari, one of the five dialects of Rajasthan, if he could check Mohan Bhopa's rendition against a transcription by John D. Smith, of Cambridge University, of a version performed in a different part of Rajasthan in the 1980s. Give or take a couple of turns of phrase, and the occasional omitted verse, the two versions were nearly identical, he said. And there was nothing homespun about Mohan Bhopa's language, he added. It was delivered in incredibly fine if slightly archaic and courtly Mewari diction.

In Yugoslavia, Milman Parry had been excited by the way that his poets recomposed and improvised their work as they recited it: each performance was unique. Yet, from what I could gather of the Rajasthani epics, they were regarded as sacred texts, their form strictly fixed. *Bhopas* such as Mohan were no more free to tamper with the text than, say, a Catholic priest was free to alter the words of consecration at the holiest moment of the Mass. In this sense, they were still like Homer's epics, for both the *Iliad* and the *Odyssey* invoke the gods at the beginning.

Mohan sang one of the most famous episodes: the Story of the She-Camels. This follows the wedding of Pabuji's favourite niece, Kelam, to his friend the snake deity Gogaji. The wedding guests give fabulous gifts: diamonds, pearls and "a fine dress of the best Deccani cloth to wear," carriages and strings of gold bells for Kelam's horses, herds of "excellent white cows" and "swaying elephants." Then comes Pabuji's turn. Instead of producing a gift, he makes a vow: "I shall plunder she-camels from Ravana the Demon King of Lanka," he says. The wedding guests all laugh, because no one in Rajasthan had ever seen a camel and they were not quite sure whether such a beast existed. Gogaji, Kelam's husband, is asked, "What kind of wedding gift did Pabuji give you?" and he replies:

O mother, Pabuji's wedding gift wanders and grazes in Lanka.
Who knows whether it is like a hill?
Who knows whether it is like a mountain?
Who knows whether it has five heads or ten feet?
But he has given me a kind of animal that I have never seen.

This episode was, incidentally, one which particularly interested Komal Kothari, because it linked the Pabuji epic with one of the great classical Sanskrit epics, the *Ramayana,* in which the hero, Lord Ram, also goes to Lanka to fight Ravana, although in the case of the *Ramayana* the hero is trying to rescue not camels, but his kidnapped wife, the goddess Sita, whom Ravana had abducted and was in the process of trying to seduce. For Kothari, the episode was an indication of how, when dealing with epics, distinctions between "classic" epics and "folk" epics had little meaning. They were, he believed, two tributaries of the same great river. The passage is also especially sacred to the Rabari cattle herders, who regard it as their myth of origin.

After Mohan had sung for a couple of hours, there was a break while the rani's guests headed off for dinner. I asked Mohan for whom he normally performed—the local landowners, perhaps? He smiled and shook his head. No, he said, it was usually camel drivers, cowherds and his fellow villagers. Their motives, as he described them, were less to hear the poetry than to use him as a sort of supernatural veterinary service.

"People call me in whenever their animals fall sick," he said "Camels, sheep, buffaloes, cows—any of these. Pabuji is very powerful at curing sickness in beasts. The farmers send a message for us to come, and we go and recite—always at night, never during the day: it is almost a sin to read the *phad* after sunrise.

"Pabuji is also good at curing any child who is possessed by a djinn," he added. "On completion of the performance at dawn, the parents light a *jyot*. Seven times they put a holy thread around the flame, put seven knots in it, then they place this *tanti* [amulet] around the child's neck. No djinns can stay after Pabu has come in this form."

"So does Pabuji enter you while you perform?"

"How can I do it unless the spirit comes?" Mohan said. "You are educated. I am not, but I never forget the words, thanks to Pabuji. It would be impossible to recite the epic without some special blessings from Pabuji. As long as I invoke him at the beginning, and light a *jyot* in his honour, all will be well. Once he comes, he forces us on to recite more, and dance more. We feel the force of him there, demanding we give everything we have. There is no trance—it is not possession. But wherever we invoke him and perform, then we feel him. And so do all the demons and evil spirits—they just run away. No ghosts, no spirits can withstand the power of this story."

Mohan smiled, and twirled the ends of his moustache. "The *phad* is his temple," he said. "The deity resides there, asleep until I wake him with the dance. Sometimes, when we recite the epic, towards dawn the lamp glows white. It happens when we reach the crux of the story—when Pabuji gives water to the stolen cattle that he has saved. At that point we know that Pabuji is pleased, that things are starting to happen, and I am empowered. It's usually around 4 a.m. Then I can glimpse the future . . . But it's very rare, and happens only when we do a complete performance. When this happens, and I complete the *phad,* there is a wonderful sense of well-being, and complete peace."

He added, "The lampblack from the lamp that glows in this way is very powerful. It can be used to heal anything."

It was the old primeval link between storytellers and magic, the shaman and the teller of tales, still intact in twenty-first-century Rajasthan. "So you are as much a healer, a curer of the sick, as a storyteller?" I asked.

"Of course," Mohan said. "But it is thanks to Pabuji. It is he who cures. Not me."

Five years after this first meeting, on the morning after Mohan's night recitation of the epic in his home village of Pabusar, the *bhopa* and I sat down on a charpoy outside his house. The bright sun of the day before had given way to massing cumulus, and a strange grey light played over the desert and the village. The sun was now the colour of steel.

Mohan had sung the epic until dawn, and had slept for only four or five hours before being woken by the visit of a neighbour, a family of bangle sellers who had dropped in for a chat. Now it was mid-morning and we sat looking out at a very rare but highly auspicious event in Pabusar: clouds massing for the winter rains. Rarer still, a few drops were actually falling on the ground.

"We call this rain the *mowat*," said Mohanji, smiling brightly. "Even a few drops are wonderful for the wheat and grain. One or two showers will give enough forage and fodder for the sheep and the goats until the monsoon. Four or five showers and even the cows will be happy."

"Aren't you tired?" I asked. "You were performing all night."

"Sleep doesn't bother me," he said. "We are friends of sleeplessness. I'll happily do another performance tonight. After all these years I'm used to it."

Chai was brought, and *parathas*, and as we sat eating our late breakfast, I asked Mohan to tell me about his childhood, and how he had first come to be a *bhopa*. As we talked, his younger children and grandchildren began to cluster around to listen.

"I was born and brought up right here," said Mohan. "For three generations my family have held this land, and this is where the family have lived and died.

"My father was a *bhopa* before me. He was very famous in his time—his name was Girdhari Bhopa. He used to be called to give performances even 300 miles away, and he made a very good living.

All my ancestors—my grandfather, his father, his father before him—all were *bhopas* of Pabuji, but it was my father who made the family famous. He had all the three different skills you need for reading the *phad*: dancing, reciting and playing the *ravanhatta*. When he performed, he was such a fine dancer people would look at his feet. When he sang, they looked at his face; and when he played, they looked at his *ravanhatta*.

"We are of the Nayak caste. Our ancestors were close to Pabu, and used to look after his horses. Ever since the time Pabuji ascended to heaven in his palanquin, we have glorified his name, and read the *phad* which commemorates him. No one can learn the epic from outside our caste—it is impossible. You have to be born to this.

"That said, not everyone born to this family has the heart—the *hirtho*—or the head, to remember the epic and to do this work. Of my five sons, only one is a practising *bhopa*. Other jobs are easier and pay better. But if you have the heart, and can perform well, then this is still a good way of making a living.

"The first step is to teach a boy to dance. He should come to as many of the *phad* readings as he can, and help to entertain the audience by dancing beside his father. By the age of twelve you can see whether the boy is suitable for further training. You can see if he has a sense of rhythm, can handle a *ravanhatta*, and if he has a good memory.

"It was my father that attracted me to become a *bhopa*. He was so good! I was very proud of him, and learned the *phad* inspired by his example. I was the youngest of four brothers and as a child this left me free to do what I wanted: to play *gindi*—village hockey—or to take my father's herd of goats out to graze. I was always with all the other boys of the village. But even at that stage in my life, when they were playing *gindi* or cricket, all I really wanted to do was to read the *phad*. I always tried to see my father's performances, and during the day, when my father was out, or perhaps was sleeping after a night of singing, I would pick up his *ravanhatta* and repeat a few songs or lines, the way we all saw him doing.

"I was too shy to play or to sing in front of him, at least at first. He was a very kind man, but he would quickly point out if I had missed a line, or pointed at the wrong image on the *phad*. I learned the epic line by line, and knew it in its entirety by the time I was sixteen. I also knew where every incident was located on the *phad*.

"The *phad* is very complex, but if you learn very young, the complexity does not become a burden: instead you learn to appreciate how wonderful and abundant and full of life it is. I love the richness of it, and a good audience appreciates the complexity too. Having so many different layers gives pleasure to the audience. But if you leave learning it too late, you may never remember it properly, and eventually give it up. Luckily, I taught Shrawan the same way my father taught me, and now Shrawan knows the *phad* nearly as well as I do.

"I got married at the age of sixteen. But I didn't start reciting the epic professionally until I was twenty, because my wife was only nine when we got married. Batasi was of course then too young to perform with me, so I had to wait until she grew up and learned the epic. At the age of twelve she was brought to my house, and from that point I kept us both busy by becoming her teacher. Although her father was also a *bhopa*, she didn't come with much knowledge of the *phad* from her parents: she had learned only a little from her mother, along with some *bhajans*. So every morning, early on, I would sing to her and she would follow me, repeating the same stanza, just as we do at a performance. She picked it up very fast, and within three years she was able to sing while I played the *ravanhatta* for her.

"In our community, we marry young. The choice of a wife is a great gamble, because at nine you can't really tell whether a woman can sing or not, yet this woman will have to be your professional partner in the reading of the *phad*, as well as your wife. A man cannot recite Pabuji's epic on his own. He needs his wife to support him, or else people will not enjoy and appreciate the performance, however good he is. My father was very lucky: my mother was a great singer and had a wonderful voice. Few women could sing as high as her, or maintain such a pitch for a long period. I was also very lucky: Batasi also had a very nice voice, though to be honest she is not quite the equal of my mother.

"As with so much in a man's life, the choice of a wife is all. Performing together gives a great opportunity for a couple to come together. We actually get into a competition as to who sings better, or picks up the transitions more cleanly. That game goes on all night, and brings love between us.

"Sadly my eldest son has not been so lucky. He wanted to become a *bhopa* but his wife turned out to be completely tone deaf, so he has had to become a manual labourer: he now works building roads. He only sings occasionally in hotels for a little extra money. There is no question that if his wife could sing, he would now be reading the *phad*, and probably earning better money. But there is nothing to be done.

"By the time I was twenty, my father's fame was such that it was easy for me to find work. People assumed that I would inherit something of my father's talents. But there were drawbacks too. When I first began to perform, everyone wanted to hear my father rather than me. Even if he was just listening in the audience, and I was performing with Batasi, still my father would be made to come up and sing a few songs. He had a wonderful voice, and I can't even begin to equal him; but I do think I have become the better *ravanhatta* player. His had only two tuning pegs and just look at the number of keys on mine!

"It is very rare that the whole *phad* is sung these days. People want to hear individual episodes, and you can sing them in whatever order you like. But it is good to have continuity in the episodes, and you have to learn to get the timing right: certain episodes should only be sung at certain hours of the night: for example the episode of Pabuji's marriage should always come at midnight, if at all possible.

"We Nayaks are from a very low caste. At some point in our history we became nomads, and so fell from the high position we once had: people never trust nomads. Still to this day we cannot eat or drink in the house of many of the people in this village. But when we recite or perform as *bhopas*, this brings us respect. I may not sit at the same level as the Rajputs or the Brahmins, but they come to see me here, they commission me to read the *phad* for them and they are happy and proud about my success and my fame in the villages nearby. They tell everyone that in Pabusar we have the best and most powerful *bhopa* in all the Shekhawati.

"Although it is our singing and performance that people talk most about, sometimes I think it is our healing powers that people are most grateful for. My father in particular found that reading the *phad* of Pabuji gave him the gifts of prophecy and healing. There was one case when a boy was bitten by a cobra. My father was fifteen miles from where this took place, but he had an insight that something had happened and he immediately stopped what he was doing, and set out in the midday sun to walk to that village.

"He passed through two villages on the way and they all called out to him: what brings you here, Girdhariji? He replied, 'Someone needs me, otherwise a calamity will happen.' When he arrived at the village in question, he went straight to the headman, saying, 'Bring the boy that is ill to me in the shrine of Pabuji immediately.' By this stage the boy was very swollen, but they brought him to my father on a stretcher, weeping and wailing as they were sure he would die. But my father took some bitter leaves from his pouch and fed them to the boy, assuring him and his family that all would be well. By the following morning, the boy was completely cured.

"There were many stories of this sort about my father. He was a great healer: headache, body ache, stomach ache, indigestion: he could cure any of these with a night reading of the *phad* and a handful of herbs.

"I am not the healer he was. But people still come to me, especially for curing their animals, and for exorcising djinns. I find this work very easy. I don't do much with the animals: just open the *phad*, give it some incense, put a *tanti* of Pabu around the neck of the animal and let Pabuji do the rest. It is the same with exorcism: it is not so much me as the *phad* of Pabu that does the work. As soon as I spread open his *phad*, all the djinns and bad spirits fly away from its power. Some djinns take longer than others, and several times it has taken a full recitation of the epic to take the spirit out of the person; but I have never yet come across any who can resist its power completely. Sooner or later, I will touch the person with the *phad* and the spirit will flee, shouting out, 'I am burning! I am burning!'

"Because of the power of the *phad*, we are careful never to treat it casually. To make sure it is never damaged, we keep it rolled up most of the time. I do not perform during the rains, in case the *phad* gets damaged with water. When I am home, I hang it rolled up above my bed, so that dogs or cats or rats cannot hurt it. That way it also blesses our family. If we ill-treat the *phad*, or make some mistake, Pabuji will usually appear in a dream and inform me of the wrong I have done. The following morning I will offer a coconut and ask for forgiveness at his temple. If it is a more serious matter, I will also offer thirteen pounds of jaggery to the cows of the village.

"Some of the more educated people in the village these days like to show off, and say they do not believe in the healing power of the *phad*. Also there is some vet in Bikaner who has begun telling people not to summon the *bhopas*, and who says that it's just superstition and faith healing. Maybe in part they are right: maybe faith and trust do play their part. But most people here just laugh if someone tells them that a doctor or a vet has more power than Pabuji. I certainly do. Ha! Show me the doctor or even the vet who could bring camels all the way from Lanka."

That evening, after sunset, Mohan continued his performance of the epic. The first night had taken the story up to the episode of Goga's wedding to Kelam. The second opened with the story of the she-camels.

Watching the epic performed in a village setting where everyone was familiar with not just the plot but the actual text of the poem was a completely different experience to seeing it done before the sort of urban, middle-class audience I had previously seen Mohan perform to.

The farmers and villagers were all sitting and squatting on a red and black striped *durree* under the awning of the tents, and were wrapped up against the cold with scarves and shawls and mufflers. Rather than sitting back and enjoying a formal performance, as the middle-class audience had done, the villagers joined in, laughing loudly at some points, interrupting in others, joking with Mohan and completing the final line of each stanza. Sometimes, individuals got up to offer Mohan a Rs 10 note, usually with a request for a particular song or *bhajan*.

Three generations of the family performed: as well as Mohan and Batasi, Shrawan was on *dholak;* the eldest son, Mahavir, also joined in with his *ravanhatta;* and Mahavir's naughty four-year-old son, Onkar, Mohan's eldest grandson, danced alongside his grandfather in a white *kurta-dhoti.* For three hours the family sang without a break, and the audience cheered and clapped.

"Because the *phad* is dedicated to our god Pabuji, we are never allowed to get up in the middle," said the village goldsmith, who was sitting next to me. "Until the *bhopaji* gets tired and stops for chai, we have to sit and listen out of respect—even until dawn."

"But now that we have TV our children don't like to listen so much," added Mr. Sharma, one of the village Brahmins, who had earlier insisted on taking me away for what he called "a pure vegetarian dinner." "The younger generation prefer the CD with the main points of the story. It takes only three or four hours maximum."

The idea that the oral tradition was seriously endangered was something I had heard repeated ever since I first began reading about the oral epics of Rajasthan. The Cambridge academic John D. Smith did his PhD on the *bhopas* of Pabuji in the 1970s. When he returned to make a documentary on the subject twenty years later, he found that many of the *bhopas* he had worked with had given up performing, and instead taken up work pedalling cycle rickshaws or sweeping temples. They told him that fewer and fewer people were interested in the performances, while the Rabari nomads who were once the main audience were themselves selling their flocks and drifting off to the cities. "Having lost their flocks," he wrote, "they lost their chief connection with Pabuji, who is above all associated with the welfare of livestock."

Another, still more serious threat that Smith identified was the DVDs and cable channels, and their broadcasting of the great mainstream Sanskrit epics, which he believed had begun to have a "standardising effect on Hindu mythology, which will inevitably weaken local variants, such as the Pabuji story." There is no question that TV and film are formidable rivals: when the *Mahabharata* was broadcast on the Indian state-run TV channel Doordashan in the early 1990s, viewing figures for the series never sank beneath 75 percent, and at one point were said to have risen to 95 percent, an estimated audience of some 600 million people. Everyone who could stopped what they were doing to sit in front of whatever television was available.

In villages across South Asia, hundreds of people would gather around a single set to watch the gods and demons play out their destinies. In the noisiest and most bustling cities, trains, buses and cars were suddenly stilled, and a strange hush came over the bazaars. In Rajasthan, audiences responded by offering *aarti* and burning incense sticks in front of their television sets, just as they did to the *bhopa's phad*, the portable temple of the *phad* giving way to the temporary shrine of the telly.

Some *bhopas* had clung to their tradition, wrote Smith, but in a bastardised form, singing snatches of the epic for tourists in the Rajasthan palace hotels, or providing "exotic" entertainment in the restaurants of Delhi and Bombay. Either way, Smith concluded that "The tradition of epic performance is rapidly dying . . . Thus a tradition that was still flourishing in the 1970s—though even then promoting attitudes that seemed to belong to a much earlier age—has almost completely lapsed."

When I had first read this, its grim prognosis sounded all too likely. But as I sat now in a tent full of enthusiastic Pabuji devotees, Smith's predictions seemed unnecessarily extreme and gloomy. During an interval in the performance, while Mohan stopped for a glass of chai, and Mahavir continued to entertain the audience with a Hindi film song, I asked Mohan what he could possibly do to hold out against Bollywood and the TV, and if he was worried about the future. Were the epics merely going to become stories watched on television and borrowed from video libraries? What could the *bhopas* do to save their audiences?

Mohanji shrugged. "It's true there is increasingly a problem with ignorance," he said. "Here in Pabusar it is still fine. But in the towns and cities the younger generation know nothing of Pabuji. They don't understand the meaning. If they listen it's because of the music and dancing. They don't know the *hunkara*—the correct responses—and they are always asking for irrelevant songs: new *filmi* ones from the latest movie that have nothing to do with the *phad*. Earlier people just wanted a pure recitation of Pabu—nothing else.

"I am always trying to improve my singing," he added. "And for the younger generation I try to put in the occasional joke when people are getting sleepy. Nothing Bollywoodish or vulgar, just enough to grab attention in between scenes. It's not easy for people to concentrate for eight hours—though here in the villages, where there are no distractions, few get up while I am performing."

I asked: "Will the *phad* survive?"

"Oh yes," he said firmly. "It will. It has to. For all that has changed, it is still at the centre of our life, and our faith, and our dharma."

This, it seemed to me, was the key, and the answer to the question of how it was that the Rajasthani epics were still living in a way that the *Iliad* and the other epics of the West were not. The poems had been turned into religious rituals and the *bhopas* had become receptacles for the messages of the gods, able to penetrate the wall—in India always a fairly porous wall—between the divine and the mundane.

Moreover, the gods in question were not distant and metaphysical beings but deified locals to whom the herders could relate and who, in turn, could understand the villagers' needs. The people of Pabusar certainly took care to propitiate the great "national" gods, like Shiva and Vishnu, whom they understood as controlling the continuation of the wider cosmos, but for everyday needs they prayed to the less remote, less awesome figures of their local god-kings and heroes who knew and understood the intimacies of the daily life of the farmers in a way that the great gods could not.

"In this village, everyone still loves the epic as much as they ever did," said Mohan. "There really is very little difference from the response I saw to my father's performances when I was a boy. It's true that some of the old customs have gone: when I was growing up, for example, if a water buffalo delivered a calf, the first milk and the first yoghurt were always offered to Pabu. These days no one seems to bother.

"And then there is a feeling that Pabuji himself is a little more distant than he used to be. When I was Onkar's age everyone in the village used to hear the noise of Pabuji riding through the village at night, circling the houses and the temple, guarding us from demons and epidemics. But it has been many years now since I heard the sound of his hooves. I don't know why that is. Perhaps because we have less faith than we used to, or because we show him less devotion.

"But you asked about the *phad*," he added. "Yes, here at least the *phad* has survived. Everyone knows it."

I asked why he thought that was.

"You see," said Mohan, "this village was founded by Pabuji, so we are all of us great devotees. We don't ignore the other gods: they are wonderful and powerful in their own way, and their own place. But here if we have a problem we naturally seek first the help of Pabu."

"Especially if it is a problem with an animal," said Mr. Sharma. "That is what he is most famous for."

"The great gods are here of course," added the goldsmith. "But Pabuji is close to us, and when we need immediate help it is more sensible to ask him."

"Pabu is a Rajput," said a man in a turban, who had also been listening in. "We people who worship Pabu are comfortable with his company. Like us, he eats meat and drinks liquor also."

"He understands us and knows our fields and our animals."

"He is a god from our own people," said Mohan. "He is like us."

"Not that the other gods are far away," added Mr. Sharma. "Gods are gods. Whatever god you worship, he is close to you."

"But it's like applying to the village *sarpanch* [headman]," said Mohan, "rather than asking the prime minister. Naturally we are closer to the *sarpanch*."

I wondered whether this lack of a devotional following was the reason that the great Indian Muslim epic, the *Dastan-i Amir Hamza*, had died out: its last recorded performance was on the steps of the Jama Masjid in Delhi in 1928. The *Hamza* epic was always understood to be primarily an entertainment, and so had died as fashions changed. But the *bhopas* and their religious rituals had survived because the needs and hungers that they addressed remained.

"Will Shrawan take on the tradition?" I asked Mohan.

"Of course," he said. "He knows the whole epic. All he lacks yet is confidence, and a wife with a sweet voice. But he loves Pabuji, and he can see that it's a good life. When the gods are asleep"—during the monsoon season—"I stay at home and look after the goats. In the other months, I travel with my *phad* wherever I want. There is still a lot of work for a good *bhopa*—all the castes around here still commission readings of the *phad* when they need something."

Mahavir and Shrawan were now beckoning for Mohan to return to the *phad* to continue the performance. Mohan smiled, and held up a single finger to indicate that he would come in just a minute. "For myself, all my life my heart has been bound up in the *phad* and its stories," he said. "I have never had any real interest in agriculture or any other work. Pabuji has recognised this, and has guarded us. We none of us have ever had a serious illness.

"Every day, I get up hungry in the morning," he said, picking up his *ravanhatta*, "but thanks to him, neither I nor my family ever go to bed on an empty stomach. Not everyone in the village could say that, even the Brahmins and Rajputs.

"It is Pabuji who does this," said Mohan Bhopa, walking back to the *phad* and strumming the first note with his thumb. "It is he who looks after us all."

Postscript

About a month after my trip to Pabusar, Mohan and Batasi came to Jaipur and we did another event together, at the literary festival there. Mohan was in his usual sparkling, mischievous form, dancing as flirtatiously as an eighteen-year-old despite his advancing years. Then a fortnight later, back in Delhi, I heard he was dead.

After his performance at the festival, Mohan had complained to a mutual friend of stomach pains, and had been taken to the main state hospital in Jaipur. Advanced leukaemia was diagnosed within a week, but owing to some bureaucratic tangle, Mohan had been directed first to a small hospital in the Shekhawati, and then on to Bikaner. At each of these he had been refused treatment, for bureaucratic or financial reasons, and sent on to another place. It is the sort of thing that often happens to the poor and powerless in India. When he died, still hospital-less, in Bikaner, ten days after the first diagnosis, he had received no medical treatment whatsoever, not even a painkiller.

His body was taken home, and he was cremated in Pabusar, with wood picked from the sacred *oran* grove of Pabuji.

In her widowhood, Batasi continues singing the *phad*, and has begun to perform with her eldest son, Mahavir, who had earlier given up performing for lack of a tuneful partner. The two, mother and son, now sing the *Pabuji ki phad* together, keeping the family tradition alive until Shrawan finds a suitable wife and succeeds in teaching her the *phad*, or perhaps until Mohan's grandson, Onkar, is ready to tell the tales of Pabuji to a new generation.

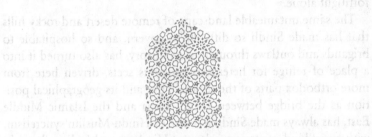

5

The Red Fairy

Rural Sindh is a province of dusty mud-brick villages, of white-domed, blue-tiled Sufi shrines and of salty desert scrublands broken, quite suddenly, by tropical floodplains of almost unearthly fertility. These thin belts of green fecundity—cotton fields, rice paddies, cane breaks and miles of chequerboard mango orchards—snake along the banks of the Indus as it meanders its sluggish, silted, café-au-lait way through southern Pakistan to the shores of the Arabian Sea.

In many ways the landscape here, with its harsh mix of dry horizons of sand and narrow strips of fertile soil, more closely resembles upper Egypt than the well-irrigated Punjab to its north; but it is poorer than either—in fact, one of the least developed areas in South Asia. Here landlords with their guns, and private armies, and feudal prisons, still rule over vast tracts of country; bonded labour—a form of debt-slavery—leaves tens of thousands shackled to their place of work. It is also, in parts, lawless and dangerous to move around in, especially at night.

I first discovered about the *dacoits*—or highwaymen—when I

attempted to leave Sukkur soon after twilight. Asking for directions to the great Sufi shrine town of Sehwan, a three-hour drive away along main roads, I was warned by passers-by huddled in tea stalls under thick shawls that I should not try to continue until first light. There had been ten or fifteen night robberies on the road in the past fortnight alone.

The same untameable landscape of remote desert and rocky hills that has made Sindh so difficult to govern, and so hospitable to brigands and outlaws throughout its history, has also turned it into a place of refuge for heterodox religious sects, driven here from more orthodox parts of the region. This, and its geographical position as the bridge between Hindu India and the Islamic Middle East, has always made Sindh a centre of Hindu-Muslim syncretism, with every kind of strange cult, part-Hindu, part-Muslim, flourishing in its arid wastes.

Much of this intermixing took place in the Sufi shrines that are still the main focus of devotion in almost every village here. For Sufism, with its holy men and visions, healings and miracles, and its emphasis on the individual's search for direct knowledge of the divine, has always borne remarkable similarities to certain currents in Hindu mysticism.

All religions were one, maintained the Sufi saints, merely different manifestations of the same divine reality. What was important was not the empty ritual of the mosque or temple, but to understand that divinity can best be reached through the gateway of the human heart—that we all have Paradise within us, if we know where to look.

The Sufis believed that this search for God within and the quest for *fana*—total immersion in the absolute—liberated the seeker from the restrictions of narrow orthodoxy, allowing the devotee to look beyond the letter of the law to its mystical essence. This allowed the Sufis for the first time to bring together Hindu and Muslim in an accessible and popular movement which spanned the apparently unbridgeable gulf separating the two religions. The teachings of Sufi poetry and song also provided a link between the devotions of the villagers and the high philosophical subtleties of the mystics. For the Sufis always wrote not in the court-Turkish or -Persian of the Muslim immigrants, but in the Sindhi, Punjabi or Hindi vernacular used by the ordinary people, drawing on simple rural symbols taken from dusty roads and running water, desert thirst, the dried-up thorn bush and the blessings of rain.

If the Sufis brought many Hindus into the Islamic fold, then they also succeeded in bringing an awareness of Hinduism to India's Muslims. Many Sufis regarded the Hindu scriptures as divinely inspired, and took on the yogic practices of the Hindu sadhus: sitting meditating before a blazing fire in the heat of summer or hanging themselves by the feet to recite prayers—a practice that is still performed by South Asian Sufis, who sometimes use the hat racks or luggage rails of trains from which to hang.

This sectarian ambiguity is particularly in evidence in the writings of the Sufi mystics of Sindh, not least that of the greatest poet of the Sindhi language, the eighteenth-century Sufi master Shah Abdul Latif of Bhit Shah. Latif came from a relatively orthodox Muslim background, but during his youth, on the rebound from a failed love affair, he set off wandering through Sindh and Rajasthan in the company of a group of Hindu sadhus and Nath Yogis, a sect of ash-smeared Shaivite mystics who invented hatha yoga in the twelfth century, and who claimed that their exercises and breathing techniques gave them great supernatural powers—to fly, to see into the future, to hear, to see over great distances and finally, if the techniques were fully mastered, to turn devotees into immortal beings, or *mahasiddhas*, who had powers greater even than the Hindu gods. The experience of travelling with these holy men profoundly altered Shah Abdul Latif's religious outlook.

One of the most famous chapters of his great verse collection, the *Risalo*, is the *Sur Ramkali*, in which he reflects on the three footloose years he spent wandering the deserts with these yogis, visiting both Hindu and Muslim pilgrimage sites. For Latif, there is no distinction between the two different faiths; the divisions, as he sees them, are between the bigoted and orthodox, on one hand, and itinerant free-thinking mystics on the other. It is these that Latif wishes to be back among:

Yogis are many, but I love these wandering sadhus.
Smeared with dust, they eat little,
Never saving a grain in their begging bowls.

No food in their packs, they carry only hunger,
No desire to eat have they,
Thirst they pour and drink.

These ascetics have conquered their desires.
In their wilderness they found the destination
For which they searched so long.
On the path of truth,
They found it lay within.

Hearing the call,
Before the birth of Islam,
They severed all ties,
And became one with their guru, Gorakhnath.

Now, sitting by the side of the road, I look for them.
Remembering these *sanyasis*, tears well up.
They were so very kind to me.
They radiated brightness.
Yogis are many, but it is these wandering sadhus that I love,
Says Latif.

A few years ago, while making a documentary on Sufi music, I visited the tomb of Shah Abdul Latif during its annual *'Urs*. The wild
and ecstatic night-long celebrations marking the anniversary of the
saint's death were almost a compendium of everything of which
Islamic puritans most disapprove: loud Sufi music and love poetry
was being sung in each courtyard, men were dancing with women,
hashish was being smoked, huge numbers were venerating the tomb
of a dead man and all were routing their petitions through the saint,
rather than directly to God in the mosque.

But for the Sindhis attending the *'Urs,* it was not they who were
the heretics, so much as the stern Wahhabi mullahs who criticised
the popular Islam of the Sufi saints as *shirk,* or heresy: "These mullahs are just hypocrites," said one old fakir I talked to in the shrine.
"Without love, they distort the true meaning of the teaching of the

Prophet. They are just interested in themselves. They should all be jailed for life."

It was while talking to the pilgrims in Bhit Shah that I heard about a Sindhi shrine, or *dargah*, that sounded even more wildly syncretic than that of Shah Abdul Latif. The *dargah* of the Sufi saint Lal Shahbaz Qalander, "The Red Royal Falcon" of Sehwan Sharif, lies barely a two-hour drive through the desert to the north of Bhit Shah. Sehwan was once a major cult centre of the great Hindu god Lord Shiva; indeed the town's original name was Sivistan, the City of Shiva. Here, sixty years after Partition and the violent expulsion of most of the Hindus of Pakistan into India, one of the *sajjada nasheens*, or hereditary tomb guardians, is still a Hindu, and it is he who performs the opening ritual at the annual *'Urs*. Hindu holy men, pilgrims and officials still tend the shrine, replenish the lamps and offer water to visiting pilgrims. I was told that it was only in the 1970s that the central Shiva lingam, long the focus of veneration in the saint's tomb, was discreetly removed to a locked annexe.

The old fakir at Bhit Shah who had ranted about the hypocrisy of the mullahs was adamant that there were two things I should not miss when I visited Sehwan Sharif. The first was the daily *dhammal*, or devotional dance to the saint, which took place each evening at sunset, after the end of Magrib prayers. The other, he said, was a famous lady fakir who lived in the shrine, and was said to be the most passionate of all the saint's devotees. Her name, he said, was Lal Peri Mastani, or the Ecstatic Red Fairy. I asked how I would find her amid the crowds.

"Don't worry," replied the fakir. "Everyone knows Lal Peri. And anyway she is unmistakable."

"In what way?" I asked.

"She is dressed in bright red, is very fat, and she carries a huge wooden club."

I arrived at Sehwan just as the sun was beginning to set over the Indus and the call to prayer was sounding through the bazaars. The *dhammal* was about to begin, so I ran through alleys thick with pilgrims to get inside the shrine before the daily dance in honour of the saint commenced.

The wide, arcaded courtyard was filled to bursting, and neatly segregated down the middle, with women on the right and men on the left. At the far end of the courtyard, between the tomb chamber and a long line of huge copper kettle drums and outsized leather-trussed camel drums, a large area had been roped off, and here the dervishes were preparing to dance.

There were men of all ages and appearances: black-robed or red-swathed, dreadlocked or shaven, hung all over with amulets and *ta'wiz,* or bound with chains and metal neck rings, their fingers heavy with cat's-eye rings. Several of the *malangs* were now bending down and tying *gungroos*—lines of dancer's bells—on their ankles. A few appeared to be practising their steps, hopping from foot to foot, like ballet dancers awaiting the curtain. One old man did this slowly and gently, while holding his granddaughter tenderly on his shoulders.

Then, with the explosion of a thunderclap, the *dhammal* began: slow at first, the drumming rapidly gained pace, and the long lines of dreadlocked dervishes began to move as they felt the rhythm pound through their bodies. Old men began to sway, arms extended or hands cupped in supplication, mouthing softly murmured prayers. As the dancers turned their eyes to heaven, smiling beatifically, they slowly began part-skipping, part-dancing, part-running on the spot.

The tempo and the volume both rose steadily, until the massed kettle drums were pounding physically through everyone in the courtyard. The dancing gradually turned from a meditative and prayerful swaying to something much more wild and frenzied and ecstatic. As a climax was reached some shouted out chants in praise of the saint—*"Dum Dum Mustt Qalander!"* ("With every breath the Qalander gets higher and higher!") or *"Jiya Jhule Lal!"* ("Long life to the Living Ruby!"). A few cried out Shia chants in praise of Ali: *"Ya Ali! Ya Haidri!"* or *"Ali Allah! Ali Allah!"* One man fell to the ground in a gesture of *namaaz,* then, amid the jumping, jerking, dancing men, stretched out full-length on the floor. The air was hot with sweat, and the rich, sweet scent of rose petals mixed with incense and hashish.

Many scholars believe that just as the Sufi fakirs of Sehwan Sharif model their dreadlocks, red robes and dust-smeared bodies on those of Shaivite sadhus, so the *dhammal* derives from the *damaru* drum of Shiva, by which, in his form of Nataraja, or Lord of the Dance, the Destroyer drums the world back into existence after dancing it into extinction. According to the sixth-century Chinese traveller Huien Tsang, Sehwan was the cult centre of a Shaivite sect called the Pashupatas, who believed in emulating the dance of Shiva as part of their rituals, using this shamanistic dancing as a way of reaching union with God. Remarkably, Sehwan Sharif seems to have maintained the ancient Shaivite dance of the Pashupatas in a thinly Islamicised Sufi form.

On the right-hand side of the courtyard, as the men danced, the women took the music in a quite different way. A few danced a little like the men: one beautiful old lady was jumping from side to side, holding her walking stick in the air. But most had gathered themselves in small groups, each one clustered around a woman in a state of trance. As their mothers and sisters supported them, the possessed women sat cross-legged, but with the upper halves of their bodies they swayed and thrashed about, their eyes rolling and long hair fanning out as they swung their heads wildly to the rhythm of the drumming. Still supported by their families, a few rose and spun around like tops.

"As soon as they hear the drumming, they have to dance," said an old man next to me. "Even if you bound them with chains they would have to dance."

"Within ten days," said another, "whatever cure these women ask for will be done. Lal Shahbaz cannot refuse his devotees."

These, explained the old man, were women who were believed to be possessed by spirits, or djinns, and who had been brought to the saint for exorcism. One teenage girl, head uncovered, sat shaking and sobbing with one of her mother's hands resting gently on her shoulders and the other supporting the small of her back. All the while, another older woman, perhaps an aunt or grandmother, kept calmly questioning the djinn she believed to possess her. "Why don't you leave?" she said. "We are in the house of Lal Shahbaz Qalander. It would be better for you to leave. Just go! Go now!"

The ecstasy of the *dhammal* is a safety valve, providing an outlet for tensions that otherwise could have no other expression in this deeply conservative society. The *dhammal* is renowned for its ability to heal, and in Sindh—as elsewhere in Sufi Islam—it is widely believed that a disease that appears to be physical, but which actually has its roots in an affliction of the spirit, can be cured by the power of Sufi music and drumming. The hope is that by sending the women into a trance, their sadness and anxiety will be calmed and, ultimately, cured.

It was while I watched the ranks of transported women that I saw Lal Peri. As my friend at Bhit Shah had indicated, she was unmistakable. In the corner of the courtyard, between the kettle drums and the shrine, was a huge, dark-skinned, red-clad woman of between fifty and sixty, dancing with an enormous wooden club held aloft in her right hand. She had silver armlets covering her forearms, and a red wimple over her head. Images of Lal Shahbaz hung from a chain around her neck. She danced with great force and a manic energy, jumping and leaping in the air, more like the male dervishes than the possessed women who were seated relatively demurely around her.

Eventually, after nearly half an hour of building, the drumming reached its final climax and Lal Peri did a last pirouette before dropping to the ground as the pounding rhythm ceased as abruptly as it had begun. She lay there panting on the marble floor, smiling an ecstatic, exhausted smile. "When I perform the *dhammal*," she said in a deep, husky voice, "I feel as if I am in the company of Lal Shahbaz Qalander himself—and alongside Ali and Hassan. I live for this moment."

I introduced myself, telling her that I had heard about her from the fakirs of Bhit Shah.

"These shrines are my home," she replied simply. "And the fakirs are my family."

"How many years have you been here?" I asked.

"I've lost count," replied Lal Peri. "Over twenty. People come and go, but many find what they are looking for here, and stay forever. This was my experience. It is *'ishq*—love—that keeps us here."

"What do you mean?"

"Once you find the love and protection of Lal Shahbaz Qalander, you want to feel it again and again and again. You never want to go anywhere else."

I asked how he showed his love.

"He protects me and gives me whatever I need," she said, shrugging her shoulders. "Whenever I am hungry, someone comes and feeds me. In his house, everything is fulfilled."

Lal Peri's full lips and very dark skin marked her out amid the relatively fair Sindhis, so I asked if she was a *siddi*—did she have African blood in her veins, like so many of the fishermen on the Makran coast?

"No," she said, smiling and revealing *paan*-stained teeth. "I am from Bihar."

"Bihar? In India?"

"Yes, from a village called Sonepur. Not far from the border with Bangladesh."

"So how did you end up in Sindh?" I asked.

"For much of my childhood there was fighting," she replied, shrugging her shoulders. "Each time, we had to leave and move on. First it was Hindus killing Muslims in Bihar: they cut people and killed them—even in mosques. Then it was Bengalis killing Biharis in what is now Bangladesh." She spat on the ground. "I can never forget what I saw."

She was silent for a while. "Sometimes I dream of my childhood in Bihar and want to go back," she said eventually. "My village was like a garden—so green, so fertile—and so different from the deserts here." She paused, chewing the clug of *paan* in her mouth. "I would come back to Lal Shahbaz Qalander—other than my mother, he is the only one who has guarded me and given me unconditional love. How can I leave him? But I'd still like to see the land of my forefathers one more time."

"Is it difficult living here on your own," I asked, "without any protector but Lal Shahbaz?"

Lal Peri thought for a second before answering. "I always talk too much, and sometimes that gets me into trouble. But I speak the truth, and if someone gives me *gali* [abuse] I have my *danda* [club]." She smiled and rapped her club on the palm of her left hand. "And

I have him, Lal Shahbaz. I am not sure the world can give you happiness, but Lal Shahbaz can. God sends many different things in this life—happiness, pain, sadness—but Lal Shahbaz makes sure it is all for the best, and that we can cope with whatever the Almighty decides. Whenever I am lonely, or feel frightened, I pray to him, and I feel I am being looked after."

Lal Peri was the sort of deeply eccentric ascetic that both the Eastern Christians and Sufis have traditionally celebrated as Holy Fools. She was an illiterate, simple and trusting woman, who saw the divine and miraculous everywhere. It was also clear that she had lived an unusually traumatic life, which had left her emotionally raw. She was in fact a triple refugee: first as a Muslim driven out of India into East Pakistan after Hindu-Muslim riots in the late 1960s; then as a Bihari driven out of East Pakistan at the creation of Bangladesh in 1971; and finally as a single woman taking refuge in the shrines of Sindh while struggling to live the life of a Sufi in the male-dominated and increasingly Talibanised society of Pakistan. The more I heard the details of her story, the more her life seemed to encapsulate the complex relationship of Hinduism with the different forms of South Asian Islam, swerving between hatred and terrible violence, on one hand, and love and extraordinary syncretism on the other.

With such a past, it was easy to see why she had found refuge in this particular shrine. For the longer I explored Sehwan Sharif, the more it became clear that, more even than most other Sufi shrines, this was a place where for once you saw religion acting to bring people together, not to divide them. Sufism here was not just something mystical and ethereal, but a force that demonstrably acted as a balm on South Asia's festering religious wounds. The shrine provided its often damaged and vulnerable devotees shelter and a refuge from the divisions and horrors of the world outside.

Lal Peri seemed to be aware of this and pointed out to me the many Hindus at the shrine: the water men at the entrance, distributing cups of free spring water to pilgrims; a Hindu *sajjada nasheen* directing the cleaning of the shrine chamber; and the many Hindu pilgrims and ascetics, in from the wild places of the desert to ask for Lal Shahbaz's blessing. The Hindus were said to regard Lal Shahbaz Qalander as a reincarnation of the sensual Sanskrit poet turned Shaivite ascetic, Bhartrihari, who in the fourth century AD renounced the pleasures of the court of Ujjain and moved to Sehwan, where he lived as an ash-smeared sadhu, and was later cremated on the site of the present shrine. The Hindus also know Lal Shahbaz by a third name: Jhule Lal, originally the Hindu water god and Lord of the Indus River. This name, and the legends that go with it, they have passed on to the Muslim devotees of the saint, some of whom still believe that Lal Shahbaz controls the ebb and flow, the angry storms and peaceful meanders of the great river of Sindh. Introduced by Lal Peri, I asked one group of Hindus if they were made to feel welcome in a Muslim shrine.

"Of course," replied their leader. "We never have any trouble in these Sufi *dargahs*. All gods are the same."

"There is one god only," agreed his wife, who was wearing the *gagra-choli* and peaked veil of the Rabari camel herders. "We are friends with our Muslim brothers and we have faith in this *pir*."

"And the Muslims do not mind you coming here?"

"Why would they mind?" said the pair, genuinely baffled by my question.

When I asked the man why he had made the effort to come all this way, from the hot deserts of the interior, he replied with the following story.

"When our child was young he became very ill," said the man. "No medicines helped. We tried everything, but our son only got weaker. Then some neighbours said we should come here. We were desperate, so we got on a bus. We brought the boy to the shrine and one of the *pirs* cured him. What could not be done by the doctors in twelve months he did in a minute."

"The child was sick, and he was made right," said his wife. "So now we believe. Each year we come back to the shrine to thank Jhule Lal."

"I tell you he is here," said Lal Peri emphatically. "People see him in the crowd. He looks after every one of his followers. No one goes away empty-handed."

The following morning I agreed to meet Lal Peri amid the date palms of the holy garden of Lal Bagh, a short distance outside the town.

Mutual friends had arranged for me to stay in the house of one of the tomb's *sajjada nasheens*. Climbing up to his rooftop in the centre of the town's bazaar early that morning, with a cup of warm green tea in my hands, I was able see a wide panorama of the shrine, the town and the belt of gardens that surrounded it. The town was slowly waking after the revelry of the night before, and from the rooftop I could hear the morning sounds familiar from any South Asian bazaar: the swishing-flicking of brooms sweeping; throats being cleared; a dog barking.

The houses of the bazaar were all of dun-coloured mud brick, though some had small white-painted prayer areas in the inner courtyards, where triple-arched *mihrabs* rose to small white *minars*, topped with flapping green flags. Lines of pilgrim shops were beginning to open up for the day, and the shopkeepers were laying out their stalls of nuts and chickpeas, sugar-ball *prasad* and rose petals, icons of the saint and cassettes of *qawwali* performances from the 'Urs. Dominating all these rooftops, and surrounded by a halo of circling pigeons, was the great gilt dome of the shrine, flanked by a pair of golden pepper-pot minarets.

On one side of the bazaar, next to an oxbow loop of the Indus, rose the old mud-brick tell of the ancient citadel that Alexander would have seen as he floated down the river in the fourth century BC. From here, in the clear early morning light, lines of leathery water buffaloes marched through the dust towards the shallow waters of the Indus.

On the other, more arid side of the town, facing away from the river and towards the desert, were the old walled tombs and graveyards, with their wind-eroded mud-brick calligraphy and crumbling tile work. Around them was a scattering of flag-topped hillocks where Lal Shahbaz Qalander and his followers once performed their austerities. Beyond lay the fans of the date palms of Lal Bagh, the walled garden where Lal Shahbaz took up residence in a hollow tree trunk.

It was here that Lal Shahbaz is said to have punished himself with great feats of self-mortification, testing his self-discipline by engaging in the Hindu ascetic practice of *tapasya*, sitting in a cauldron over a fire, so turning his skin red. It was also here, according to his devotees, that the saint transformed himself into a falcon—the other legend which gave the saint his name. On one occasion he flew to Mecca to perform evening prayers at the Ka'ba; another time he flew off to the aid of his friend Sheikh Baha ud-Din Zakariya, who was in mortal danger from the King of Multan. Lal Bagh was also the scene of another of his celebrated miracles: producing the springs of sweet water which to this day irrigate his holy garden.

Lal Shahbaz Qalander was originally born near Tabriz, in northwest Iran, and walked to Sindh around the same time as Marco Polo was setting off from Venice to China, at the end of the thirteenth century. Known during his life as Sheikh Usman Marwandi, the saint was probably part of the same wave of humanity that brought the greatest of all Sufi poets, Jalal ad-Din Rumi, from Afghanistan to Turkey—the great diaspora of refugees set in motion by the advance of the Mongol armies, who in turn destroyed both Balkh, the home of Rumi, and Tabriz, the home of Lal Shahbaz.

In his lifestyle, however, Lal Shahbaz Qalander was a much more extreme figure than Rumi. For all his theological free-thinking, Rumi was in fact a prominent *maulana* in a mosque in Konya and so a respected local divine. In contrast, Lal Shahbaz was a Qalander, or holy fool, "an unruly friend of God" who, enraptured by the love of the divine, followed a religious path that involved rejecting the material world, the constraints of convention and the strictures of the Shariah, and looking instead for humiliation and blame from society as a proof of sanctity. As part of this quest, Lal Shahbaz is said to have moved from Lal Bagh into the brothel area of Sehwan. This of course horrified the clerics of the local ulema, but Lal Shahbaz Qalander in time converted the prostitutes, who soon became his most ardent devotees. He also encouraged his followers to dance their way to God—a Persian poem ascribed to him describes his ecstatic Qalanders as dancing in the fire and on the gallows of life.

These traditions have continued at the shrine, and many of the Qalanders of Sehwan still embrace a radical inner path and a lifestyle that, like that of the Hindu sadhus and Tantrics, completely rejects convention. They are often strange and disquieting figures, *bi-shar*—"outside the religious law"—who have chosen a life of wandering and calculated impropriety, seeking God on the road and in the Sufi shrines through a regime of self-punishment and celibacy, while trying to generate a state of religious ecstasy with the aid of music and dance and hallucinogens.

For these Qalander dervishes, who today live in and around Lal Bagh, Lal Peri is very much the uncrowned queen of Sehwan, and as a single woman who lives on her own in this male-dominated society she is perfectly placed to defy more conventions than most.

I found her the following morning, sitting telling the beads of her *rudraksh* and cowrie-shell rosaries on a prayer rug next to a hollow tree said to be that in which Lal Shahbaz once lived. She called over to a young dervish, whom she introduced as her disciple, to bring us tea, and we settled on the rush mat that she laid out in the cool shade beneath a palm-thatched canopy decorated with calendar images of the saint. Then, between sips of green tea, she began to tell me how a girl from Bihar, in eastern India, had ended up in a Sufi shrine in Sindh, on the west side of Pakistan.

"I was born in a small village called Sonepur in Bihar," said Lal Peri. "Hina was the name my mother gave me.

"Our village was on the edge of the jungle. The soil was very fertile, and although we were poor, as children we never went hungry. My earliest memories are of plucking fruit from trees: mangoes, *jamun* and guavas grew so thickly there, and dates and sweet coconuts too. You didn't have to buy fruit from shops: it was always there, twelve months a year, completely free. My father grew a little rice and some vegetables on our land, and there were always wild antelope and deer in the jungle—if my father went in there to hunt with a bow and arrow, he was sure to come back an hour later with a deer, and then we would have venison for dinner. He was a very good hunter, and would always distribute a little to the other villagers, especially his friends, and his cousins, and the poor.

"Before the fighting began, I had a very happy childhood. I used to help carry coconuts in big baskets from the trees. In our village, the men did the work in the paddy, and the women only helped with the coconuts. We were Qureshis, from a good family, so the women were not allowed to work in the fields and they generally stayed inside. But as children we were always out, running around. I remember skipping with a rope, and playing hide and seek in the bamboo. We were a big family—and all my mother's family were around too, so there were always cousins to play with, and we all loved each other.

"When I was small, it seemed as if the Hindus and Muslims were like brothers and sisters. There were many Hindus in the village and we would play with them without thinking about religion: my best friend was a Brahmin girl, and my father's best friend was a Hindu too. There was a mosque and a temple not far from each other, and if people wanted something, they would usually go to both. We had all grown up side by side, and I can't remember any difficulty until much later.

"Our house was of bamboo and thatch, and had a sloping roof. Looking back, it was quite a primitive life. There was no power or electricity, no pukka roads. I have heard that now Bihar is quite developed and there are roads and even electricity, but in those days there was nothing. Nothing except water—that was everywhere. People here in Sindh get very excited about a small spring of clear, sweet water, and people will walk miles to drink there; but in my village, water was so common that no one thought twice about it.

"The first troubles came when my father died. He caught TB, and died after a year of illness—I remember him getting thinner and thinner, and spitting blood. When your father dies, you realise that you have no shelter and no protector. The day after he was buried, my paternal uncle grabbed our land, and my mother, brothers and I had to take shelter with my maternal uncle. We were all very upset, but what could we do? The following year my mother remarried, and my stepfather took a dislike to me. He said I was ugly, and why should he work to feed me? He was good to my mother, but cruel to me, and to my brothers too. Twice, when he was drunk, he tried to beat me. But my mother protected me, and made sure I always had enough food to eat. She truly loved me. Sometimes she still comes in my dreams and tries to help me.

"In my village there was a small shrine between the banyan tree and the well, and there was a fakir with black robes and long hair who used to sit there. He would always sit cross-legged and chant, *'Mustt! Mustt! Mustt!'* I would go to him, and he would teach me prayers, and would make me meditate on the *Kalimah*, and to say, *'Allah hoo! Allah hoo! Allah hoo!'* There were many other things he said that I didn't understand then—I was too young—but I was fascinated by that man, and increasingly drawn to fakirs. Whenever I saw one, I would go and talk to him.

"It was soon after I met the fakir, when I was thirteen years old, that everything began to go wrong. First, my best Hindu friend took poison and killed herself: she was in love with a Muslim boy, and her family would not let her marry him. Then the Hindus began to be angry with us because of politics. There were many stories of Hindus being mistreated over the border in East Pakistan, and some of the Hindu politicians began to say that we should pay the price for this, and that the Hindus should kill all the Muslims in Bihar in revenge. We didn't know anything about what was happening in East Pakistan, but they said that we were Muslims, so we must take the blame. There was a song they used to sing:

> I will cut down the Muslims, and I'll make a bridge,
> Then I will cross the Rupsha River
> And I will bathe in the blood of the Muslims.

Things steadily got worse. There were isolated murders: Hindus killed a Muslim, then the Muslims killed a Hindu. But our village was majority Muslim so we were never that worried, and we were sheltering the family of my father's Hindu friend, rather than living in fear ourselves. We felt in no real danger.

"Then one day, there was a big attack on the village. A large party of *gundas* came to Sonepur one Friday, when all the men were in the mosque during midday prayers. They had daggers and long staves and they surrounded the mosque and dared the men to come out, shouting insults, calling them all circumcised cowards. Eventually, when they set fire to the roof of the mosque, our men rushed out, but they were unarmed and completely surrounded, and they were all killed. That was how I lost my stepfather, my paternal uncle—the one who took our land—and my cousin.

"As chance would have it, none of us children were in the mosque that day—we were all out playing in the bamboo. When we saw people running and the smoke rising from the mosque, we ran into the jungle. Our mother eventually found us hiding there. She was with her brother, my uncle, who had also been out in the fields, and so had managed to escape. He dug us a small pit in the jungle, in the middle of a banana plantation, and covered it with palm thatch. We hid there for fifteen days, creeping back to our house at night on a couple of occasions to get food.

"Eventually, the family decided that we would cross to East Pakistan, and seek shelter with some cousins of my mother who lived just over the border, until things blew over. I was very excited at the prospect of the journey, and was looking forward to meeting some new cousins. After the fear of living in the pit, it was a relief just to head off. I didn't think for a minute it would be permanent.

"We left late one evening, and walked for several days through the jungle towards the border, carrying whatever goods we had managed to salvage from the village. My uncle had bribed one of the border guards, and we stayed the evening with him just before the crossing. The guard's family was kind to us, and gave us dal and rice. Then just before dawn, he rowed us across the river, and left us on the river bank next to a field on the far side. He pointed us in the right direction and told us to run. I remember running across the field. I was very scared as he had said we might get shot; but he had said don't cry, just run, run, run, so that was what we did.

"The following evening, we finally reached my cousin's village. The village was much larger than the one we came from, and our cousins were very good to us, and made us feel welcome. They built us a new house in the middle of a garden, and we had all the fruits and trees we could wish: mangoes, coconuts, bamboos, betel nuts, grapes, pomegranates. They even put me in a school—the only one I ever went to. My cousins were powerful people locally, and we feared no crime.

"In fact for the first year, the only fear we had was of the floods. The fields of the village were very rich, but every monsoon they would become inundated and the river would burst its banks so that we had to take shelter on makeshift platforms up in the trees. In the branches we would be safe—but the river swept away everything, including all our belongings. The houses we had made were *kucha*, made of bamboo and mud and palm thatch, and they could not withstand the floods. Everything was spoiled by the water. So we had to start again, and this time we built an embankment around the village. But the following year, during the rains, the same thing happened again.

"That year was 1971; a very bad year indeed. The West Pakistanis were fighting with the East Pakistanis, and the Biharis sided with the West Pakistanis against the Bengalis. We knew nothing about this, and the violence did not come to our village. But we heard that many people had been killed in towns nearby, and that both sides were murdering each other in every way they could. We also heard that Biharis were being kidnapped by Bengali militias and made to work as slave labour. Others were kidnapped, then beheaded. Many of our people took refuge in camps, but then died for lack of food. Things were so bad that we stopped eating fish from the river because there were so many bodies rotting in the water. Everyone was frightened, and no one knew what to do, or even what it was really about. We could just about understand why Hindus might want to kill Muslims, but why would Muslims want to kill Muslims? It seemed as if the whole world was soaked in blood.

"Then, just when things had become unbearable, the Pakistanis announced that any Bihari in Bangladesh who wanted to come to Pakistan could have land in the southern Punjab. We didn't know anything about the Punjab, but we had heard it was very rich so were tempted, especially as Bangladesh was very, very poor after the floods and the war.

"In the end, the family split. My mother stayed in Bangladesh with her cousin, saying she was too old to move again, and that she would take her chances with the Bengalis. But my younger brother and I took the offer of some land in Pakistan. Bihari volunteers from a camp near Khulna organised our journey. They gave us documents and took us in trucks first to Calcutta, then to Delhi. From there we crossed into Pakistan and were put in a camp near Lahore. Finally they took us to a cotton factory near Multan. There was no land when we got there, but at least we were given a small room, and a job.

"For all of us, it was very strange. We couldn't speak Punjabi, and none of us knew how to work ginning cotton. We were used to fish and rice, and all we were given was meat and *roti*. But at least we were safe, and for every eight-hour shift in the factory we were given Rs 15. When I was not working, I spent my time visiting shrines in Multan, and talking to the fakirs. It was at this time that I first began to think that one day I too might become a wandering Sufi.

"For ten years I lived this life, and even got used to the work in the factory. My brother always looked after me. But then my brother died in an accident in the factory, and his wife misbehaved with me, saying that I was stupid and cursed, that I had always lived off my brother's money and given nothing in return, and it was my bad luck which had caused the death. She said she didn't want to live with me any more. On the fortieth day after his death, when all the ceremonies were complete, I decided to leave. How could I stay after what had happened, after all the words that had been spoken?

"The day before I left, I visited the shrine of Sheikh Baha ud-Din Zakariya and prayed for guidance. That night I had a dream. I saw an old man with a long beard who came to me in my sleep. He was sitting in a great courtyard, and he said, 'Now you are all alone. I will be your protector. Come to me.' In my dream, I replied, 'But I don't know who you are or where you are.' He said, 'Just sit on a train, and it will bring you to me. But leave all your money, and do not pay for a ticket, or for food. I will provide.'

"I did as I was instructed. I didn't even tell my sister-in-law I was leaving. I caught the first train that pulled into the station at Multan, and just as the man in my dream had said, the ticket inspector didn't ask for a fare—instead he shared his food with me. The following day, when the train reached Hyderabad in Sindh, a great crowd of pilgrims and fakirs were on the platform. Some were beating drums, and one them shouted, *'Dum Dum Mustt Qalander!'* I looked out at what was going on, and I must have caught the eye of the fakir, for through the bars of the train he handed me an amulet, saying, 'This will protect you—keep it!'

"I looked down and saw that on the *ta'wiz* was a picture of the man in my dream. I ran out of the train and chased after the fakir, asking him who the old man was. 'It is Lal Shahbaz Qalander,' he replied. 'We are on our way to his *'Urs*.' I asked whether I could come too, and he agreed. We all caught a bus together, and when we arrived, I recognised that the shrine was the place in my dream. The courtyard where Lal Shahbaz was sitting in my dream was the one where the *dhammal* takes place every day.

"That was more than twenty years ago. Since then I have never left this shrine, except for once a year when I go to the *'Urs* at the shrine of Shah Abdul Latif in Bhit Shah. The first year I slept in the courtyard at the *dargah*. In those days I was not a fakir or a *malang*—just an ordinary homeless woman. But I did the *dhammal* every day, and gave water to the thirsty pilgrims, and swept the floor of his tomb chamber. The longer I stayed, the more people got to know me. They accepted me, and I became part of the family of this shrine. I took a *pir*, who taught me how to live as a Sufi, and eventually I moved here to Lal Bagh, to the place where Lal Shahbaz lived and meditated. I've been here ever since, and now I have disciples of my own.

"This place is very peaceful, but has a strong power. Anywhere else it would difficult to live alone as a woman, but here I am protected, and accepted—no one bothers me. My food is provided by the *pirs* of the shrine. There are other holy women who come occasionally, for a week or a month, but I am the only one who permanently lives here. My *pir* and the other *malangs* have taught me how to live this life. They have told me all I know about Lal Shahbaz and Shah Abdul Latif, and the ways of a Qalander. Lal Shahbaz has become like a father. He is everything to me. Shah Abdul Latif is like my uncle. Though I am a stranger here in Sindh, and am not educated, what Latif says in his poetry speaks to me. I think he understands the pain of women.

"These days, however, I sometimes feel that it is my duty to protect both these saints, just as they have protected me. Today in our Pakistan there are so many of these mullahs and Wahhabis and Tablighis who say that to pay respect to the saints in their shrines is *shirk*. Those hypocrites! They sit there reading their law books and arguing about how long their beards should be, and fail to listen to the true message of the Prophet. Mullahs and Azazeel [Satan] are the same thing. My *pir* once taught me some couplets by Shah Abdul Latif:

> Why call yourself a scholar, o mullah?
> You are lost in words.

> You keep on speaking nonsense,
> Then you worship yourself.

> Despite seeing God with your own eyes,
> You dive into the dirt.

> We Sufis have taken the flesh from the holy Quran,
> While you dogs are fighting with each other.

> Always tearing each other apart,
> For the privilege of gnawing at the bones.

Lal Peri was not alone in her fears of the advance of the Wahhabis, and what this meant for Sufism in the region.

Islam in South Asia was changing, and even a shrine as popular and famous as that of Sehwan found itself in a position much like that of the great sculpted cathedrals and saints' tombs of northern Europe 500 years ago, on the eve of the Reformation. As in sixteenth-century Europe, the reformers and puritans were on the rise, distrustful of music, images, festivals and the devotional superstitions of saints' shrines. As in Reformation Europe, they looked to the text alone for authority, and recruited the bulk of their supporters from the newly literate urban middle class, who looked down on what they saw as the corrupt superstitions of the illiterate peasantry.

Where this process differed from sixteenth-century Europe was in the important role played by colonialism. Religiously conservative Hindus and Muslims both suffered the humiliation of colonial subjugation and had to watch as their faith was branded degraded and superstitious by the victorious colonisers and their missionaries. In both faiths, reform movements re-examined and reinvented their religions in reaction to the experience of conquest; but while Hindu reformers tried to modernise their diverse spectrum of theologies and cults to more closely resemble Western Christianity, Islamic radicals opted instead to turn their back on the West, and return to what they saw as the pure Islamic roots of their faith. In the aftermath of the brutal massacres by the British following the Great Uprising of 1857, Islamic radicals left the ruins of Delhi and the demolished Mughal court, rejecting both the gentle Sufi traditions of the late Mughal emperors and the ways of the West.

Instead, disillusioned refugees from Delhi founded a Wahhabi-like madrasa at Deoband which went back to Quranic basics and rigorously stripped out anything European from the curriculum. One hundred and forty years later, it was out of Deobandi madrasas in Pakistan that the Taliban emerged to create the most retrograde Islamic regime in modern history, a regime that in turn provided the crucible from which emerged al-Qaeda, and the most radical fundamentalist Islamic counterattack the modern West has yet had to face. In the al-Qaeda training camps of Kandahar, Deobandi currents of thought received a noxious cross-fertilisation with ideas that emerged from two other intellectuals forced to rethink their faith in reaction to the West: the intellectual fathers of the Egyptian jihad, Hassan al-Banna and Sayyid Qutb.

If it is the Islamists' assaults on India and the West that has understandably absorbed the Western press, it is sometimes forgotten that the Taliban are also at war with rival comprehensions of Islam. This had been made especially clear by the 2009 dynamiting of the shrine of the seventeenth-century Pashto poet-saint Rahman Baba, at the foot of the Khyber Pass in the North-West Frontier region of Pakistan.

By chance, this was a shrine I knew very well. As a young journalist covering the Soviet–mujahedin conflict in the late 1980s from

Peshawar, I used to visit the shrine on Thursday nights to watch Afghan refugee musicians sing songs to their saint by the light of the moon. For centuries, Rahman Baba's shrine was a place where musicians and poets had gathered, and Rahman Baba's Sufi verses in the Pashto language had long made him the national poet of the Pashtuns—in many ways the Shah Abdul Latif of the Frontier. Some of the most magical evenings I have ever had in South Asia were spent in the garden of the shrine, under the palms, listening to the sublime singing of the Afghan Sufis.

Then about ten years ago, a Saudi-funded Wahhabi madrasa was built at the end of the track leading to the *dargah*. Soon its students took it upon themselves to halt what they saw as the un-Islamic practices of the shrine. On my last visit there, in 2003, I talked about the situation with the shrine keeper, Tila Mohammed. He described how young Islamists now regularly came and complained that his shrine was a centre of idolatry, immorality and superstition. "My family have been singing here for generations," said Tila. "But now these Arab madrasa students come here and create trouble."

"What sort of trouble?" I asked.

"They tell us that what we do is wrong. They tell women not to come at all, and to stay at home. They ask people who are singing to stop. Sometimes arguments break out—even fist fights. This used to be a place where people came to get peace of mind. Now when they come here they just encounter more problems, so gradually they have stopped coming."

"How long has this being going on?" I asked.

"Before the Afghan war there was nothing like this," replied Tila Mohammed. "But then the Saudis came, with their propaganda to stop visiting the saints and to stop us preaching *'ishq*. Now this trouble happens more and more frequently."

Making sure no one was listening, he leaned forward and whispered, "Last week they broke the *saz* of a celebrated musician from Kohat. We pray that right will overpower wrong, that good will overcome evil. But our way is pacifist. As Rahman Baba put it:

I am a lover, and I deal in love. Sow flowers,
So your surroundings become a garden.

Don't sow thorns; for they will prick your feet.
We are all one body,
Whoever tortures another, wounds himself.

The end came on 4 March 2009, a week before my visit to Sehwan.
A group of Pakistani Taliban arrived at the shrine before dawn, and
placed dynamite around the squinches of the dome. No one was
hurt, but the shrine chamber was completely destroyed. The Taliban
issued a press release blaming the shrine for opening its doors to
women, and allowing them to pray and seek healing there. Since
then several other shrines in areas under Taliban control have been
blown up or shut down, and one—that of Haji Sahib Turangzai,
in the Mohmand Tribal Federally Administered Tribal Region of
Pakistan—has been turned into a Taliban headquarters.

Behind the violence lies a theological conflict that has divided
the Islamic world for centuries, albeit one dramatically radicalised
by the aftermath of the anti-Soviet jihad. Rahman Baba, like Lal
Shahbaz in Sindh or Rumi in Anatolia, believed passionately in the
importance of the use of music, poetry and dance as a path for
remembering and reaching God, as a way of opening the gates of
Paradise. But this use of poetry and music in ritual, and the way the
Sufis welcome women into their shrines, are some of the many
aspects of Sufi practice that have attracted the wrath of modern
Wahhabis, and their South Asian theological allies, the Deobandis
and Tablighis. For although there is nothing in the Quran that
specifically bans music, Islamic tradition has always associated
music with dancing girls and immorality, and infections from Hinduism, and there has been a long tradition of clerical opposition.

In the long story of the complex three-cornered relationship
between Hinduism, Sufi Islam and Islamic orthodoxy—in which the
determination of the Sufis to absorb Hindu ideas and practices has
always clashed with the wish of the orthodox to root them out as
dangerous and deviant impurities—Sehwan has historically played
an important part. It was the home of the great Sufi philosopher-
poet Mian Mir, who in turn became the *pir* of the seventeenth-
century Mughal prince Dara Shukoh, the ruler who arguably did
more than anyone else to attempt to bring together the two great
religions of South Asia. Dara was taught by his Sehwan-born

pir that there was an essential unity of the Islamic and Hindu mystical paths. Heavily influenced by Mian Mir's philosophy, Dara would go on to write, in his great treatise on Sufism *The Compass of Truth*:

> Thou art in the Ka'ba at Mecca,
> as well as in the [Hindu] temple of Somnath.
> Thou art in the monastery,
> as well as the tavern.
>
> Thou art at the same time the light and the moth,
> The wine and the cup,
> The sage and the fool,
> The friend and the stranger.
> The rose and the nightingale.

Dara also had the *Bhagavad Gita* and the *Upanishads* translated into Persian as *The Mysteries of Mysteries,* and he wrote a comparative study of Hinduism and Islam, *The Mingling of Two Oceans,* which emphasised the compatibility of the two faiths and the common source of their divine revelations. In it he speculated that the essential nature of Islam was identical to that of Hinduism, and following the Quranic injunction that no land had been left without prophetic guidance, became convinced that the *Vedas* constituted the mysterious concealed scriptures mentioned in the Quran as the ultimate scriptural spring of all monotheism. In the end, however, Dara's Sehwan-influenced speculations proved too radical for the Muslim elite of India, and while Sufism has always had a large following, its influence among the Islamic ulema has always been controversial and frequently challenged. What is happening today is only the latest round of a much more ancient and intractable theological conflict within the Islamic world, albeit one super-charged by modern politics and weaponry.

Now the same madrasas which had so radically and successfully challenged the Sufi traditions of the Frontier were beginning to spread their web around rural Sindh. Lal Peri had told me about a new Deobandi madrasa that had just that month opened on the edge of the Sehwan bazaar, so after leaving her at Lal Bagh that evening, I went and met its director, Maulana Saleemullah.

The madrasa was located in an old *haveli*, recently renovated at some expense in gleaming marble, but still only semi-furnished. The twenty or so children in residence were still sleeping on mats and bedding on the floor, and the only furniture in the classrooms where the kids sat cross-legged chanting the Quran was a single desk for the teacher.

Saleemullah turned out to be a young, intelligent and well-educated man, who received me warmly. He was articulate in debate; but there was no masking the puritanical severity of some of his views.

For Saleemullah, the theology of the dispute between the Sufis and the orthodox was quite simple. "We don't like tomb worship," he said. "The Quran is quite clear about this, and the scholars from the other side simply choose to ignore what it says. We must not pray to dead men and ask things from them, even the saints. In Islam we believe there is no power but God. I invite people who come here to return to the true path of the Quran. Lal Shahbaz is dead, I tell them. Do not pray to a corpse. Go to the mosque, not to a grave."

"Do the people here listen to you?" I asked.

"Sadly this town is full of *shirk* and grave worship," he replied, stroking his long, straggling black beard. "It is all the Hindu influence that is responsible. Previously these people were economically powerful in this area, and as they worshipped idols, the illiterate Muslims here became infected with Hindu practices. All over Pakistan this is the case, but Sindh is much the worst. It is like what happened with Moses and Pharaoh. The children of Moses were influenced by the children of Pharaoh, and when Moses left them to go and speak to God, a magician made an idol of a calf, and the children of Moses began to worship it. Our job is to bring the idol and grave worshippers from *kufr* [infidelity] back to the true path of the Shariah."

"And what about the drumming and the music and the *qawwalis* they play in the shrine?"

"Music is also against the law of Islam," he replied. "Musical instruments lead men astray and are sinful. They are forbidden, and these musicians are wrongdoers. With education we hope they will change their ways."

"So you think there is nothing Islamic about what goes on in the shrines?"

"Sufism is not Islamic," replied Saleemullah. "It is *jadoo*: magic tricks only. It has nothing to do with real Islam. It is just superstition, ignorance, perversion, illiteracy and stupidity. This town is full of fools—if people here were less stupid we could have filled this madrasa. We can accommodate 400 here, but only ten families have sent their children. Have you talked to the fakirs in the shrine? They are all illiterate. Really—what do they know of the Quran? Yet the people go to them and seek their opinion as if they were scholars. We have a long way to go here. At the moment only the poor will send their children to us, and then only because we feed them. We just have to be patient and explain to the people here that their superstition leads to Jahannam—hell—but the path of true Islam leads to Jannah—Paradise."

"And what of the Sufi idea that Paradise lies within you?" I asked. Here it seemed, lay a small but important clash of civilisations, not between East and West, or Hinduism and Islam, but within Islam itself. Between the strictly regulated ways of the Wahhabis and the customs of the heterodox Sufis lay two entirely different conceptions of how to live, how to die and how to make the final and most important, and difficult, journey of all—to Paradise.

"Paradise within us?" said Saleemullah, raising his eyebrows. "No, no: this is emotional talk—a dream only. Is there evidence for this in the Quran? There is nothing in the Quran about Paradise within the body or in the heart: the heart is too small for God. Paradise is outside, a physical place in the heavens which God has created for his people. According to our beliefs there will be many levels of Paradise, eight in all, with a place for each believer. There will be couches to lie in the shade, and rivers of milk and honey and cool, clear spring water. To get there you must follow the commands of the Almighty. Then when you die, *Insh'Allah*, that will be where your journey ends. On Judgement Day the seas and oceans and earth will be turned into hell, but those Muslims who follow the law and do good deeds will be transported up to Paradise."

He paused and stroked his beard again. "Real Islam is a discipline," he said. "It is not just about the promptings of the heart. There are rules and regulations that must be followed: how to eat, how to wash, even how to clip your moustache. The heart and ideas of love–these are all irrelevant if you fail to follow the rituals and practices commanded by the Holy Prophet."

Saleemullah's organisation, he said, ran 5,000 madrasas across Pakistan, and were in the process of opening a further 1,500 in Sindh. These figures seem to be just the tip of the iceberg. According to one recent study there are now twenty-seven times as many madrasas in Pakistan as there were in 1947: from 245 at Independence the number has shot up to over 8,000. Across Pakistan, the religious tenor has been correspondingly radicalised: the tolerant, Sufi-minded Barelvi form of Islam is now increasingly out of fashion, overtaken by the rise of the more hard-line and politicised Deobandi forms of Wahhabism, which many now see as an unstoppable force overwhelming the culture of the country.

"I am full of hope," said Saleemullah. "Look what has happened in Bhit Shah. We have a large madrasa there and seven mosques in the control of the Deobandis. At first the people clung to *shirk* and resisted the truth. But slowly the children went back home and educated their parents. Now every day our strength is growing."

I got up to leave. "Mark my words," said Saleemullah as he showed me out, "a more extreme form of the Taliban is coming to Pakistan. Certainly there are many challenges. But the conditions in this country are so bad. The people are so desperate. They are fed up with the old ways and the decadence and corruption. They want radical change–a return to the Caliphate."

"And what is your role in that?" I asked.

"Most of the work is being done by the government and the [intelligence] agencies. Whatever they say to the Americans, we know that really they are with us. But our role? That is to teach the people that only our Islamic system can provide the justice they seek. We are the only people giving the poor education. We give the knowledge that the Islamic groups in Pakistan are using to change this country forever."

"And do you plan to take the battle to the shrine here?"

"For the time being we cannot challenge the people directly in shrines. We have no wish to invite trouble, or to fight. All we can do is to befriend people, tell them what is right and wrong, educate their children and slowly change their minds. If we can get children away from their homes to board here with us we can influence them more thoroughly. With education, we hope the appeal of *shirk* and Sufism will fade, and that there will be no need for punishment."

"But if you get your Caliphate?"

"When the Caliphate comes," he said, "yes, on that day there is no question. It will be our duty to destroy all the *mazars* and the *dargahs* [Sufi shrines]—starting with the one here in Sehwan."

No one knows if the Sufis of Sindh can fend off the chill winds of Wahhabism that are currently blowing so strongly; but Lal Peri, for one, was certain that the mullahs would gain no following in Sehwan. To prove it, she said I should come and talk to her *pir* at his retreat in the desert. His name was Sain Fakir, and he was, she said, a great poet and scholar, who knew by heart the entire *Risalo* of Shah Abdul Latif. No one, she said, was a greater defender of the Sufis than he.

The following day, my last in Sehwan, I picked up Lal Peri at Lal Bagh at 7 a.m. She got into the car, her *ta'wiz* clanking and her club banging against the ceiling of the car. Then we drove out, past the belt of tombs, into the scrub beyond.

Three miles out of the town, we passed a placid blue lake, with egrets, kingfishers and flamingos nesting round the edge. A black swan flew overhead. Lal Peri pointed out some small thatched houseboats moored at the edge: "Those belong to the fishermen," she said. "They are great devotees of Lal Shahbaz Qalander. They believe that it is he who provides them with their fish."

From there we drove out into the open desert. To me, the dry ridges and arid scree-strewn scrub, bare of vegetation, were stark and lowering, but Lal Peri regarded it all with a sort of rapt veneration. I asked what she was looking at.

"Everywhere has its own beauty," she said. "The sand, the foothills, the mountains in the distance: these are all different manifestations of God."

"In what way?" I asked.

"Every place has the name of God in it. Each has its own meaning. God says in the Quran, 'I have my signs everywhere: in the rocks, the trees and the landscape.' But most people don't realise these things are there."

As we drove, I thought over the previous day's conversation at the madrasa. Maulana Saleemullah seemed so confident, yet it seemed there were good reasons to hope that the sane and beautiful madhouse of Sehwan, and the shelter it still offers to people like Lal Peri, might yet survive. For just as Italy and Spain never underwent the Reformation that swept through northern Europe with a wave of iconoclastic image breaking and shrine destruction, so Sindh is a very different place to the North-West Frontier, with a very different variety of Islam practised there. Here in the deserts of Sindh it seems that Sufi Islam, and the deeply rooted cult of the saints, with all its borrowings from the indigenous religious traditions of the area, may yet be able to act as a powerful home-grown resistance movement to the Wahhabis and their jihadi intolerance of all other faiths.

An hour's drive through a low dry valley brought us at the end to a small oasis. We passed through a belt of graves and then came to a small plantation of date palms, and in the middle, a modest *dharamsala* for pilgrims heading on the *yatra* to Lahut. Beside it was a walled garden, bubbling with spring water.

"This is the Garden of the Panjethan, the Five Sacred Personalities," said Lal Peri. A small boy was sitting looking after his goats on the mud bank of an irrigation runnel leading from the spring in the garden, and Lal Peri called to him by name, telling him to go and fetch his grandfather. After a few minutes, Sain Fakir appeared, hobbling on a stick, and directed us to a shady trellised shelter in the middle of the garden. Nearby a group of dreadlocked *malangs* on their way to Lahut sat silently smoking chillums of hashish, as a family of mynah birds chattered around them.

Sain Fakir was a venerable, frail, hawk-nosed old sage in his eighties, with liver spots under his eyes and fabulously gnarled hands. He sat down cross-legged on the mat, and before long was talking of his veneration of the two great saints of the region.

"I am the *murid* [disciple] of Lal Shahbaz Qalander," he said, "and the *talib* [student] of Shah Abdul Latif. In Sindh we don't really differentiate between the two. The two are inseparable, like Allah and the Holy Prophet."

Saying this, he suddenly launched into a verse of the *Risalo*, singing with a surprisingly strong and melodic voice for a man of such age. As he completed each verse, Lal Peri cried out, "*Haq!*" ("Truth"), "*Jiya Latif!*" ("Victory to Latif"). When he was finished he smiled, and lay back, accepting the *paan* that Lal Peri had rolled for him.

"My ancestors were all followers of Lal Shahbaz," he said. "But it is the poetry of Latif that has always set my heart aflame. We believe that his verses are more than poetry—they are the essence of the spirit of the Quran. The Quran is not always easy to understand, and as a result we Muslims fail to take the real message of the Prophet. Only the Sufis teach the true path, the path of love."

"What about the mullahs?"

"The mullahs distort the Prophet's message for their own purposes," said Sain Fakir. "Men so blind as them cannot even see the shining sun. Their creed is extremely hard. It doesn't understand human weakness."

"It excludes everyone," said Lal Peri. "Even other mullahs, at times."

Sain Fakir shrugged his shoulders. "In this world, everyone commits sin. The Sufis have always understood this. They understand human weakness. They offer forgiveness, and people will always love those who forgive."

"So you're not that worried when you hear about the Taliban blowing up Sufi shrines elsewhere in Pakistan?" I said, and then told him about my meeting with Saleemullah.

"It is certainly true that they want to destroy all tombs and Sufi shrines," said Sain Fakir. "Just like the Wahhabis did to the tombs of the Companions of the Prophet in Mecca. And of course we worry about that."

"With this new madrasa, they will try to poison the people here against us," said Lal Peri.

"But as a result of this, God's wrath is upon them," said Sain Fakir. "Latif had a saying: 'Deal only with things that are good. If you trade coal, you will be covered in black soot. But if you trade musk, you will smell of perfume.' Good deeds have good effects. Bad deeds have bad effects. See how these Wahhabis are always killing each other: at the Lal Masjid in Islamabad, in Swat, in Afghanistan, in Iraq. Now is the beginning of the end for them. I truly believe that."

"So you think what happened at Rahman Baba's shrine couldn't happen here?"

He shook his head. "No," he said firmly. "They'll never be able to destroy the shrines here in Sindh. The Sindhis have kept their values. They will never allow it."

"Lal Shahbaz Qalander will protect us," said Lal Peri. "And we will protect him."

"And what would you say to the mullahs and Wahhabis who say that what happens in Sufi shrines is not Islamic?" I asked.

"The Wahhabis are traders who sell their faith for profit," said Lal Peri angrily. "They are not true Muslims—just fuel for the fires of hell."

"A lot of it is about power," said Sain Fakir, more gently. "The Sufis are a threat to the mullahs because we command the love, loyalty and faith of the ordinary people. No one is excluded. You can be an outcaste, a fallen woman, and you can come and pray at the shrine and the Sufi will forgive you, and embrace you."

"You don't even have to be a Muslim and you will be welcomed," said Lal Peri.

"What difference does it make if you call Allah by his Hindu names—Bhagwan or Ishwar?"

"These are just words from different languages," said Lal Peri.

"The mullahs are always trying to fight a jihad with their swords," said Sain Fakir, "without realising that the real jihad is within, fighting yourself, achieving victory over your desires, and the hell that evil can create within the human heart. Fighting with swords is a low kind of jihad. Fighting yourself is the greater jihad. As Latif said, 'Don't kill infidels, kill your own ego.' "

"Jiya Latif!" cried Lal Peri.

We talked all morning about the Sufism of Sindh, and Sain Fakir's belief that it would never succumb to the Wahhabis. One of Sain Fakir's sons brought green tea, and we sat in the shade beside a bubbling rill of spring water as the midday desert sun beat down, sipping tea and tearing great flaps of newly cooked naan. Every so often father and son would burst into song, illustrating some theological point with a verse or two of the *Risalo*.

"You must understand," said Sain Fakir, putting a hand on his heart, "everything is inside. This is what we believe. Both hell and Paradise—it is all within you. So few understand . . ."

"There is a story about Lal Shahbaz Qalander, which Sain Sahib once taught me," said Lal Peri. "One day Lal Shahbaz was wandering in the desert with his friend Sheikh Baha ud-Din Zakariya. It was winter, and evening time, so they began to build a fire to keep warm. They found some wood, but then they realised they had no fire. So Baha ud-Din suggested that Lal Shahbaz turn himself into a falcon and get fire from hell. Off he flew, but an hour later he came back empty-handed. 'There is no fire in hell,' he reported. 'Everyone who goes there brings their own fire, and their own pain, from this world.' "

6

The Monk's Tale

"Once you have been a monk, it is very difficult to kill a man," said Tashi Passang. "But sometimes it can be your duty to do so."

We were standing on a platform of the Tsuglag Khang, the temple attached to the Dalai Lama's residence-in-exile in Dharamsala, high above the Kangra Valley and the dusty plains of the Punjab. All around us Tibetan pilgrims were circling the open-air ambulatory, around the prayer hall on the topmost terrace of the temple. Some, in their ankle-length sheepskin *chubas*, were clearly new arrivals, nomads and pastoralists from western Tibet, fresh across the high snowy passes; others were long-term residents of this Tibet-in-exile: red-robed refugee monks performing the thrice-daily *parikrama*, or circumambulation, of the Dalai Lama's temple-residence. There was a strong smell of incense and burning butter lamps, and the air was filled with the low murmur of muttered prayers and mantras.

"I knew that if I stayed in a monastery under the Chinese there was no point in being a monk," continued Passang. "They wouldn't let me practise my religion. So, to protect the ways of the Lord Buddha, the Buddhist dharma, I decided to fight."

The old monk had a wide leathery face, broad shoulders and an air of quiet calm and dignity. He wore enveloping maroon robes, a jaunty knitted red bonnet and thick woolly socks. Despite his age, his brow was unfurrowed and his face almost unlined. "Non-violence is the essence of the dharma," he said. "Especially for a monk. The most important thing is to love each and every sentient being. But when it comes to a greater cause, sometimes it can be your duty to give back your vows and to fight in order to protect the dharma."

Standing talking on one side of the circling pilgrims, we seemed to be the only stationary figures in a great roundabout of religiosity. Some pilgrims paused on their *parikrama* to spin the line of brass-plated prayer wheels mounted in a recess on the outside wall of the shrine chamber; others performed formal prostrations, a few of them on wooden pallets laid out for the purpose. The pilgrims faced in the direction of the great gilt images of the Buddha and the Bodhisattva Avalokitesvara that could be glimpsed, gleaming dimly in the light of a thousand lamps, through the great open doors of the temple. They stood up, facing the images, and with their hands clasped in a gesture of prayer, sank to their knees. Then they fell forward on to the pallet, measuring it with their full length, palms together, fingers outstretched before them, before slowly rising again to a standing position. They repeated this exercise over and over again, even though many were craggy octogenarians who between prostrations shuffled painfully around the temple, spinning their prayer wheels and bowing with visible effort before the images.

Later, we sat in the winter sunlight of the temple tea stall, high above the corkscrewing mountain paths of Dharamsala. Passang talked easily, almost abstractedly, about his youth as a nomad on the Tibetan plains; of his time studying in a now destroyed monastery; and of his ambition to become a hermit, living alone in a cave. He also described how quickly those hopes had evaporated with the coming of the Chinese. Their attempts to impose their atheistic creed on a Tibet whose values could not have been more different, and their campaign to close down the monasteries, had, he said, ended that life forever.

But more surprising was what Passang said of his eventual decision to give up his monastic vows and take up arms to resist—something which seemed to go against all the usual preconceptions about the non-violence of Tibetan monks.

"It was not that I wanted to murder individual Chinese soldiers," he said. "And it was certainly not blood lust, or because I took any pleasure in killing." He paused, unsure of how to explain, twirling his prayer beads pensively between thumb and forefinger. "I knew that the Chinese soldiers were committing the most sinful of all crimes—trying to destroy Buddhism. And I knew that it is written in our scriptures that in certain circumstances it can be right to kill a person, if your intention is to stop that person from committing a serious sin. You can choose to take upon yourself the bad karma of a violent act in order to save that person from a much worse sin."

"So inspired by these teachings," I asked, "you took up a gun and fought the Chinese?"

"I tried," replied the monk. "But we were just fools. Though we acquired some old guns, we were outnumbered and knew nothing of fighting. All we knew was how to pray, not how to kill. As soon as we came across the Chinese troops they put us to flight. It was a total fiasco."

Eventually, he said, after fleeing Tibet and spending many years with a special Tibetan unit in the Indian army, he had retired to a small wooden hut in Dharamsala, intent on spending his last years atoning for the violence he had committed. Here he began trying to earn merit, by making wooden blocks and printing prayer flags. Finally, encouraged by a sermon of the Dalai Lama, and along with several other former monks, he had once again taken up his old monastic vows and robes, a full thirty years after he first renounced them.

"Every day now, I recite the mantras of repentance," he said. "We are told that when you really regret your actions, and repent, and bow towards the Buddha, it is possible for the bad karma to be removed. After all, the Buddha himself forgave a mass murderer.

"There was a man named Angulimala who had killed 999 people, and hung a finger from each around his neck on a garland. He hoped the Buddha would be his thousandth victim; but instead, on meeting the Lord, he converted and became a monk. Many were critical of this decision, but the Lord Buddha insisted his repentance was genuine, and that he should be allowed to atone for his misdeeds. If he can be forgiven, then maybe so can I . . ."

Passang smiled, his broad face lighting up momentarily. "Since I retired I have gone and repented before many lamas. I have visited many temples, pledging not to do such things ever again. I have prayed for the souls of the men I have killed, and asked that they have good rebirth. But still I worry."

The prayer beads were whirling nervously around his fingers again. "The lamas told me that if my motivation was pure, and I had done violent acts to help others at the expense of my own karma, then I can still be saved. But every sentient being has life and even the thought of killing makes me unhappy. In truth I don't know how much forgiveness I have gathered. I don't know yet whether on my deathbed I will feel calm and satisfied. Maybe I will never know . . ."

Passang sipped at his butter tea, warming his hands around the sides as he did so: "In the scriptures it says that one who lives in the dharma sleeps at ease in this world, and also in the next; but I still have a feeling that I did a terrible thing. When you take up arms, you have to follow orders—you have no right to act as you wish. Sometimes you are told to kill. Still sometimes the dreams come. At night, I hear the noise of war . . ."

The monk broke off, and fell silent, looking into his empty cup. "Come and see me tomorrow," he said, rising suddenly, "and I will tell you how all this came about."

McLeod Ganj, the Tibetan settlement above the north Indian town of Dharamsala, is a miniature Tibet-outside-Tibet. It is the place to which countless displaced lamas and landowners, refugee peasants and farmers, exiled townsmen and traders have made their way, clustering like barnacles on a rock around the temple-residence of the Dalai Lama.

The complex crowns a saddle on one of the higher ridges of the town. Above, in the grey wintery light, loom the black rock walls and fault lines of the Himalayas, rising to a series of gleaming white snow peaks glowing strangely with refracted light at the level of the clouds.

Below, rutted roads and cobbled footpaths lead down to the Tibetan Parliament, which despite its grandiose name is in reality little larger than a village scout hall. On one side is the equally modest yellow ochre Tibetan Home Ministry; to the other a library and archive. Farther below still, through steep slopes of cedar and deodar, and below the slowly circling eagles, is a stutter of foothills. These lead down to the foggy floor of the Kangra Valley, where the hilltops emerge from the flat blanket of winter morning mist like the humps of a school of whales rising from the deep.

The old people's home for Tibetan veterans where Passang had finally found shelter lay a short walk below the library, on a projecting ledge of rock in the lee of a small temple. It was late afternoon when I arrived. The old veterans who had been sitting silently on benches in the sun, playing cards or watching the light rake down the peaks, now found themselves in shade, with the temperature dropping rapidly. So they gathered their shawls around them, and adjusted their knotted mufflers and bonnets. Then they began to shuffle inside to drink their evening butter tea before heading up to the temple for their evening prayers. I later learned that of the 150 inmates in the home, no fewer than thirty had, like Passang, been monks who had given back their vows to fight in the ill-fated Tibetan resistance.

Passang led me to his room, a warm and snug space at the back of the home, in the shadow of the cliffs. This he shared with one other monastic army veteran. On a shelf at the end of the room lay a line of doll-like images of Tibetan saints and rinpoches. A butter lamp burned in a brass brazier, and a red electric light mimicked the flickering of a candle below a framed image of the Dalai Lama. Above the door, Passang had hung some fatty yak meat to dry on an improvised framework of skewers.

For a few minutes the old man fiddled around with a primus, making chai, which he poured from a saucepan into small cups. He passed me one, then proceeded to sip noisily from his own. Only when he had finished did he begin to talk.

"I was born in 1936 in the Dakpa country of Kham province," said Tashi Passang. "Like many in eastern Tibet, my family lived a semi-nomadic life. Although we were small landowners with a stone three-storey house, we also had many yak and *dri*. The herd numbered almost 100, and in summer it was the job of the boys of the family to help my grandparents and my uncles to take the animals up to the high summer pastures.

"As a young child, I would watch my elder brothers go off with the herd, and feel sad to be left behind. But the valley where we lived was very beautiful in summer. The trees were all in blossom and there were so many wild flowers—cornflowers, poppies, deep purple gentians—that I couldn't name even half of them. There was a big river leading to a lake near our house, and in summer red crane and white duck would come in their thousands, and build their nests. They laid their eggs by the side of the lake and my parents would warn me not to go near the nesting area, in case I touched the eggs. Then the mother would smell a human and abandon them, and the young would die—something my mother said was a sin and which would bring bad karma on all of us.

"In autumn the birds would fly south, and we would begin to prepare the butter lamps to light us during the cold and darkness of winter. I remember helping my father roll the cotton for the wicks, hold it in the centre of the bowl and pour in the melted butter, then put it aside to settle. As we did so, my father would quietly chant mantras, as if it was some sort of religious ceremony.

"Soon after, winter would come, and both river and lakes would freeze over. It was very, very cold and the blizzards would bring a covering of thick snow. The ice on the river was so hard that you could walk or even skate on it. We each had a pair of flat wooden skates that my mother kept in a special box, and would produce only when she was sure the ice was hard enough to take our weight.

During this season the yaks were all sheltered in a covered enclosure, and it was only at the beginning of the thaw that we would take out the young beasts and pierce their noses so we could put a rope through and harness them for ploughing.

"When I was twelve, I asked my parents if I could accompany the herds to the mountains for the summer. Finally, after much pleading, they agreed. For me this was a totally new way of life. That part of the year we all slept in a single round *ba* made of skins. Inside there were no partitions, and a fire in the centre; the smoke would escape through a small hole in the roof. My mother would pack *tsampa*—roasted barley—and butter, cooking vessels and lots of bedding, and load them with the tents on the back of the yaks.

"Five families would collect their herds, and head together into the mountains. We would walk all the way, driving the animals in front of us. Yaks are very good-tempered, and I always felt safe with them. They seemed to enjoy the journey and my grandmother was especially good at handling them. She knew them all by name and would talk to each one as she milked them in the evening. Every evening, all the families in the migration would gather together to have dinner, and recite prayers to the goddess Tara.

"Once we reached the summer pastures the different families would separate and we would each head to our own camp. My job would be to take the yak up to the high green pastures each morning, and to stop the mountain wolves from attacking them. At first I was scared of the wolves, but it soon became clear that they were more scared of us than we were of them—at least during the day. Only when they were hungry in winter were they really dangerous. All you had to do was to shout, and maybe fire a warning shot, and the entire pack would run away. Occasionally I would have to fire at them, but I was too young to handle a rifle in those days, and I never managed to hit one. There were stories of yetis up in the mountains, but I never saw one. A much bigger threat were the *dremong*—fierce brown bears—which sometimes attacked the yaks, usually as you led them down for the night.

"On my third summer in the mountains, my great-uncle came with us. He was a monk, though he no longer lived within a monastery, and it was he who persuaded me to become a monk too.

My mother had taught me to read and write a little Tibetan, and he thought that I was a promising boy who might benefit from a monastic education. Every day he would sit with me and teach me to write on a slate, or on the bark of a dwarf oak, as of course there was no paper in the mountains. He also loved history, and was very good at telling stories. As we tended the animals, he would tell me long stories about Songtsan Gampo and the kings and heroes of Tibet.

"But his main love was the dharma, and he told me that if I continued to lead the life of a layman I might acquire many yaks, but would have nothing to take with me when I died. He also said that married life was a very complicated business, full of responsibilities, difficulties and distractions, and that the life of a monk was much easier. He said that it gave you more time and opportunities to practise your religion. I was always a religious child, and I thought about what he said.

"By the end of the summer I had decided that I would like to try monastic life. I thought that if I really dedicated myself to religion I would have a better chance of a good rebirth in my next life, and have the opportunity to gain Nirvana. My uncle and I guessed that my parents would forbid me from becoming a monk, so we decided that I should join the monastery first, and only later inform the family. At the end of the summer, when we came down from the passes, my uncle and I went ahead to Dakpa monastery, and there he handed me over to the abbot.

"I was worried I would miss the freedom of the mountains. But as it turned out, in the monastery I was happier than I had ever been. In my life as a herdsman, I had to worry about the wolves, and my yaks, and to look after my grandparents—life was full of anxieties. But as a monk you have only to practise your prayers and meditation, and to hope and work for Enlightenment.

"Also, the life in the mountains, for all its beauty, was quite lonely. In Dakpa there were nearly 500 monks, and many boys of my own age. Very soon I made many friends. I knew I had made the right decision. Before long even my parents became reconciled to what I had done.

"How you start your life as a monk can determine the rest of your life. One of our scriptures says, 'Men who have not gained spiritual treasures in their youth perish like old herons in a lake without fish.' I worked very hard at memorising the scriptures and proved to be good at remembering them.

"The main struggle, especially when you are young, is to avoid four things: desire, greed, pride and attachment. Of course you can't do this completely—no human being can—but there are techniques for diverting the mind. They stop you from thinking of yaks, or money, or beautiful women, and teach you to concentrate instead on the gods and goddesses. The lamas who taught us trained us to focus on these things. We were taught how to concentrate—to stare at a statue of the Lord Buddha or Guru Rinpoche, and to absorb the details of the object, the colour, the posture and so on, reflecting back all we knew of their teachings. Slowly you go deeper, to visualise the hand, the leg and the *vajra* in his hand, closing your eyes and trying to travel inwards. The more you concentrate on a deity, the more you are diverted from worldly thoughts. As it says in our scriptures:

> The quivering, wavering mind,
> Hard to guard, hard to check,
> The wise one makes straight,
> Like the bowman his shaft.

It is difficult, of course, but it is also essential. In the Fire Sermon, the Lord Buddha said: 'The world is on fire and every solution short of Nirvana is like trying to whitewash a burning house.' Everything we have now is like a dream, impermanent. You can see it: this floor feels like stone, this cupboard feels like wood, but really it is an illusion. When you die you can't take any of this, you have to leave it all behind. We have to leave even this human body.

"The training to be a monk was very rigorous. For three years we were given text after text of the scriptures to memorise. It was a very slow process. First we had to master the Tibetan alphabets. Then we had to learn a few mantras, and then slowly we were taught the shorter versions of the scriptures. Finally we graduated to the long versions, and learned the techniques of debating. When I couldn't remember the words, the teachers would be very disappointed. Sometimes I would try to fool them by taking a peek at the texts. Once I was so frustrated by my inability to remember more that I tore up one of the texts, and the teachers were very angry with me.

"Finally, after three years, we were each sent off to a cave for four months to practise praying in solitude. We were supposed to master the art of being a hermit, of being alone. There were seven other boys nearby, in the same cliff face, but we were not allowed to speak to each other.

"Initially I was apprehensive. The cave was cold and dark, and I thought there might be evil spirits lurking there. But once I got into a routine of praying and meditating I became more confident. I made a small altar, and I placed the image of Guru Rinpoche that I had brought from the monastery upon it. I made flower offerings and lit a butter lamp. I used to rise at one o'clock in the morning and until 6 a.m. I was praying and prostrating, until my knees were so sore I could prostrate no more. At 6 a.m. I would make butter tea and take a break for half an hour. Then it was back to meditating on the roots of compassion, until a small lunch of *tsampa* at midday. At 7 p.m. I would have some rice, rest for an hour, and was asleep by 8 p.m.

"Initially I felt like a failed monk. I was lonely, and scared, and had a terrible pain in my knees from the number of prostrations— we were expected to do 4,000 a day. But by the end of the first fortnight, I began to see my way. It was only then that I began reflecting deeply on things, and really began to see the vanity of pleasures and ambitions. Until then I had not really sat and reflected. I had done what I had been taught and followed the set rhythms of the monastery.

"In the cave I felt I had found myself, and for the first time was practising the true dharma. I discovered a capacity for solitude I hadn't known I had, even in my days in the mountains. My mind became clear, and I felt my sins were being washed away with the austerity of the hermit's life; that I was being purified. All my worries began to disappear and there were no distractions. I was happy. It is not easy to reach the stage when you really remove the world from your heart. That took place in the cave, and ever since then

I have always had a desire to go back and to spend more time as a hermit.

"But it was never to be. Soon after I returned from those four months of solitude, the Chinese appeared."

The Chinese invaded Tibet in the summer and autumn of 1950. They rolled across the Drichu River, and split their forces into three, quickly overwhelming and encircling the antiquated and primitive Tibetan army with their speed, efficiency and numbers.

A year later, in May 1951, with more than 40,000 People's Liberation Army (PLA) soldiers lined up outside Lhasa, the Chinese pressured the Tibetans to sign the Seventeen Point Agreement. This was supposed to safeguard some Tibetan freedoms in return for giving the Chinese the right to guide and reform the Tibetan government. In reality, it allowed the Chinese to station troops all over the country, build supply routes and entrench Chinese Communist rule in Tibet.

"The Chinese invasion of our country had taken place even before I joined the monastery," Passang told me. "I was twelve or thirteen when I first saw them—long lines of soldiers streaming through our valley with their guns and their horses. In those days there were no roads for trucks or cars. I had no idea why they were there, or what they wanted, but initially there were very few of them, and they never really impinged on our life.

"Then one day the Chinese troops came to the monastery. There was a colonel, and about fifty or sixty soldiers with guns. Without asking anyone, they put up posters of their president on the walls and erected loudspeakers in the courtyard so that we would have to listen to what they said. Their colonel wore spectacles. He was polite at first. He said they had come to help Tibet be self-reliant and they would return back home when they had taught us to be modern. He said they had come to bring justice, and to help the poor, and to make Tibet a good country, like China. He said that China was like our big brother, and that it would be good for us if we accepted their authority until the people of Tibet were ready to govern themselves in a modern, Communist way. The colonel even told us he had come to liberate us. To this the abbot replied that he could not liberate us, as the Lord Buddha had showed us that it was up to each man to liberate himself. The colonel just made a face—I don't think he really understood what the abbot meant.

"After that, the Chinese came to the monastery every month or so and gave us a lecture—they called them indoctrination meetings. Sometimes the posters they put up were blasphemous—insulting the Lord Buddha and saying that the monks were trying to keep the people of Tibet poor and ignorant. Slowly the lectures became ruder and more pointed: they said that everything the monasteries did was wrong, and that there was no other option but to accept the changes the Chinese were making. Even when the Chinese were nice and polite—giving free seeds and yaks to the poor people and so on—we always felt we could not trust them. Even from the seclusion of the monastery we could see that they were bringing in more and more of their people to build roads, and more and more troops. I realised something was wrong, even though they tried to make it look as if they were our friends. I sensed that something bad would come—that something evil was creeping behind their smiles.

"As the programme of lectures progressed, I began to have sleepless nights, thinking about what was happening to Tibet, and how these Chinese people—and Chinese *lay* people at that—kept telling us what we should do in our own monastery. I didn't want to be under their rule, but I couldn't see any other option. Some of the monks began to talk about fighting, saying that the Chinese were out to destroy Buddhism, and that we should not simply surrender to what they wanted. Some nights as I lay awake, I wondered if maybe these monks were right.

"Then, in the summer of 1954, rumours began to spread that the Chinese had killed many monks and bombed a monastery at the other end of our Kham province. We also heard that there had been a rebellion among some of the Golok and Khampa nomads. It was said that when the rebels took shelter in the monastery of Lithang the Chinese had bombed it, killing everyone there. Then we heard that the same had happened closer to us, at Changtreng Gompa, and that the monastery had been first bombed and then desecrated.

"There were other stories too: that the Chinese made some of the monks in Kham get married, and others they forced to join the PLA, to build roads for them or even to work in slave labour camps. Some said that parents who refused to send their children to Chinese schools were tied to posts and had nails driven through their eyes.

"Shortly after we began hearing such things, the Chinese army came to our monastery and asked us to give them all our guns and swords from the monastery armoury. The abbot said that these things had been given to us by our forebears and parents, and that the Chinese had no right to take them. But they ignored him, and searched the monastery and took away all the arms they could find.

"After this, we had a meeting—not just the monks, but many lay people from the villages nearby. The monks were unanimous that we must fight, as the Chinese were now clearly intent on destroying the Buddhist dharma and so were *tendra*, Enemies of the Faith. We had heard that many fighters—some said 15,000—had gathered in Lhokha to the south and founded a resistance movement called the *Chu-zhi Gang-drung*, or Four Rivers, Six Ranges. Many said we should all leave and join them there.

"So we went to the abbot and before him we renounced our vows. We simply said that we could not continue as monks. Now we had to fight to protect the dharma. There was no ceremony; the abbot just said, 'All right. You have my permission to give up your vows. Now go.' We weren't sure whether this really did release us from all our promises; it seemed so perfunctory, especially as we were all still wearing our robes. But there was no time to worry about these things at that moment, though it was something which greatly exercised us later when we had to take up arms.

"Many went off on horseback—a number of the monks were from the village at the foot of the monastery and their families gave them horses to go and join the resistance. As for me, I took the gun I had used as a shepherd from the place where I had hidden it, and left the monastery as well; but I had no horse. I went on foot, on my own, with my gun. All I really wanted to do was to go to my home and see my family again. But the PLA had built a small camp next to our land, and I knew it would not be safe. So taking my gun with me, I headed back in the direction of the camp in the mountains where we used to pasture the yak and *dri* in summer.

"What I didn't know was that the monastery was full of informers. As soon as the Chinese heard that I had taken my gun and gone to the hills, they came to our house and began beating my mother, asking her for details of where I was. They were very cruel. They beat her feet, and dragged her by her hair so that she was almost bald, and stayed that way for months. They tied her to a stake outside our house, stripped her and threw cold water over her. They left her there overnight so that the water froze to her and she nearly died of exposure.

"They came back every day, each time beating her and devising new tortures so that she would say where I had gone, or so that I would come and give myself up. But I was up in the mountains, and it was over a month before I came to hear of what had happened to her."

By the time Passang had reached this part of his story, it was very late, and he needed to retire for the night: he had to rise at 3 a.m. to begin his round of prayers and meditation.

The following morning, Passang said he had to go and visit the Home Ministry about his allowance, so I offered to help him down the hill. We wandered down together, and while he was there I took the opportunity to visit the library and archive which stood next door. This contained some of the most precious texts and artefacts that had been smuggled out of Tibet. Like the Parliament building which it abutted, it was modest in scale, but built in the style of a Tibetan *gompa* with sloping walls and wooden pillars vaguely modelled on those of the Potala Palace. Inside, the walls were closely lined with books, while one room contained shelves of ancient Sanskrit and Pali texts, wrapped up in yellow cotton dust covers.

Browsing around the books, I asked the scholar who kept the manuscripts to explain to me the rules governing a monk who wished to renounce his vows. In answer he produced from the shelves a series of old leather-bound volumes of Max Müller's translations of the earliest Buddhist texts on monastic rules and conduct, the *Vinnaya Sutra* (in Sanskrit, literally, "The Text on Taming"), said to have been collected together in 499 BC at the great council which convened after the death of the Buddha; before then the rules had been passed down orally from the Buddha to his disciples. He also brought down the celebrated commentary on the *Vinnaya Sutra* made by the monk Tsonawa in Debung monastery in the fourteenth century, and a translation of the *Pratimoksha Sutra* (literally, "The Path Which Leads to *Moksha*"), the fundamental Buddhist text on vows.

From these it was clear that there was a long tradition of monks being able to give up their vows in case of emergency. Unlike ordination, for which very detailed ceremonial instructions were given, the renunciation of vows was a very straightforward matter. As long as strict criteria were met—notably the need for the monk to fight for the dharma—then the monk merely approached a rinpoche or senior lama, or if none was available, a statue of the Buddha, and explained what he wanted to do, and that his intention was to defend rather than damage the dharma.

There were also many examples in Tibetan Buddhist cosmology and history which justified violence in the defence of the dharma: most notably the very popular Bodhisattva of Wisdom, Manjushri, who changed into his terrifying and wrathful form to become the most violent and destructive of all Tibetan deities, Yamantaka, the Conqueror of Death. In 1984, as an eighteen-year-old backpacker fresh from Scotland, I had first come across this fearsome god on a visit to the monastery of Alchi in Ladakh. Now part of India, Ladakh had been for most of the Middle Ages an important region of western Tibet. At this time the great Tibetan emperors like Songtsan Gampo had ruled from Bengal and the borders of Kashmir through the whole of China as far north as Mongolia.

In Alchi, a huge mural of Yamantaka was placed above the doorway in the Sumtsek of the monastery. The god was shown sitting naked but for a tiger skin, surrounded by a flaming halo in a graveyard strewn with filleted and decapitated human corpses. He was depicted fanged, blue-skinned, six-headed and six-armed, clutching in his claws his sword, bow and mace, as well as his strangler's noose and disemboweller's hook, his hair decorated with the skulls of his victims and his neck garlanded with snakes. Seven hundred years after it was painted, it still had the power to make you shudder.

Yamantaka is not alone in Tibetan cosmology. There is also, for example, the four-headed, six-armed Chakrasamvara, who is shown in murals dancing on his prostrate demonic enemies. Engulfed in flames, roaring with rage, yet strangely poised and balletic, he is crowned and garlanded with skulls, brandishing thunderbolts and skull-headed sceptres; over his head he holds the stretched skin of a dead elephant. Such angry and violent protectors are common in Tibetan Buddhist art, and correspondingly popular in Tibetan devotion; they use their powers for the good of humanity, warding off demons and the creatures of darkness, subverting the ancient warrior imagery of Tibet and utilising it for peaceful ends. Even the most benign figures, such as Guru Rinpoche, are believed to have the power to transform themselves into terrifying killers who can perform acts of great violence in order to protect Buddhism and defeat its enemies, both human and demonic.

Nor is this tradition of violence to protect the dharma solely the preserve of religious tracts and iconography. The great secular epic poem of King Gesar tells how the ruler of the legendary Tibetan Kingdom of Ling killed hundreds of thousands of enemies of the dharma. If these figures could take up arms to protect their faith, then so could the monks. The Dalai Lama's message has always been one of strict *ahimsa* (from the Sanskrit for "to do no harm"), and was reinforced after his arrival in India by his reading of Mahatma Gandhi; but it is clear that in the 1950s some monks looked as much to their ancient Tibetan warrior traditions as they did to their Buddhist heritage of non-violence.

As I walked Passang back up to his home later that afternoon, I asked him how he had felt about taking up arms after so long practising non-violence. "There is a teaching story about this in our *Jataka* Tales. Let me tell it to you.

"There was once a rinpoche of the highest mental state, who was very near Enlightenment. One day he was travelling across the Ganges along with 500 of his brethren in a boat. The captain of the boat was an evil man who hated the Buddhist dharma, and in particular hated the monks who lived and protected it. Secretly he planned to take this boatload of monks to the middle of the river, overturn the boat and drown them all. But because of his spiritual gifts, the rinpoche was able to read the man's mind, and realised what he was planning. So after hesitating and praying for guidance, he decided to throw the man into the river before he was able to carry out his plan. He did this, and the man was pulled under the waves and drowned almost immediately.

"The other monks were horrified and asked: 'Rinpoche, you are a most senior monk, the reincarnation of a great soul, and an example to us all. How could you do this? How could you perform an act of such violence and kill a man?' The rinpoche explained what the man was planning and said that he was willing to take responsibility for his actions, and the bad karma that would accrue through the killing, in order to save the lives of 500 monks. He was supremely unselfish, sacrificing himself and his place on the wheel of rebirth for the sake of the dharma so that the other monks could continue on the path of Enlightenment. I often think of that rinpoche's sacrifice, and wonder whether he was right to make it. I think he was."

When I asked how he had actually ended up fighting, Passang told me he had been in the mountains for a month, successfully avoiding the search parties the Chinese sent to look for him, when news first reached him of what had happened to his mother. His uncle the monk came up to the mountains to bring him the news that she had been tortured. He asked that Passang surrender his gun in order to save his mother, and of course he immediately did so. The uncle then took it to the Chinese, who eventually released Passang's mother. Passang meanwhile made contact with several of his brethren who were also hiding in the hills, and decided to walk with them to Lhasa to warn the monks there of what was happening, and to try to galvanise some resistance.

"For seven or eight months we walked," he said as we headed up the hill back to the veterans' home, Passang ahead and me puffing a little behind, struggling to keep up with this man forty years older. "At first we travelled only at night, but after a while, when we began to near Lhasa, we felt more secure walking during the day. There were many checkpoints, but there were lots of other pilgrims and monks on the roads. We told anyone we met that we were pilgrims heading to Lhasa for the Monlam ceremony, when the Dalai Lama addresses all the people with sermons for two weeks.

"When we finally reached Lhasa, the streets were crowded with pilgrims and the atmosphere was very tense. But our government had no real soldiers, and there was little they could do to stop the Chinese doing exactly what they wanted. I and my fellow monks planned to take shelter in Sera monastery, our mother house, because although we had tried to renounce our vows, we were still wearing the robes of monks and still really thought of ourselves as monks. Sera lies to the north of the city, where the Lhasa plain meets a great arc of mountains. There we found to our pleasure that several of our brother monks had already arrived before us.

"I was sure that the Chinese would come to Sera too, as I could see the army camps already established around the outskirts of Lhasa, and I was determined not to bow down to the Chinese. I told the other monks about the Chinese, how they were very strong and very cruel, and how we had to stand up to them. We said the monks should take their guns while they still had them, and join the rebels. But the older monks wouldn't listen. They thought our government could still protect us, and that the magical powers of the Dalai Lama would keep the Chinese away. We replied that if this was the case, why were the Chinese here, even on the outskirts of Lhasa, and not the other side of the border?

"Then word reached Lhasa that my mother had died. She was not old—no more than fifty. But she never recovered from the beatings the Chinese gave her, and she died as a result of the internal injuries she received for what I had done."

Passang looked down, and for a moment his face crumpled; but he stopped himself. "Of course, I wept when the news came. For long days after that I was too paralysed with sadness to think of anything else. But I was worried too, because I now felt a real hatred for the Chinese. Violence may be justified by our scriptures in certain circumstances, but anger and hatred are always forbidden. I knew I was now in mortal danger of real sin, but this only made me hate the Chinese more."

For the next fortnight, while he turned these issues over in his mind, Passang performed the elaborate round of prayers prescribed in Tibetan Buddhism for the souls of the dead. By the time they had been completed, it was early March 1959, and Lhasa was in crisis.

The following morning, Dharamsala dawned dark and threatening, with black thunderheads massing above the town and blotting out the snow peaks.

I had arranged to meet Passang again at the tea house below the temple after he had finished his morning *parikrama*. The weather had turned, and as it was now bitterly cold we sat inside and ordered tea, *momos* and a bowl of *thukpa* to warm us.

As we ate, Passang described how the tension in Lhasa had reached crisis point during the first week of March, when the Chinese invited the twenty-five-year-old Dalai Lama to attend a theatrical performance in the army camp outside Lhasa. The invitation came when the Tibetan leader was debating in the great Jokhang Temple. Two Chinese officers barged through the crowd and demanded to see His Holiness immediately, breaking all rules of Tibetan protocol. They said that, contrary to custom, the Dalai Lama should bring no bodyguards when he came to their camp to see the performance.

Word of this suspicious invitation soon got out, and the population of Lhasa, along with the crowds of pilgrims who had come to Lhasa for Monlam, converged around the gardens of the Dalai Lama's summer palace of Norbulingka, in an attempt to prevent his attending and—it was widely suspected—being abducted to China.

"On the evening of 15 March, I and twenty-five other monks of Sera were told to get ready as we were going to meet His Holiness," said Passang. "Ahead of us, leading the party, went two senior monks on the back of donkeys. The rest of us walked. We assumed we were going to join the crowds gathering at Norbulingka, and I was excited as I hoped we would get to hear His Holiness give one of his public teachings. But we didn't stop at Norbulingka; instead we headed off into the darkness. We crossed the wide Tsangpo River in a small boat, and for the next two days we walked and walked, through empty plains, with only hard balls of *tsampa* to eat. The monks who were leading us refused to tell us where we were going or what we were doing, and as we were all very junior monks we had no option but to obey.

"Finally, at the village of Chi Thu Shae, we stopped to rest and to eat. We had only been there two hours when a party of Khampa horsemen turned up at the inn. Among them, to our amazement, was His Holiness, with a rifle strapped to his back. At first none of us recognised him, as he was dressed as an ordinary guard, but it was his spectacles that gave him away. He had fled Lhasa in disguise, and we were told that it was our job to escort him. None of us knew that he was heading into exile. I am not sure even he knew at that stage. All we knew was that we had to escape from the Chinese, and to stop their soldiers seizing the Dalai Lama. Of course we were very excited, and very honoured. We realised this was a great responsibility.

"We walked for several more days through very harsh country, struggling to keep up with His Holiness, until we reached Lhuntse Dzong. It was here that we met a rinpoche in the street. We asked him to release us from our vows a second time, as we were still wearing our monastic robes, and it was clear that our duty was now to take up arms to defend His Holiness, and to slow down the PLA if they tried to follow and capture him. We obviously couldn't do this while still wearing the robes of monks, and we felt strongly that we must end this ambiguity. The first ceremony of giving back our vows at Dakpa had seemed very inadequate and hurried, and we were not sure what our exact status was: were we monks or not?

"So the rinpoche gave us a long lecture, almost a sermon, and said that just because we were giving back our vows didn't mean we could indulge in loose living and worldly affairs. We were doing this to protect the Dalai Lama. If we needed to, we must fight the Chinese and even kill; but he warned us—'Don't do anything else which will go against your monastic vows.'

"We shed our robes and were given ordinary *chubas* to wear, and guns to use. His Holiness had already left, hurrying on to escape the Chinese, who were expected at any moment. We remained behind with the Khampa fighters of the *Chu-zhi Gang-drung* movement, vowing to stop the Chinese if they attempted to follow him. We were very proud to do this work, and planned to make a heroic stand, and to die fighting for His Holiness. But that is not what happened.

"Only a single day passed before a huge force of Chinese arrived. There were hundreds of them, with trucks and tanks and artillery and machine guns. Worst of all they had two fighter planes, and we were completely outnumbered. I'm ashamed to admit it, but when the planes began to strafe us, we fled into the hills after firing only a few shots, heading in the direction of the Mango-la Pass. Without food or arms or supplies it seemed pointless to stay and die. We could not fight, so we fled. Some of the *Chu-zhi Gang-drung* volunteers died fighting at Lhuntse Dzong, but almost all of us monks took to our heels and ran, hoping that on another occasion we might be able to redeem ourselves and do a better service to His Holiness.

"In fact, I think we did do him a service just by running, though that wasn't really our intention. For the Chinese patrols followed us, perhaps thinking His Holiness was with us. Many of the people I was with were shot dead. The planes were out searching for us. We hid during the day and travelled only at night, and even then the Chinese sent up flares, and shelled anyone they could see.

"When we got higher we found ourselves trudging through heavy snow. By that time we were reduced to eating the donkeys that had died—we had nothing else—and the snowfall was very heavy. There was nowhere to shelter, and it was very cold. We lost so many on the way, zigzagging through the shells in thick snow red with blood. We were frozen, and our feet and hands were numb and senseless. By the end we were reduced to just six people, half-walking, half-sleeping.

"After ten or fifteen days of this we finally reached the Indian border. Only then did we hear that our Precious Jewel, the Dalai Lama, had escaped. But we also heard there what had happened in Lhasa—that the Potala and Norbulingka Palaces had been shelled, and that thousands had died when the Chinese sent their tanks into the Jokhang Temple.

"In my heart I knew that we must get our country back, and if I had to learn to fight to do so, then so be it. This had happened before, at the time of the Thirteenth Dalai Lama, when the Chinese invaded for the first time, and after a while those who fled returned, and the Chinese went back to their own country. I never guessed it would take so long this time. Not only me; most Tibetans thought that in a year or two we would be back."

I asked: "Did what happen damage your faith? Did you wonder how it could happen that such a catastrophe could overtake Tibet?"

"On the contrary," said Passang, "I gained more faith. How else could we have survived, despite the entire PLA following us? I wore amulets with religious texts to guard my life and when the bullets came, they just travelled right past me. On one occasion, when we were being shelled at night, a shell landed very close to me. For a moment in the sudden blinding light I thought I saw the protector goddess, Palden Lhamo. Though the shell landed only a few feet away from us, no one was hurt. So, no, my faith was not affected. I felt completely protected.

"We Buddhists believe in karma, and in cause and effect. An action has consequences; we are the consequences of our acts. Perhaps because there was a time in the seventh century when we Tibetans invaded China and tortured the Chinese, so we are suffering this torture now. It is our turn to suffer for what we did in previous lives."

For a while Passang waited at the border, to see if the resistance needed him, and he could return.

"We had a plan to return to Tsona, which we had heard was still free," he said. "We thought that we'd fight the Chinese from there. But we had no food and no bullets. We thought that we'd give it a go, that someone must come and support us, and that they'd give us some supplies. We waited for two weeks, but nothing came and no one was there to organise us into a fighting force. We hesitated to enter India. We were scared that we had lost our country, and were angry that we couldn't go back and fight. Eventually there was no alternative: it was starvation that forced us across the border. But when we decided to cross, we did so only because we thought it the most likely way for us to be able to continue the fight for the dharma."

In time, the Indian government gave the refugees places to stay, and was especially generous to those who had joined the resistance: Passang was lodged with other members of the *Chu-zhi Gang-drung* in an old British bungalow. It was only in the months that followed, when so many former monks and fighters were forced to join Indian road gangs in order to eat and survive, that the full implication of what had happened sank in.

"It felt awful," said Passang. "It was the lowest point in my life. At night we would talk about how everything was over. We had lost our country. We were in exile, dependent on others, with no will or right to do what we wanted. We hoped that someone would arm and help us, so that we could recapture Tibet, but nothing happened. Our only hope was in following His Holiness."

In time the refugees were divided up, and Passang was sent to the new Tibetan settlement that was created at Bylakuppe in the forests of Karnataka in southern India. Here Passang was taught to make carpets and handicrafts, and for two years he lived by selling these. It was not destitution; but it certainly seemed a dead end.

However, the fortunes of the Tibetan resistance changed radically two years later, in 1962. When China attacked Indian positions in Aksai Chin in the brief 1962 Sino-Indian war, seizing the disputed border region linking Kashmir and Tibet, it left Nehru's policy of appeasement of China in tatters. It was realised in India that the Tibetan refugees contained a large body of potential troops who would willingly fight against China and who were, moreover, accustomed to fighting at high altitude. Recruiters were sent to the Tibetan refugee settlements, and Passang was among those who were enlisted in the Indian army.

Along with many of his former monastic brethren, Passang was persuaded to join a Tibetan unit in the Indian army known as the Special Frontier Force, or Sector 22. This secret force was jointly trained by India and the CIA in a camp near Dehra Dun. Like all the other Tibetans, Passang was assured that he and his fellow monks would be parachuted back into Tibet to fight for their country and their faith.

"We were told that we would train for a few months and then be sent back to Tibet to begin a revolution. We signed up as we thought this was the way to get our land back and re-establish the Buddhist dharma. Clearly making handicrafts in Karnataka was not going to do that, and this seemed the help we had been waiting for ever since we fled Lhasa."

But the promise was never realised. Instead, after many years, first of training under American officers in high-altitude warfare, then guarding the high passes and glaciers for India, and occasionally being sent over the Assam border into Tibet to do low-level intelligence work, Passang and his brethren were sent to fight in the war that led to the creation of Bangladesh.

"The first time we really saw action was the 1971 war," said Passang. "From Dehra Dun they flew us to Guwahati, and then drove us in trucks up into Manipur. We crossed a river into Bangladesh, and managed to surround the Pakistani army from three sides. It was a great victory, at least as far as the Indians were concerned. But for me, it felt like a total defeat.

"I had to shoot and kill other men, even as they were running away in despair. They would make us drink rum and whisky so that we would do these things without hesitation and not worry about the moral consequences of our actions. Every day I saw corpses. Sometimes even now at night I see them—the whole scene: people shooting, others being shot, airplanes dropping bombs and missiles, napalm, houses burning and men and women screaming. War is far worse than you ever imagine it to be. It is the last thing a Buddhist should be involved in.

"Despite all this, we tried to behave as much like monks as we could. We brought our short Buddhist texts with us and recited our mantras, even in battle. In between the fighting we continued praying—when we were marching, when we were fighting. If anything I prayed more in the army than I did as a monk. Even when we were digging trenches in the jungle we carried holy images in our packs, and lit butter lamps to honour them.

"But within my heart, I knew I was going against *ahimsa*, and the most important Buddhist principles—it was not to fight the Pakistanis that I gave up my monastic vows. I knew that I wouldn't free Tibet, however many Pakistanis I killed. It was for the Tibetan cause and to defeat China that I joined the army; but it occurred to me that now I was no better than the Chinese. They also blithely shot people with whom they had no argument. It was only their guns and bullets that gave them power. The same was true of us in Bangladesh.

"We weren't happy doing this fighting, but what could we do? It is almost impossible to leave the army once you are signed up. I used to feel I would not get a good rebirth, as I wasn't doing any good with my life—just learning to kill, and then putting those skills to use, actually killing people. And I felt sorry, because the war didn't seem to be about right and wrong, and it certainly wasn't about the dharma. It was because of some high politicians in Delhi and Islamabad that people had to suffer and to kill."

I asked if he felt he had been misled by the Indians into joining the army.

"For refugees like us who had no rights, the Indian army was a life commitment, though of course we didn't really realise that when we first joined up. My conscience was very troubled by what I had seen, and by what I had done in Bangladesh. On my annual leave, in expiation, I had begun touring the Buddhist pilgrimage sites of India and Nepal, searching for peace of mind. I went to Bodhgaya, Varanasi, Sarnath and Lumbini. There I spent my time praying and meditating, performing prostrations in an attempt to gain back some of the merit I had lost. I went to the place where the Lord Buddha lived, to where he was born, to where he attained Enlightenment, and where he preached his first sermon. And I swore that the very day that I was able to leave the army I would try to make up for what I had done as a soldier.

"It was not until 1986 that my papers came. I retired and caught a bus the same day to Dharamsala. As chance would have it, I arrived in the middle of the Monlam ceremony, when the Dalai Lama gives his public teachings—the same ceremony I had seen in Lhasa in 1959, nearly thirty years earlier. As I listened to the sermons, I wondered what I could do to make up for all I had done. Then I saw some prayer flags attached to the temple, and thought, this is something I can do: I can make prayer flags.

"Compared to Tibet, there are relatively few prayer flags in India, even in Dharamsala, and many are very badly printed: you can't read the mantras, and often they are not correctly written. I knew all the mantras from my training as a monk and I decided I would try to make well-printed prayer flags. I decided I would really take trouble over them so that they earned good rather than bad merit. In this way I could help the Lord's dharma and do service to the community. I thought I could live a calm and peaceful life, and also make a little money to supplement my army pension.

"I found a small wooden hut in which to live. It had a tin roof and was mounted on four small wooden chocks. I also found an old lama who taught me the techniques of printing. As part of my penance and reparation for what I have done, I have made it a point that every single flag should be perfect, that every word should be correct and legible. When someone buys my flags they are putting their faith in them, and I don't want to cheat them. It is like when we used to draw *thangka* paintings when I was a boy in the monastery in Dakpa. If you miss something, or have the wrong number of fingers, or give the wrong Bodhisattva the wrong mudra, we were told that that would be a great sin. So when I make the flags, I try to think of the person who will buy them, and of the merit they will earn by flying them, and I always pray that they may find the right path and not make the same errors as me.

"Finally, in 1995, I decided to become a monk again. It wasn't a difficult decision. I only gave back my vows so that if the need came I would be able to kill to protect the dharma. But in my heart I never really gave up my vows. I was always a monk in my heart—it was just that sometimes my duty led elsewhere. I talked about it with several of my old army colleagues, including two who had been monks with me in Dakpa, and we decided to take our habits again together. His Holiness gave us our vows, and gave us new names to signal the new beginning we were making, even though it was so late in our lives.

"The period since I rejoined the religious life has been the happiest time—at least the happiest since my days as a nomad in the mountains, or when I went to the cave in Dakpa to live as a hermit. It may seem odd: many people think that old age is an affliction. But from youth I have always accepted that I had to grow old—it comes to everyone. I now have the time to read all the scriptures, which I could never do in the army. What is done is done, and I can't undo my actions in Bangladesh. But I feel very fortunate that I had this second chance. Now at least I can die as a monk. It may be more difficult to memorise and learn by heart the scriptures than when I was young; but there are many less distractions in old age, and concentrating becomes easier. It is tough getting all the readings for the day done at my age—I have to start at 3 a.m. or I don't finish, but at least my mind no longer goes off like a yak that has escaped its herder.

"The veterans' home is a good place, and almost like a monastery. Certainly there is some loss of freedom, but I know that if I get sick now I will be looked after. Everything is taken care of, and you can concentrate on your prayers. Like in the old days, I get up at 3 and pray and meditate until 6:30. At 8:30 I go to the temple here. Then we have tea, and after that I do the first circumambulation of the Dalai Lama's residence. Two others follow in the afternoon and evening.

"For the first time in thirty years I feel that I spend my day practising the dharma again. I have no material goods, and no temptations. I think of the time I will die and how best to embrace this. I am here in Dharamsala, near His Holiness. Whenever the Dalai Lama preaches, I can attend, and listen to him, and learn from his wisdom.

"And I am especially fortunate that of late I feel I have conquered the hate I used to feel for the Chinese. His Holiness is always preaching that it is not the Chinese, but hate itself that is our biggest enemy. Ever since the Chinese tortured my mother, I felt a deep hatred for them, and was always striving for violent retaliation. Whenever I saw a Chinese restaurant in India, I would want to throw stones at it. Even the colour red could make me boil with anger at what the Chinese have done. But after I heard His Holiness say we must defeat hatred, I determined that I would try to eat a Chinese meal in a Chinese restaurant to try to cure myself of this rage. I wanted to wash my anger clean, as His Holiness puts it, to wash clean the blood.

"So one day when I was on pilgrimage in Bodhgaya, I saw a small Chinese restaurant by the roadside. It was run by two Chinese women—an old woman of seventy and her daughter, who must have been around forty. I went in there one evening and ordered some noodles. I have to say that they were delicious. After I had eaten, I thanked the mother and asked her to sit down with me, so we could talk. I asked, 'Where are you from?' and she replied, 'Before the Communists, I was from China.' It turned out her father had been tortured and killed by Mao's soldiers at the Cultural Revolution, and her relations had fled to Hong Kong and from there to Calcutta. By this stage, she was weeping: crying and crying as she told me what her family had suffered. I told her, 'Before the Communists, I was from Tibet, and my mother was also tortured, and died from what Mao's soldiers did to her.' After that, we both burst into tears and hugged each other. Since then I have been free from my hatred of all things and people Chinese.

"There is another reason I feel very fortunate. Three years ago, I was doing the *parikrama* when I saw a man from my village. I hadn't seen him for over fifty years but I recognised him immediately. He had only just come to India from Tibet, and he was able to bring me news of my family, and told me that one of my elder brothers was still alive. Even more than that, he knew his telephone number.

"The next day I rang home. After thirty years I was able to talk to my brother, though I couldn't understand very much, as he was crying so much. He told me all my other brothers had died, and it was just the two of us who were left. He said that the Chinese had taken the family house, and our land, and all the yak and *dri*, saying that we were landowners and so Class Enemies. They gave the yaks to a collective farm and made the family live in the yak shed. But that was all I could really hear. My brother kept sobbing and asking me to return. 'Just come back, come back, and everything will be all right.' I wondered whether I should. But then I thought: what help could I be at my age? I will just be a burden."

As we walked back to the veterans' home in the evening light, with the sun setting behind the peaks, the crows were calling to roost, wheeling and croaking in the deodar slopes around us. Passang was silent, so I asked: "But wouldn't you like to go back to Tibet, even just to see it one last time? Isn't that where you should be ending your days?"

He didn't answer immediately. "I always thought I would return to Tibet in this life," said Passang eventually, as we climbed down the path to the home for the last time. "That was why I joined the army, to fight for it. India is still a foreign land for me, even though I have been here forty years and the people have been very hospitable."

I could see the prayer beads whirring in Passang's hand—always the sign that he was thinking hard.

"And of course," he continued, "I am sad that I have been separated from my country and my family, and that even now, in old age, I am not back home. I am sad that there has been so much violence and suffering in my life. I am now seventy-four. I am still in exile, and Tibet is still not free.

"I still hope that one day Tibet will be free, and who knows? Even the Chinese do not believe in communism any more, so maybe in time the dharma will spread from Tibet into China? Maybe before I am finished, I will get to go back home. That is my last wish, to go back to Tibet and die there."

Passang looked down the wooded slopes to the Kangra Valley, far below the veterans' home. "But you know . . . I have always felt that all of us fled together, and I should wait until a time came when we could all go back together.

"It wouldn't be right to go back alone," he said. "After all this time, it just wouldn't be right."

7

The Maker of Idols

The gods created man," said Srikanda Stpathy, "but here we are so blessed that we—simple men as we are—help to create the gods."

Rain was coming down in sheets, and we were sitting looking out onto the downpour from the veranda of Mr. Krishnamurthy's house. Men in white lungis bicycled past, their right hand on the handlebars and their left holding up an umbrella. Rickshaws sluiced through the flooded streets, their wheels cutting wakes through the ankle-deep water, like motorboats on a canal.

Earlier, Mr. Krishnamurthy had seen me caught in the downpour and had beckoned me over. While we waited for the rain to end, and the annual procession of the village gods to begin, he had introduced me to his friend. Srikanda, explained Mr. Krishnamurthy, was a Brahmin and an idol maker, or Stpathy: the twenty-third in a long hereditary line stretching back to the great bronze casters of the Chola empire, which had ruled most of southern India until the end of the thirteenth century. His workshop was a short distance away in the great temple town of Swamimalai. There he and his two elder brothers plied their trade, making gods and goddesses in exactly the manner of their ancestors.

Srikanda was a plump, middle-aged man with a side parting and a slightly slow left eye. He wore a freshly laundered white lungi and a long baggy white shirt which nearly, but not quite, hid the swelling bulge of his rice stomach. On his left breast he wore a small enamelled star which, he explained proudly, was his badge of office as president of the Swamimalai Lions' Club; our host, Mr. Krishnamurthy, who was the proprietor of the Sri Murugan Hotel, and also headed the local temple committee, was his vice president. It was Mr. Krishnamurthy who had commissioned Srikanda to cast the new pair of idols that were about to be processed around the village for the first time, before being taken off to visit the great Murugan temple in Swamimalai.

I had arrived in Tamil Nadu only a couple of days before. It was the week of Tamil New Year, and I had come to see one of the many temple chariot processions which each year mark the occasion. The monsoon had not yet broken, yet already the humidity was high, and the rains which fell late each afternoon were heavy and insistent. Sheet lightning quaked sourceless beyond the distant thunderheads. For an hour each day, the dark archipelagos of cloud bank massing over the Kaveri Delta let loose a great white waterfall that flooded the rice fields and washed clean the dusty fronds of the palm trees, ran down the tumbling eaves of the temple *gopuras* and soaked the palm thatch of the village huts.

The village, when I finally found it, did not look as if it was about to celebrate its annual festival. It was true that an improvised *rath,* or chariot, constructed from a farm cart topped with a brightly coloured wooden canopy, was parked outside the temple, under a makeshift rain shelter of bamboo and palm leaves, and that inside the chariot were the dressed, anointed and garlanded images of the village's deities. But although the procession was due to set off at 5 p.m., when I arrived only half an hour earlier no crowds had assembled in the wet village street, and there was no Brahmin there to supervise. Instead, the area outside the temple was deserted except for a kneeling calf, a pair of wet black goats drinking from puddles and several roosters who strutted around, eyeing up a nearby gaggle of hens. Farther up the road, a group of barefoot children were playing cricket in the rain, with a broken stool for a wicket.

Mr. Krishnamurthy, however, was confident that, despite the downpour, the festival would go ahead and the procession would take place: "No problem," he said. "Pundit will come. Time is there."

As we waited for the rain to end, we talked about Srikanda's business, and he told me the story of his family. The Stpathys, he explained, had been sculptors of stone idols in Vellore before being called to Tanjore to learn the art of bronze casting at the time of Rajaraja I (AD 985–1014), one of the great kings of the Chola empire. After assisting in the construction of the two greatest Chola temples, at Tanjore and Gangakondacholapuram, they settled in Swamimalai in the thirteenth century. This happened after one of his ancestors discovered by accident that clay made from the especially fine silt at the bend in the Kaveri on the edge of the town was uniquely well suited to making the moulds in which the bronzes were cast. The bronze idol business had now kept them in work for nearly 700 years. "It is with the blessings of the Almighty," he said proudly, "that we have taken this birth, and are able to make our living in this way, creating gods in the form of man."

In fact, added Srikanda, business was very good at the moment, and the workshop had a backlog of orders that would take at least a year to clear. There was a growing market for what he called "show pieces" for tourists and collectors, but the family's main work was idols created in exactly the manner laid down by the ancient Hindu religious texts, the *Shilpa Shastras,* and specifically designed for temple worship. These days, he said, most of the orders were no longer from the Kaveri Delta, their traditional market, nor even from Tamil Nadu, so much as from the new temples springing up wherever the Indian—and especially Tamil—diaspora had settled around the world, from Neasden to New Jersey. Their largest order ever had been from Iskcon, the Hari Krishna headquarters in California.

As we sat sipping a cup of hot, sweet south Indian coffee brought by Mrs. Krishnamurthy, I asked Srikanda what it was like to forge the idols that other men worshipped.

"When I see one of the idols that I have made used in a temple, or in a procession," replied Srikanda, "I try not to think that this is something made by me, or even something made by man. I don't even think this is a good or bad statue. I think: this is a deity.

"Of course I do feel very proud," he added. He smiled, and slowly wobbled his head from side to side. "That is only human.

"God is inside us," he said. "It is from our hearts, our minds and our hands that god is formed, and revealed in the form of a metal statue. My statues are like my children. As we say, *silpi matha, pitha shastra*: the sculptor is the mother and the sacred *shastras* are the father. Usually I want to keep them, but this is my profession, so sooner or later they must leave me, just as a daughter leaves her father when she is married. Once the eyes are opened by having their pupils chiselled in with a gold chisel, once the deity takes on the form of the idol and it becomes alive, it is no longer mine. It is full of divine power, and I can no longer even touch it. Then it is no longer the creation of man, but a god only."

"It contains the spirit of god? Or it is a god?"

"It is a god," he replied firmly. "At least in the eyes of the faithful."

"What do you mean?"

"Without faith, of course, it is just a sculpture. It's the faith of devotees that turns it into a god."

It seemed to me that Srikanda had mentioned three quite different ways in which an inanimate statute could become a god: by the channelling of divinity via the heart and hands of the sculptor; a ceremony of invocation when the eyes were chipped open; and through the faith of the devotee. I pointed this out to Srikanda, but he saw no contradiction; all that mattered was that at a certain point a miracle took place and the statue he had made became divine.

"Our mind should never go back to what it was or how it came into being," he said. "It is the same as with a baby, or a small child. When it is young you play with it, but once it has grown up you treat it differently—as an adult, with more respect and more reverence."

Outside in the street the rain had almost stopped. As we talked, a large, burly, bare-chested Brahmin, hair cut into a topknot, clambered up onto the temple *rath*. He began to take the old garlands off the two idols, and from a big, bulging plastic shopping bag he produced a fresh set: red hibiscus for the goddess and white jasmine for the god. These he placed reverently over the deities, then applied a new sandalwood-paste tikka to the forehead of each. As he was working, a temple elephant ambled along the street, a mahout on his back and his tail swishing from side to side; bells rang from around his neck. Within a few minutes, the street had begun to fill with curious onlookers; even the cricket players left their game to see what was happening.

The festival was in honour of Valli, the second wife of Murugan, who was believed to be a girl from this village. She was born from a deer made pregnant by the glance of the sage Sivamurti, and was adopted by the king of the hunters, Nambiraja. Valli was the most beautiful girl in all Tamil Nadu. One day, when she was out in her father's fields, guarding the millet with her slingshot, Lord Murugan, the son of Shiva, happened to pass that way, and immediately fell in love with her.

To test her, he assumed the form of a feeble old man. First, he asked her for a drink of water, which she gladly gave him. He then asked for some food; this too she gave. Finally the old man asked for her hand in marriage, at which Valli of course hesitated, saying that how could she, such a young girl, marry such a very old man, and in any case she could only marry the man her father chose for her.

Realising that he needed some help, Murugan prayed to his brother Ganesh and immediately the latter appeared in the millet field, taking the form of a crazed wild elephant. Valli was terrified, and embracing the old man, promised him that she would indeed marry him if he saved her from the trumpeting elephant that was about to charge her and trample her underfoot. With a single wave of his outstretched hand, Murugan drove the elephant away, but once it had gone, Valli again hesitated, saying she could only marry a man her father chose. So Murugan prayed to Ganesh a second and then a third time, but each time Valli agreed and then hesitated about marrying such a very decrepit old man.

Only on the fourth occasion did Murugan finally reveal himself in all his divine beauty, and immediately, and inevitably, Valli fell in love. All this, said Mr. Krishnamurthy, had taken place in the fields of this very village and the festival they were holding today was to celebrate the divine marriage. Murugan and Valli were already waiting for the marriage ceremony in their temple at Swamimalai. It was the traditional privilege of this village to escort Valli's family from their home to the great temple in town. Previously the villagers had had to take a pair of very simple iconic stone idols on the *barat* procession to the wedding. Now, thanks to Srikanda, they had glistening new bronze idols, the equal of any in Swamimalai.

"Normally we have to go to the temple to pray to the gods," said Mr. Krishnamurthy, "but today they come to us in our houses in the village. For us it is the most auspicious day of the year."

"If you pray here today," added Srikanda, "your prayers will certainly be successful."

"More than on other days?"

"Of course," said Srikanda. "God is everywhere, but just as we feel that an idol can be the focus for a god's power, so there are certain days when your prayers are more readily heard and fulfilled."

It was, I thought, a lovely idea: that just as there were sacred images and sacred places there were also pools of sacred time. For faithful Hindus it was as if a window momentarily clicked open in the heavens, allowing devotees direct access to the divine.

As we were talking, there was a roll of drums and a fanfare on the *nadeswaram*, the giant Tamil oboe whose raucous notes fill the air with a noise like the screech of peacocks. Two musicians whom I had earlier spotted sheltering from the rain in a nearby hut now appeared between the chariot and the elephant, and as they struck up the music, the street quickly filled with people, including a number of fruit and balloon vendors who had appeared, as if by magic, with carts displaying their wares.

By now the rain had completely stopped and the evening light was beginning to filter through the clouds. Farther up the street, the girls of the village were busy sweeping the fronts of their houses and making *rangoli* patterns with rice powder on their doorsteps. In twenty minutes the mood had completely changed—not for nothing are such festivals known as *"utsavas"*–"that which drives away sorrow."

As I watched, Srikanda walked up to the chariot and presented a silver *thali* plate of offerings to the Brahmin: inside were coconuts, pieces of jackfruit, two bananas, some incense sticks and a small pile of *ladoo* milk sweets. The Brahmin cracked the coconuts on the side of the cart, then lit the incense sticks and circled the plate of offerings in front of the two idols.

From every house devotees, most of them women, now emerged holding *thali* plates, jasmine garlands and other presents for the deities. For twenty minutes coconuts were cracked and offerings made. Then the Brahmin shouted out a word of command, and all the cricket players and their equally ragged sisters began pushing the chariot from behind, while the fathers and uncles of the village pulled at the ropes that had been attached to the front. As the chariot began to creek slowly up the street with the elephant in the lead, the goats and chickens scattered and some of the villagers went down on their knees before the idols. Despite the damp and puddles, a few even performed full-length prostrations in the street.

I asked Srikanda if he shouldn't be taken in the chariot alongside his gleaming new idols, as I heard happened during certain festivals. "Not on this occasion," he said. "They are deities. I am not on their level, so I cannot have equal rank. But if we give a new chariot to a temple, then the Brahmins there will give us new gold rings and turbans and we are given a round—a *parikrama*—of the four gates of the temple in the chariot we have built. On that occasion only we are given the same level of respect as an idol."

"Now," he added, "I will only walk alongside them."

In the end, we walked together. At one point, the top of the chariot pulled down an illegal electricity connection that was strung across the road to draw power from the grid, and there was a small stampede to avoid the fizzing wire; but otherwise the procession made slow and stately progress past the byres and hayricks and cowsheds of the village, stopping briefly to pay respects at the small shrine of the other protector deity of the village, Mariamman. Every twenty or thirty yards the temple chariot came to a standstill so that the deities could receive the offerings of each new group of householders.

"Look at all the people honouring the gods," said Srikanda happily. "It is very good for me to leave the workshop occasionally to see such festivals. We get so buried in the daily detail of our work that sometimes we forget that idols are the base of our Hindu worship: everything else is built on top of this. Without a *murti*, there could be no *puja*, no temples, nowhere for people to come with their prayers and their problems. Really—a devotee can tell an idol secrets they can't tell even to their wife or children."

Srikanda gestured to the devotees now surrounding the chariot on all sides. "All these people have a lot of worries—about money, about family, about work. But when they come to the god in a temple, or a festival like this, for a while their problems vanish and they are satisfied."

He smiled. "When I see the worshippers praying to a god I helped bring into being, then my happiness is complete. I know that though the span of my life is only eighty or ninety years, the images live for a thousand years, and we live on in those images. We may be mortal, but our work is immortal."

There are few places in the world where landscape and divinity are more closely linked than in southern India.

In the sacred topography of the south, every village is believed to be host to a numberless pantheon of sprites and godlings, tree spirits and snake gods, who are said to guard and regulate the ebb and flow of daily life. They are worshipped and propitiated, as they know the till and soil of the local fields and the sweet water of the wells, even the needs and thirsts of the cattle and the goats of the village.

If the villages are the preserve of godlings and obscure village goddesses, then in the prosperous temple towns that dot the plains of the south many of the features of the landscape are animated with stories and myths which link them with the great pan-Indian gods Shiva, Vishnu and the Devi: on this shoreline, by this temple, the Devi does penance, waiting until the end of the great Cosmic Flood, after which she will finally celebrate her marriage; that rock was an evil elephant who attempted to trample the town's Brahmins to death before being turned to stone by Lord Shiva; this temple marks the place where a peahen with beautiful eyes in its tail was revealed to be the goddess Parvati in disguise; the river there was created by Lord Murugan to quench the thirst of one of his wedding guests who had developed an unbearable craving for water after too much salty rice.

Lying in the centre of these towns, the great temples of Tamil Nadu are conceived as the palaces of the gods. But the gods of this country are understood to be jealous and territorial deities, and instead of sitting in their temple-palaces, their devotees believe that they like to oversee their domains. It is for this reason that on the great festivals they are taken out from the temples, robed, jewelled and garlanded, put on a palanquin or temple chariot, offered betel leaves and areca nuts, and then, like a raja surveying his dominions, given a tour so that they can establish their sovereignty, and be taken along a circuit of the borders of their kingdom.

Here in the streets and fields they receive tributes and offerings, while their devotees and subjects—including those of the lower castes who were traditionally not admitted to the temples—can see them, and make *darshan*, so giving the gods pleasure while at the same time providing spiritual merit for the devotees. Such expeditions sometimes end with the god taking a bath at the mouth of the delta of a sacred river, or taking a trip on a boat in a temple tank. On return the idols are bathed in milk, curds, butter, honey and sugar, before being anointed with sandalwood paste and dressed in the finest silks.

When these temples were first built, the large stone idols of the temple sanctuaries were often found to be too large to move around. It was for this reason that in the tenth century the first portable bronze deities began to be cast in southern India. The art seems to have begun in the court of the Pallava monarchs of Kanchipuram, but it was under the patronage of their nemesis, the Chola kings of Tanjore, that the sculptors of this region brought the art to perfection. On the completion of their great dynastic temple in Tanjore in 1010 AD, the Cholas donated to their new structure no fewer than sixty bronze images of deities, of which about two-thirds were given by Rajaraja I, while the rest were given by his sisters, queens, officials and nobles. According to Srikanda, the Stpathy who oversaw all this casting was his direct ancestor Kunjaramalla Rajaraja Perunthatchan.

Exquisitely poised and supple, these Chola bronze deities are some of the greatest works of art ever created in India. They stand quite silent on their plinths, yet with their hands they speak gently to their devotees through the noiseless lingua franca of the mudras—gestures—of south Indian dance. For their devotees, their hands are raised in blessing and reassurance, promising boons and protection, and above all, marriage, fertility and fecundity, in return for the veneration that is so clearly their divine right.

It is the Nataraja, Shiva as Lord of the Dance, which is arguably the greatest artistic creation of the entire Chola dynasty. On one level Shiva dances in triumph at his defeat of the demons of ignorance and darkness, and for the pleasure of his consort. At another level—dreadlocks flying, haloed in fire—he is also dancing the world into extinction so as to bring it back into existence in order that it can be created and preserved anew. With one hand he is shown holding fire, signifying destruction, while with the other he bangs the *damaru* drum, whose sound denotes creation. Renewed and purified, the Nataraja is dancing the universe from perdition to regeneration in a circular symbol of the circular nature of time itself.

In Western art, few sculptors—other than perhaps Donatello or Rodin—have achieved the pure essence of sensuality so spectacularly evoked by the Chola sculptors, or achieved such a sense of celebration of the divine beauty of the human body. There is a startling clarity and purity about the way the near-naked bodies of the gods and the saints are displayed, yet by the simplest of devices the sculptors highlight their spirit and powers, joys and pleasures, and their enjoyment of each other's beauty.

In one idol in the Tanjore Museum, Lord Shiva reaches out and fondly touches the breast of his consort, Uma-Parvati, who is naked but for anklets, bangles and waistband supporting a thin and diaphanous silk wrap. In another he nuzzles the back of her naked shoulders or touches the lobe of her ear. It is a characteristically restrained Chola way of hinting at the unmatched erotic powers of a god whose iconic image is a phallic symbol, and who is celebrated in the scriptures for his millennia-long bouts of Himalayan lovemaking. In some Tamil temples, the last act of the priests, before they close the doors of the inner shrine, is to remove the nose jewel of the bronze idol of Shiva's consort lest the rubbing of it irritate her husband when they make love—an act, so the priests will tell you, that ensures the preservation and regeneration of the universe.

Elsewhere, Hindu devotional sculpture can often be explicitly and unembarrassedly erotic: across India can be found medieval Hindu temples whose exterior walls contain graphic scenes of oral and group sex—most famously, and inventively, at Khajuraho and Konarak. This same sensuousness is also there in the startlingly beautiful Tamil poetry of the period:

> Her arms have the beauty
> Of a gently moving bamboo.
> Her eyes are full of peace.
> She is faraway,
> Her place not easy to reach.
> My heart is frantic
> With haste
> A ploughman with a single ox
> On land all wet
> And ready for seed.

Or again:

> My Love
> whose bangles
> glitter, jingle,
> as she chases crabs
> suddenly stands shy,
> head lowered,
> hair hiding her face;
> but only till the misery of evening
> passes, when she'll give me
> the full pleasure
> of her breasts.

To some extent, none of this is a surprise. Sexuality in India has always been regarded as the subject of legitimate and sophisticated inquiry. Traditionally it was looked upon as an essential part of the study of aesthetics: *sringara rasa*—the erotic *rasa*, or flavour—being one of the nine *rasas* comprising the classical Hindu aesthetic system. The Judaeo-Christian religious tradition, which tends to emphasise the sinfulness of the flesh, the dangers of sexuality and the idealisation of sexual renunciation and virginity, begins its myth of origin with the creation of light. In contrast, the oldest scripture of the Hindu tradition, the *Rig Veda*, begins its myth with the creation of *kama*—sexual desire: in the beginning was desire, and desire was with God, and desire was God. In the Hindu scheme of things, *kama* remains one of the three fundamental goals of human existence, along with dharma, duty or religion, and *artha*, the creation of wealth.

What is perhaps more surprising is that the same erotic concerns found in the secular poetry of classical India are equally evident in the devotional and religious poetry of the period: Kalidasa's poem *The Birth of Kumara*, for example, has an entire canto of ninety-one verses entitled "The Description of Uma's Pleasure," which describes in graphic detail the lovemaking of Lord Shiva and his divine consort. The poetry of the Tamil saints, who walked from temple to temple in the region during the early centuries AD, singing and converting the local Jains and Buddhists, likewise dwells at length on the sensuous beauty of the deities they adore. The boy saint Sambandar, for example, was especially taken by the loveliness of Uma-Parvati, who, it was said, had taken human form and suckled and comforted him when, as an infant, he was left crying on a temple ghat, while his father went off to bathe:

> Smooth and curved,
> her stomach
> like the snake's
> dancing hood,
> her flawless gait
> mocks the peacock's grace.
> With feet soft
> as cotton down
> and waist
> a slender creeper.

Nor was it just the female deities who were imagined as magnificently sexual beings. The saint Appar, a convert from Jainism, wrote with equal sensuousness of Lord Shiva in his incarnation as the Enchanting Mendicant, a form of the god particularly popular with the Cholas and sculpted on the walls of many of the great Chola temples. In this poem, Appar imagines himself as one of the girls who falls in love with Shiva in this form of the beautiful beggar, whose stunning good looks could entrap any woman whom he approached with his begging bowl:

> Listen my friend,
> yesterday,
> in broad daylight
> I'm sure I saw
> a holy one.
>
> As he gazed at me
> my garments slipped
> I stood entranced,
> I brought him alms
> but nowhere did I see
> that Cunning One—
> If I see him again
> I shall press my body
> against his body
> never to let him go,
> that wanderer
> who lives in Ottiyur.

If Chola poetry is sometimes explicit, then in Chola sculpture the sexual nature of the gods is strongly implied rather than directly stated. It is there in the extraordinary swinging rhythm of these eternally still figures, in their curving torsos and their slender arms. The figures are never completely naked; these divine beings may embody human desire, but unlike the sculpture at Khajuraho, the Chola deities, while clearly preparing to enjoy erotic bliss, are never actually shown in flagrante; their desire is permanently frozen at a point before its final consummation.

The distinctly sensual charge of the bronzes is not just a modern reading: devotees from the Chola period who viewed images of the gods enraptured by their consort's beauty left inscriptions asking the deities to transfer the sensual ecstasy they experience to their less fortunate followers. There is reason to believe that some of the images of goddesses were modelled on actual Chola queens—a Parvati in the Tanjore Museum is one example—and physical grace and sexual prowess seem to have been regarded among the Cholas not as private matters, but as vital and admired attributes in both god and ruler. When the dynasty was first established in Tanjore in AD 862, the official declaration compared the conquest of the town to the Chola monarch's love sport: "He, the light of the Solar race, took possession [of the town] . . . just as he would seize by the hand his own wife who had beautiful eyes, graceful curls, a cloth covering her body, in order to sport with her." What was true of rulers was also true of the gods, and there are many *bhakti* devotional poems apparently inspired by the feelings of a poet-devotee lost in an intense sensual-spiritual swoon before the beauty of an idol in a temple:

> So my mind touches the lotus feet of Ranga's Lord,
> Delights in his fine calves, clings
> To his twin thighs and, slowly,
> Rising, reaches
> The navel.
>
> It stops for a while on his chest,
> Then, after climbing
> His broad shoulders,
> Drinks the nectar of his lovely face.

Hinduism has always held that there are many paths to God. Yet for many centuries there has been a central tension between the ascetic and the sensual. The poet-prince Bhartrihari of Ujjain, who probably lived in the fourth century AD, oscillated no fewer than seven times between the rigours of monastic renunciation and the abandon of the courtly sensualist. "There are two paths," he wrote. "The devotion of the sage, which is lovely because it overflows with the nectarous waters of the knowledge of truth" and "the lusty undertaking of touching with one's palm that hidden part in the firm laps of lovely limbed women, with great expanses of breasts and thighs."

"Tell us decisively which we ought to attend upon?" he asks in the *Shringarashataka*: "The sloping sides of the mountains in the wilderness? Or the buttocks of a woman abounding in passion?"

In the sculpture of the Cholas, and those like Srikanda who have kept its flame alive in the Kaveri Delta ever since, this tension is at least partially resolved. More than in any other Indian artistic tradition, the gods here are both intensely physical and physically gorgeous. The sensuality of a god was understood as an aspect of his formless perfection and divine inner beauty. Celebrating and revelling in the sensuality of a god was therefore central to the devotee's expression of love for that deity.

In this conception of theology, it was not considered necessary to renounce the world to gain Enlightenment in the manner of the Jains or the Buddhists or the Hindu sadhus; nor was it necessary to perform the bloody animal sacrifices or fire ceremonies laid down in the *Vedas*. Instead, intensely loving devotion and regular *pujas* to images were believed to bring salvation just as effectively. For if the gods were universal, ranging through time and space, they were also forcefully present in certain holy places and most especially in the idols of the great temples. Here the final climax of worship is still to have *darshan*: to actually see the beauty of the divine image, and to meet the eyes of the god. The gaze of the bronze deity meets the eyes of the worshipper, and it this exchange of vision—the seeing and the seen—that acts as a focus for *bhakti*, the passionate devotion of the devotee.

The idea of the bronzes as the devotional focus for a religious rapture in which God is often envisaged as a lover is something that would have been entirely familiar to the ancient Babylonians, Greeks and Romans, but which is as far as it is possible to go, theologically, from the three Abrahamic religions, with their scriptural suspicion of idols and graven images, and their deep misgivings about sexual pleasure.

As Srikanda later put it to me, "What is so strange about the statues being beautiful and attractive? The erotic is part of human life—the secret part—and the idol is the human form of God, God in the form of man. If it was unattractive and ugly, would anyone pray to it? The *Shilpa Shastras* that guide us as sculptors lay down certain norms about the correct proportions for each god. We believe that unless these proportions are exactly perfect, the god cannot live in the idol. As sculptors, we struggle to become master craftsmen just so that we can begin to convey the beauty of the deity.

"Only then," he said, "will a deity attract devotees. And it is only then that we as sculptors begin to do justice to the tradition we have inherited from our forefathers."

Swamimalai, where the Chola tradition of idol making has survived in the workshops of Srikanda Stpathy's family, lies a couple of hours' drive from the small airstrip at Trichinopoly, which itself lies a bumpy forty-minute flight in an old-fashioned twin-prop from Madras.

Returning to the area two months after my first visit, as the plane banked and emerged below the monsoon clouds, I could see for the first time the rich soils of the Kaveri Delta spread out below: a flat plain, the essence of green, broken into a mirrored patchwork of flooded paddy fields, each square glinting with a slightly different refraction in the light of the late afternoon sun. Through the middle ran the thin silver ribbon of the Kaveri, winding its way slowly through an avenue of palms that line the banks of this rich delta, before looping itself around the island temple of Srirangam and the great smooth rock of Trichinopoly.

Other parts of India may be leaping aggressively forward into the new millennium, but for a visitor at least, rural Tamil Nadu still seems deceptively innocent and timeless. On the way from Trichy airport, the villagers spread their newly harvested grain on the road to be winnowed and threshed by the wheels of passing cars. The villages appear like those in R.K. Narayan stories, with roadside shops full of sacks of dried red chilli and freshly cut stalks of green bananas. Buffaloes are wallowing on the sandbanks of the Kaveri, and bullock carts trundle along red dirt roads, past village duck ponds and the tall, rain-wet fans of banana trees. Old women in blue saris sit out on their verandas, while their granddaughters troop along the roads with jasmine flowers in their hair. The cattle are strong and white, and their long horns are painted blue.

Overlooking this landscape for miles in every direction is the *vimana* pyramid-spire of the great Tanjore temple. It rises 216 feet tall above the horizontal plain, dominating the flat-roofed village houses and the farmland round about as completely as the cathedrals of the Middle Ages must once have dominated the landscape of Europe: like Chartres or Cologne, this was the tallest building in the country when it was built. The temple was created by the great Rajaraja I, whose rule was in many ways the Golden Age of Tamil culture, and the occasion for a renaissance of Tamil literature, scholarship, philosophy and poetry. He sent embassies to China and war fleets as far as Bali; conquered Sri Lanka, the Maldives, Kerala and the Deccan, exerted hegemony over Java and made Tanjore the capital of southern India.

Only at the end of his reign did Rajaraja erect his magnificent temple to commemorate his glory. A massively self-confident and imperial statement, it was five times the size of any previous Chola shrine, yet built entirely without mortar. The top finial at the apex of the pyramid is of solid stone and weighs eighty tons; it was hoisted into place by the erection of a ramp four miles long and pulled up to its socket at the very top by thousands of bullocks.

Entering the great temple today, and passing over the warm flagstones through two magnificent courtyards, each reached through a monumental gateway, you see on every side oiled black stone images of gods and demons, saints and hermits, and in particular of Lord Shiva and his consorts. In front of some, pilgrims prostrate themselves full-length; in front of others, small offerings of flowers are placed, or the flames of small camphor lamps are lit.

The Cholas fell from power in the thirteenth century, yet the classical Tamil Hindu civilisation that they cultivated in the south still survives partly intact. Some of the rituals you see today in the Tanjore temple are described in the *Rig Veda*, written when both the

Pyramids and Stonehenge were still in use. Yet Sanskrit, the language of the *Vedas*, is still alive, and while Zeus, Jupiter and Isis are all dead and forgotten, Lord Shiva is now more revered than ever, and the great Chola temples at Chidambaram and Tanjore are still thriving and bustling.

Moreover, the devotional world which brought the Chola bronzes into being is still, just, intact. On my way from the airport to see Srikanda's workshop in Swamimalai, I arranged to meet in the temple courtyard Shankara Narayana, one of the last professional singers of *Thevaram* devotional songs. These are the seven volumes of devotional hymns written by Appar, Sambandar and the other great Tamil saints, and first performed in this temple over a thousand years ago. I asked Shankara Narayana what it was like to sing in front of one of the temple's great bronzes. "As singers, we try to lose ourselves in the beauty of Lord Shiva," he replied. "The bronzes allow us access to his beauty, and in turn our words help give life to the idol."

It was these *Thevaram* hymns—the widespread oral memory of which is only now beginning to be endangered—that created the intense, mystical and often sensual *bhakti* world which needed the Chola bronzes as focuses for devotion. The direct family link between the Chola bronze casters and Srikanda's family workshop in Swamimalai is only one aspect of a much wider continuity of Tamil theology and devotion.

On arrival at Swamimalai, I found Srikanda hard at work in his small family factory on the main street of the temple town.

No longer was he wearing the smart laundered lungi I had seen him wearing on my previous trip. Now he sat in an old stained vest and waist-wrap, unshaven yet with a smear of ash and sandalwood paste at the centre of his forehead. He was concentrating fixedly on a small idol of Mariamman, the mother goddess and principal deity of many of the villages of the region, gently chipping away at her with a hammer and chisel. While he finished his work, I looked around the workshop.

The smartest rooms were those closest to the street. Here, two air-conditioned offices contained piles of order books and a huge old-fashioned typewriter out of which sprouted several sheaves of carbon paper. It was manned by a matron in a stiff white sari who tap-tapped away at it with the regularity of a metronome. A few cuttings from newspapers were framed on the walls, as was a large photograph of Srikanda with his father and two brothers, receiving some award from Mr. Karunanidhi, the sunglasses-wearing former screenwriter who was now Chief Minister of Tamil Nadu.

The next room was the workshop proper. On one desk was the abandoned arm of a goddess, moulded in fresh beeswax and tree resin; beside it was a small basin of wax warming on a brazier, along with a knife, a scalpel and a litter of pellets and shavings which some craftsman had left lying there while taking a tea break. A second basin, filled with water, contained a collection of finished but detached body parts, as if from the casualty unit of a Victorian field hospital.

Next to it was another desk, where one of Srikanda's elder brothers was busy kneading, smoothing, cutting and rolling a length of wax into what would soon be a deity's arm. The moulding took place with incredible speed, and with the ease of a child playing with plasticine. It seemed to be done entirely from memory: no pattern book or model lay open to guide him. When it was nearly done, and the fingers worked into the appropriate mudra, Srikanda's brother held it in his left hand and began to finish modelling its curves with a hot scalpel. This he replaced every few minutes from a selection of chisels up-ended in a charcoal fire-pot at the edge of the workbench. As he gently caressed the wax with a series of quick strokes from the flat, hot blade it first liquefied, then vanished, with a sizzle of wax and a puff of fragrant resin.

On the floor at the other side of the room sat eight cross-legged workers, all stripped to the waist, chipping, filing, finishing and decorating the cast bronzes. One boy was busy polishing with a bottle of Brasso and an old rag; another rested the head of a nearly completed goddess on a wooden chock while he worked on her bangles and armlets. All around the workers were ranks of gleaming bronze idols in various stages of finish, some dull and leaden-looking, fresh from the furnace, others shiny and brassy new, while a few were of the same darkly muted gunmetal grey as those in museums.

The room beyond—which opened onto a yard and a cow byre at the back—was the part of the workshop that contained the furnaces, and was surrounded on all sides by a litter of slag and broken moulds. Here two men were calmly engaged in covering one of the wax models in a clay mud pack, while a third was embalming a finished mould in a lattice of wire, ready for firing.

Opposite them, only a short distance away, a pair of sweating dark-skinned and barefoot workers were stoking a furnace set in the mud floor, while a third worker fired it up with a pair of enormous bellows. Into this ever-hotter furnace, the two stokers were shoving old scrap—a series of crushed bronze *lota* pots, pieces of copper wire and brass plates. The temperature was very high, and orange, green and pale yellow flames shot out as the inferno was fed.

Then, as I watched, one of the two stokers took a crucible of molten metal from the furnace and poured it into the mouth of the waiting mould, the glowing green liquid metal pouring as easily as water from a kettle. To one side of this furious furnace scene lay a garland of fresh marigolds, remnants of the *puja* which had preceded the beginning of the casting, while beyond, two cows were chewing the cud.

Srikanda joined me there, explaining that the cows' role was to provide milk for *pujas* and to create an auspicious and appropriately Hindu environment. He then demonstrated the lost-wax process by which the bronzes were made. He showed me how, just as his ancestors used to do, he first made a perfect model of a god in a soft and pliable mixture of beeswax and resin; how the model was encased in a fine-grained clay made from the Kaveri alluvium, tinctured with charred coconut husks and salt, then left to dry in the sun for a week. The clay mud pack, he explained, was then buried and heated in such a way that the wax ran out, leaving a mould into which the molten bronze was then poured—a process he compared to conception, with the mould taking the place of the womb for the future god, and the slag that of the blood and afterbirth, with the sculptor as midwife and wet nurse. Ten minutes later, the mould was broken open and the sculpture of the god was waiting, ready for the beginning of the process of finishing.

As he spoke, the two workers who had poured the liquid metal into the mould now placed it into a vat of water to cool it. Then they began to break the mould open. "This is the most magical bit," said Srikanda as we watched, "and the most unpredictable. You do not know whether the casting has worked until this moment.

Gently tapping with their hammers, the two men broke away the clay, so that the head, leg and trident of an image of Kali began to take shape amid the mess of fused mud. It felt slightly like watching an archaeological excavation, as a familiar object emerged from the earth through the careful prodding of the specialists. "The finishing which follows this is the most arduous part of the process," said Srikanda. "For a large idol, this alone can take as long as six weeks."

This, he added, was the only point at which he believed their technique diverged from those of the Chola master casters: so fine and skilled was the work of their Chola forebears, said Srikanda, that their pieces needed virtually no finishing after they emerged from their moulds. Today, he said, somehow there were always flaws, and the idols emerged from the casting in need of much smoothing and polishing before they would be ready for the eye-opening ceremony. Somewhere along the generational line of Chinese Whispers, the secret of flawless casting had been lost.

The whole process, explained Srikanda, was itself encased in a fine mould of ancient ritual: only on a new moon or a full moon could a model be begun or cast; no work except finishing could be done while the moon was waning. The idol's eyes must be carved open between 4 a.m. and 6 a.m., when there was no sound or disturbance which might upset the deity; no meat or alcohol could be consumed while a bronze was being made; a series of ancient Sanskrit incantations—the *Admartha Slokas*—must initiate the process, and another set—the *Dhyana Slokas*—must be spoken while the work was in progress. All prayer and thought should be focused on the deity who was to be asked to take possession of the idol. All the proportions, gestures and sacred geometry were exactly laid down by tradition, and only the most elite families of Stpathy Brahmins, literate in Sanskrit and all the appropriate *shastras*, were allowed to work on pieces intended for worship.

"Our workshop should be like a temple," Srikanda said. "Every second is holy. Some people think that what we do is an art, but we think of it mainly as an act of devotion. For us art and religion are one: only when there is prayer can the artist make a perfect sculpture. Even the wax models we create have a little of God's *jivan* [life] in them, so we give even that reverence, and as we work we think only of God, saying the appropriate mantras as we carve and model.

"These idols are reflections of our minds and spirits, so while we are at work on a sculpture we must behave as if we were in a holy temple: we must speak only the truth, and be kind and polite to everyone. Until the sculpture is finished, for weeks we must follow all the rules and regulations that have been laid down."

It was true, he said, that there were other workshops in Swamimalai which did not follow these traditions. They didn't know Sanskrit, so they were unable to read the *Shilpa Shastras,* and broke many of the sacred rules and conventions. They employed Dalits—untouchables—and atheists, and regarded making idols principally as a business, aimed at selling to tourists. "Some of their work is very good technically," he said. "Art lovers will be satisfied, but I do not think their idols are divine. No respectable temple will touch bronzes made in this way. That kind of work never moves or touches me. As an outsider you may not be able to see the difference, but we can. It may seem unjust today, and we all respect talent, whatever caste it is born into. But the rules of the *shastras* are quite clear, and we believe God will only be there if the particular image is made exactly according to the rules."

I asked whether the gods remained in the images forever. Srikanda explained that Hindus believe that, like humans, the idols of deities also have a defined life span: that the *jivan* will not stay in a sculpture forever, though it may do so, if properly and faithfully worshipped, for as long as 850 years, the faith of the devotees in effect keeping the idols alive in their old age. But as the idol heads for its millennium, the *jivan* in even the most adored and carefully tended idols will start to fade and disappear.

If the idol was not properly tended to, the *jivan* could ebb much earlier, and if stolen or abused, the deity would leave the statue immediately. Such was the case with all the idols in museums, none of which was now alive. Each sculpture has a birth star, and according to its size and proportions, the *shastras* give elaborate astrological formulations by which the life of a sculpture can be determined, in the same manner as it is believed that the life of a human being can be determined by a carefully calculated horoscope. If the god was intended for private *puja* in a home, the horoscope of the husband and wife would be taken, and the proportions of the god subtly altered to best suit the stars of that family.

As we chatted, Srikanda was chipping away with his chisel at the rounded breasts of the goddess. I asked whether it was ever difficult or distracting for the sculptors having to deal with such deliberately sensuous forms. Srikanda acknowledged the problem: "We have to look at these idols as a goddess," he said. "Never as a human body."

He smiled. "Once when I was installing one of my idols in the Murugan temple in London, I visited the waxworks at Madame Tussaud's. There I saw an image of Aishwarya Rai, and of course you immediately think of all the love films you have seen her in. When you are making an idol of the Devi you must always fight such thoughts, and instead concentrate on your prayers."

He paused. "Self-discipline is the most important thing in this job. It is just as important as skill. Many have lost their skills through lack of self-control. If a god is in the heart and that heart becomes corrupted, the deity cannot flow through that sculptor into the idol. Good Stpathys—some of the best artists, unique artists—have lost their abilities in this way. You need to maintain not just your skills, but also your discipline."

When I came back at 9 a.m. the following morning, Srikanda had already been at work for five hours: his day began when the workshop opened at 4 a.m.

As he chipped away with his chisel, now finishing a large idol of the mountain god of Kerala, Lord Ayappa, I asked him about his childhood. "I don't remember when I first visited my father's workshop," said Srikanda. "It was probably as a baby. I spent much of my childhood there, and even before we went to school my father encouraged us to play there, making toy animals with the wax and resin. First I made a snake, then an elephant. All this came in the same way that a fish knows how to swim, without having to be taught. It is in my blood."

Srikanda said that it was while watching a procession of the gods through Swamimalai that he thought for the first time that he had to become a sculptor like his grandfather, father and uncles.

"It was the festival of Kartika," he said, "and huge crowds were pouring into the village to watch the procession of Murugan through the town. Many were carrying pots of milk on their head with which to bathe the idols. It is said that if you go to the temple on that day whatever you wish for will be accomplished.

"Everyone was decorating the front of their house, and my father had put hundreds of bronze idols from his store out on the shop front. Eventually the temple chariot passed our shop—it was much smaller in those days—and as it passed my father whispered to me that our forefathers had made the image of Murugan and donated it to the temple. I was so proud, and realised that these skills we pass down are the gods' gift to this family. Ever since then my only ambition has been to be a master craftsman and to try to equal the skills of my father and uncle.

"I trained by watching my father. At the same time my grandfather would teach us all Sanskrit for three hours a day so that we could read and understand the complex sacred geometry of the *Shilpa Shastras*, and comprehend the nature of each deity. From the age of eighteen, once we had got places at college, we were allowed to begin our formal training in the college holidays. First we were taught to work wax and make the wax models, with our father overseeing our work. Only then were we allowed to graduate to engraving and finishing all the jewellery and ornamental articles on the bodies of the deities. Making the faces and hands, finishing them, and the whole process of casting: these are the most difficult skills. The chiselling is the most painful part to accomplish: if you work hard even for one day you can get a bad pain at the back of your shoulders.

"In the house, my father was very free. He played with all of us, and just smiled if we made a noise, or if we three brothers fought with one another. But in the factory he was completely different. If we made any noise or didn't concentrate on our work he could be very severe and very angry—everything was about rules and regulations. He wanted us to treat our work like yoga, and lose ourselves in a trance of total concentration.

"Every month or so he would take us to the Tanjore Museum, where they have on display the greatest collection of Chola bronzes in the world. Even the museum in Delhi does not have their equal. My father used to say that this was our university. He would make us look at each piece very carefully, and when we got home he would make us try to copy the statue in wax. It was the best training I could ever have had. The work of our ancestors has never been equalled, and they are still the best teachers.

"Once when there was the Festival of India in New York, the government asked my father to make a copy of the greatest masterpiece in the museum—Shiva as Vrishabhavahana, the herdsman, from the hoard of buried bronzes that were unearthed in Tiruvengadu in the 1950s. Many people regard it as the finest bronze in the world. My father moved into the museum and he took us with him as his assistants. We lived there for six weeks and when the replica was finished no one could tell the difference between the two. The Archaeological Survey of India were so anxious about its perfection that they made my father write REPLICA in large letters on each side of the plinth, then placed it in a vault in their headquarters in Madras in case anyone tried to switch the two. Even today when we export our idols they are frequently seized by customs officers who think we are smuggling Chola originals.

"In 1984, at the age of twenty-two, soon after we had finished at the museum, my father decided I had learned enough to begin working on my first idol. He determined that I should begin my career by making the goddess of our village, Vikkali Amman. I worked night and day to get the wax model exactly correct, then to make a good mould. We fired the mould after three weeks of work, and I then spent three further weeks finishing the model. When it was done I presented it very formally to my father, as a *chela* to his guru. I was very nervous, as he was not easily pleased.

"He looked at it very carefully in silence for a long time. Then he gave some small suggestions for corrections where some of the jewellery was not done exactly right. He said nothing more. I made the corrections as he asked, and the following week we had the eye-opening ceremony.

"The god or goddess only fully enters a new idol when we open his eyes and carve in the pupils—the final piece of carving—and when the appropriate *puja* is performed. This is the most important and most intense moment. I am human: hard as I try, many times when I am carving I think of sales tax, family problems, getting the car repaired. But when the eyes are opened, and the appropriate mantras are chanted, I forget everything. I am lost to the world. I go into a state approaching meditation. Sometimes the devotees who sponsor the idol become possessed by the goddess, and dance around, speak in strange voices, or go shaking and shivering into a full trance. The priest has to wake them by putting *vibhuti* on their forehead and lighting a camphor light. This happened only last week: six or seven people who came for the ceremony were possessed, and one of them announced, 'I am the goddess and have come to solve your problems.'

"On this occasion it was especially intense. My father acted as the priest, invoking the deity to enter the statue, slowly chiselling open the eyes, and I sat there in a state that was part nerves, part excitement and part intense devotion. Only when the ceremony was finished and the deity was awakened did my father say that my workmanship had been perfect, and that he was very proud of me.

"Since then, I have been working continuously for twenty-five years, and still get satisfaction from each and every piece I work on. I never get bored. Sometimes, with a large piece, it can be hard, long, difficult work. My father used to say that the chisel was his teacher. It moves in a way that even we cannot control—the heart is its driver, and God is in the heart. With every piece I try to improve my skills and to design more beautiful images, within the strictures of the *shastras*. I still have much to learn, and don't feel that I am yet the equal of my father, still less even comparable to my ancestors. Even now I am adapting the way we do the casting in an attempt to find a way to achieve what they were once able to.

"Of course every human life has its problems, and there are stressful moments. But in general this is a peaceful life. It is also a good business, though I never think of it like that. No one can equal our skills, and so we almost have a monopoly, even though some of our rivals charge half what we do. We are now three brothers and I think forty-eight assistants. Each week we deliver four or five finished idols, and we have a one-year backlog on our books. Even if we were to do only urgent ones we would be busy for three months."

I asked about the future: would the tradition continue?

"Ah," he said, his face falling. "That is my only real worry: who knows what will happen after my generation has passed away? My son is saying that he wants to become a computer engineer in Bangalore, and that he will give up the family business, so breaking our lineage. His cousin—my elder brother's boy—is much the same. He knows the skills here, and can make a decent sculpture, but he is not a master craftsman. I suppose he's about halfway there. He studied computer science and is now doing a course in business administration. We hope he will come back here, but he's more interested in the Internet and what I think he calls online sales. He wants to expand the business, but is not really interested in making idols himself.

"When I was a boy my father told me that I would be a Stpathy. It was almost incidental that I wanted to be one myself. He did not give me a choice. I will not do that to my son. You cannot do that today. My son is obsessed with computers—he is always in front of the screen, always playing computer games. Certainly I will make sure that he has this skill—and already he can make good wax models. But if he gets good grades, and has the opportunity to study computer engineering at college, it would be unfair for me to deny him the opportunity he wants. Our work here is very hard. Computer work is not so difficult, and it pays much more."

I said: "That must worry you very much, after all these generations."

"I would be telling you a lie if I said I wasn't upset," he replied. "We are inheritors of an unbroken tradition, generation after generation, father to son, father to son, for over 700 years. That's part of what makes a difference with our sculptures. I do feel there is something special in the blood. At some level this is not a skill which can be taught. The blood itself teaches us our craft, just as a fish's blood teaches it to swim, or a peacock's blood teaches it to spread its tail. In the West you say art is all about inspiration, not lineage, and it's true that God can touch anyone, from any background. I've seen that with some of our assistants. But you cannot ignore blood, and all those countless generations of skill passed down. Somehow the gods guide us. When he was small—no older than six—my son did a drawing of Shiva of such power it made us all shake. I had very, very high hopes for him.

"Still, every day, I pray to our family deity, Kamakshi Amman, to change his mind and preserve the lineage. I have even promised to renovate her temple if my prayers are answered. But I know that if my boy gets high marks he will certainly go off to Bangalore—and it looks as if he will do well in his exams. For some reason all the Brahmin boys do well in maths and computer exams. Maybe that's in the blood too—after all we've been making calculations for astronomy for 5,000 years.

"I don't know," said Srikanda, shrugging his shoulders. "It's all part of the world opening up. After all, as my son says, this is the age of computers. And as much as I might want otherwise, I can hardly tell him this is the age of the bronze caster."

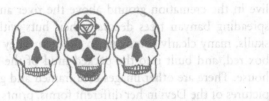

8

The Lady Twilight

Before you drink from a skull," said Manisha Ma Bhairavi, "you must first find the right corpse."

We were sitting in a palm-thatched hut amid the dark woods and smoking funeral pyres of the cremation ground at Tarapith in Bengal—a *shakti pith*, one of the most holy places in India, and said to be the abode of the Devi's Third Eye. It is also the home of the great goddess Tara.

Tarapith is an eerie place, with a sinister reputation. In Calcutta I had been told that it was notorious for the unsavoury Tantric rituals and animal sacrifices which were performed in the temple. Stranger things still were rumoured to take place after sunset in the riverside burning ground on the edge of the town, outside the boundaries of both village life and the conventions of Bengali society.

Here the goddess is said to live, and at midnight—so the Bengalis believe—Tara can be glimpsed in the shadows, drinking the blood of the goats slaughtered day after day in an effort to propitiate her anger and win her favour. In this frequently vegetarian country, where blood sacrifice is growing rarer and rarer, the worship of the goddess at Tarapith is an increasing oddity, a misweave in the weft of things, where can be found scenes almost unknown elsewhere: at least twenty goats a day are dispatched here to satisfy her hunger.

Tara is believed to be especially attracted to bones and skeletons, and for this reason the dreadlocked and ash-smeared sadhus who live in the cremation ground above the river and under the great spreading banyan trees decorate their huts with lines of human skulls, many clearly belonging to children. They are painted pillar-box red, and built into the packed mud of the threshold of each house. There are other images too: framed and garlanded calendar pictures of the Devi in her different forms, prints of the great saints of Tarapith, and tridents strung with garlands of marigolds; but it is skulls and bones that dominate, and not just human ones, but those of creatures of the night such as jackals and vultures, and even snakes.

"So how do you go about finding the right skull?" I asked Manisha.

"The Doms who administer the cremation ghats find them for us," she replied matter-of-factly. "They keep them for us and when we need them, they give them to us. The best ones are suicides," she added. "When someone has drunk poison or hanged themselves, their skulls are especially powerful. So are the skulls of innocent and pure *kumaris*—virgin girls."

"And then?"

"Well, once you have a good skull, the next thing is to cure it. You must bury it in the earth for a while and then oil it. If you only want to use it for drinking, then it's ready; but if you wish to use it as a decoration, then when it's completely dry, you can paint it red. That way they don't go mouldy in the monsoon."

For all the talk of what might elsewhere be considered black magic, in the daylight at least, the cremation ground that surrounded Manisha's little hut made an oddly domestic scene. The Tantric sadhus who live here were all sitting around, ash-smeared, naked or half-naked, sipping tea and playing cards, as if living in a skull-filled burning ghat was the most normal thing in the world. While we talked about curing skulls, Manisha's dreadlocked partner, Tapan Sadhu, was sitting at the back of the hut, with a radio clamped to his ear, and occasionally interrupting with the latest score from South Africa. "England are 270 for four!" he shouted excitedly at one point.

Nor was Manisha in any sense a fearsome or sinister figure. Despite her matted, dreadlocked grey hair and ragged saffron robes, she was a large, warm woman in her sixties, quietly spoken, with gentle, vulnerable eyes. Her dark-brown skin was disfigured with large, creeping patches of white, the result of a skin disease. She attended dutifully to the devotees who came to her for blessings, looked after the sadhus who passed by, offering them water and chai, and was gentle and affectionate towards Tapan.

"Whatever people think," she said, "this is not an evil or frightening place. People imagine all sorts of things about us—but we look after one another much better than people who live in proper houses in the cities. In Calcutta, if you fall sick, none of your neighbours may notice you've gone. Here if one of us is ill, the others make sure he is all right. When the floods come during the rains and the river rises to submerge our homes, we come to the aid of one another. If someone is ill, we all help pay for the hospital. If one of us dies, we all contribute to their cremation."

Manisha shrugged. "People who don't know what we do are afraid of Tantra," she said. "They hear stories about us abducting girl-children and killing them. Sometimes *gundas* come to the graveyard and insult us, or knock about the sadhus when they see them in the bazaars. Many times I have been called a witch."

I had read a little about this in the newspapers: according to one report I had seen, Tantra in Bengal was now under threat from the ruling Communist Party, which occasionally sent out members of what were called "Anti-Superstition Committees" to persuade people to reject faith healers, embrace modernity and return to more mainstream and less superstitious forms of Hinduism. This often involved attacking—rhetorically or otherwise—the Tantrics of the area, whom they depict as perverts, drug addicts, alcoholics and even cannibals. In the press in West Bengal there have also been reports of the persecution of poor, widowed and socially marginalised women, who are accused of practising witchcraft and "eating the livers" of villagers, particularly when some calamity befalls a community; indeed they are still occasionally put to death, like the witches of Reformation Europe and North America.

"Several of my Tantric friends to the west of here in Birbhum have been badly beaten up," said Manisha. "But I am not worried. Our local Communist MP may tell his followers that what we do is superstition, but that doesn't stop him coming here with a goat to sacrifice when he wants to find out from us what the election results will be. He was here only a fortnight ago. He is just afraid that people will come to the goddess and get power from her, and not from him. In his heart he believes."

"But why live in a cremation ground in the first place?" I asked. "Isn't it asking for trouble? Surely there are better places to lead a holy life? In the Himalayas, or at the source of the Ganges . . ."

"It is for her that we people inhabit this place," said Manisha, cutting me short. "Ma Tara pulled us here, and we remain here for her sake. It is within you that you find the loving *shakti* of the Mother. This is a place for its realisation, for illumination."

As we spoke, a devotee approached and bowed his head before Manisha, who stopped her story to give him a blessing, and to ask how he was. As he left, the man slipped a few coins on to the cloth that was laid out for offerings in front of the largest skull.

"Every night we believe she reveals herself here, just before dawn," continued Manisha. "At that time you feel her very strongly. If she did not bless us in this way we would not be here. She takes us in. She takes care of us. She gives us help. Anyone who comes here and calls on her will overcome their difficulties. She is everywhere in Tarapith: in the leaves of the trees, the buds of the rice, in the sap of the palms, the clouds that bring rain. All we do is to light some fires in her honour, chant a few mantras, perform some rituals. She does the rest."

"But aren't you scared to live in a place like this?" I asked.

"Tara loves us," replied Manisha. "So no, I am not scared." She paused, then added, "And anyway the dead do not stay here in the burning ground. Only the bodies are here. The dead take birth again."

Manisha smiled. "We have been fetched by the Mother," she said. "She has taken us away from the humdrum of normal life. She arranges everything for us: the gifts that come to us, the alms which allow us to survive. I feel her presence here. This is her home."

"Have you actually seen the goddess?" I asked.

"The Mother has many forms," she replied. "All the forms of Tara cannot be numbered. Recently, I saw a jackal—her vehicle. Sometimes in my dreams I glimpse her, but she has never yet appeared to me in a vision. I hope one day she will. If you call her from your heart, one day you will see her, floating before you."

Manisha fingered the beads of her *rudraksh* rosary. "Maybe I am not worshipping her in the right way. Unless you call her from within, in a truthful manner, she will never hear you. It is a long struggle, and it's not easy. But if you stay here, getting up at 2 a.m. to pray, and if you persist and do not give up, then surely you will see her."

I asked about the skulls that littered the graveyard: what did they actually do?

"We cannot speak of everything," she replied. "But the skulls give us power and charge our prayers with their *shakti*. The spirits help bring them to us, and they remain with the skull. We take good care of them, and feed them with rice and dal. Then they protect us, keeping us away from evil and death. They help us to awaken the goddess."

From the way that Manisha spoke, it was clear that for her the goddess was not something terrible. She talked intimately of her as Ma Tara—Mother Tara—as if she were a benign matriarch, quite a different image from that on the popular prints that I had seen in the bazaar on the way there. Here, it is true, Tara was sometimes shown as a nursing mother or enthroned in the Paradise of Kailasa or on the Isle of Gems. But usually she was depicted almost naked with matted hair and a blood-red lolling tongue and sitting upon a tiger's skin with four arms, wearing a garland of freshly severed heads. She wielded a blood-smeared cleaver as she stood victorious, dripping with blood, over a dead corpse with an erect phallus. To my eyes she was unambiguously terrifying, weird and ferocious. I said as much to Manisha.

"Ah," she said. "This is true. This is her wild side. But all this just means she can fight the devils on your behalf."

"But she looks herself almost as much a demon as a goddess."

"Tara is my mother," replied Manisha simply. "How can your own mother evoke fear? When I first came here in a distressed condition, Ma protected me. I had been beaten by my husband, rejected by my mother-in-law and had lost my home and my three daughters. It was she who brought Tapan Sadhu to protect me and give me love. In this place of death, I have found new life. Now I don't want to go anywhere. To me, Ma is all. My life depends on her."

Tarapith lies in a great planisphere of flat, green country: fertile floodplains and rice paddies whose abundant soils and huge skies stretch out towards the marshy Sunderbans, the Ganges Delta and the Bay of Bengal—a great green Eden of water and vegetation.

The road from Shantiniketan is raised on a shaded embankment and passes through a vast patchwork of wetlands: muddy fields of half-harvested rice give way to others where the young green seedlings have been transplanted into shimmering rectangles in the flooded fields. Through all this runs a network of streams and rivers and frog-croaking, fish-filled, lily-littered duck ponds. These are surrounded by fishermen with bamboo fishing cages and lines of village women with earthen pitchers. Kingfishers watch silently from the telegraph wires. Rising from the ripples of this flat waterland are raised mounds encircled with windbreaks of palm, clumps of bamboo, and tall flowering grasses. On these stand small wattle villages of reed and clay, with their bullock carts and haystacks, their thatched bus stops and the occasional spreading banyan tree. Sometimes, to one side, rises the brick estate house of the local grandee.

From a distance, Tarapith looks like just any other Bengali village, with its palm-thatched huts, and still, cool fish pond. But here one building dominates all the others: the great temple of the goddess. Its base is a thick-walled, red-brick chamber, broken by an arcade of arches and rising to a great white pinnacle, like the snow capping of a Himalayan peak. Inside, below the low-curving Bengali eves, stands the silver image of the goddess with her long black hair, half-submerged beneath marigold garlands and Benarasi saris, and crowned and shaded by a silver umbrella. On her forehead is a patch of red *kumkum* powder. Onto this the temple priests place their fingers, then transfer the red stain onto the foreheads of the devotees. In gratitude the pilgrims then kiss her silver feet, and leave her offerings of coconuts, white silk saris, incense sticks, bananas and, more unexpectedly, bottles of whisky.

Yet in Tarapith, those who live here are quite clear that Tara's preferred residence is not the temple, but the cremation ground which lies above the ghats of the river on the edge of the village. Tara is, after all, one of the most wild and wayward of Hindu goddesses, and cannot be tamed and contained within a venerated temple image. She is not only the goddess of supreme knowledge who grants her devotees the ability to know and realise the Absolute, she is also the Lady Twilight, the Cheater of Death, a figure of horror and terror, a stalker of funeral pyres, who slaughters demons and evil *yakshis* without hesitation, becoming as terrible as they in order to defeat them: in the tenth-century hymn of a hundred names from the *Mundamala Tantra*, Tara is called She Who Likes Blood, She Who Is Smeared with Blood and She Who Enjoys Blood Sacrifice. And while Tara has a healthy appetite for animal blood, the *Mundamala Tantra* explicitly states that she prefers that of humans, in particular that taken from the forehead, hands and breasts of her devotees.

Tara means "star" in Sanskrit, and some scholars trace the origins of her cult to the Mesopotamian goddesses of the stars, Ishtar and Astarte: indeed the modern English word "star" and "Tara" are almost certainly linked through a common Indo-European root, via the Persian *Sitara*, the Greek *Aster* and the Latin *Stella*, all of which have the same meaning. It is even possible that the modern Catholic cult of Our Lady Stella Maris, Star of the Sea, may be part of the same tradition. Moving eastwards in the early centuries AD, the cult of Tara quickly became central to Mahayana Buddhist cosmology, where the great goddess was worshipped as the consort of the Bodhisattva Avalokitesvara and came to represent primordial female energy. As such, it was believed that she enabled her devotees to surmount all forms of peril and danger.

In her Hindu form, which re-entered Bengal from the Himalayas via Buddhist Tibet, and hence is sometimes known as "Chini Tara"—Chinese Tara—the goddess has always been perceived as a more volatile figure than her Buddhist devotees understood her to be. According to the *Mantra Mahodadhi* of Mahidhara, the great medieval Sanskrit work on Tantra, Tara can be found "sitting on a white lotus situated at the centre of the water enveloping the entire universe.

With her left hand she holds a knife and a skull and, in her right hands, a sword and a blue lotus. Her complexion is blue, and she is bedecked with ornaments ... She is decorated with three beautiful serpents and has three eyes. Her tongue is always moving, and her teeth and mouth appear terrible. She is wearing a tiger skin around her waist, and her forehead is decorated with ornaments of white bone. She is seated on the heart of a corpse and her breasts are hard ... [She is] the mistress of all three worlds.

In this frightening aspect, she is not alone, but instead part of a sisterhood who encompass a range of visions of the divine feminine at its most terrible: a brood of dark-skinned and untameable Tantric divinities who are worshipped in Bengal, and who here take precedence in popular piety over the more familiar male gods: Brahma, Vishnu and Shiva. These goddesses, known as the Ten Mahavidyas, are attended by jackals, furies and ghosts. They cut off their own heads, and are offered blood sacrifices by their devotees. In the miniatures which illustrate the Tantric texts, they prefer to have sex with corpses than living men or gods, straddling them on a burning cremation pyre and bringing the dead to life through the power of their *shakti*. These goddesses, embodying all that would normally be considered outrageous or even repulsive, lie at the shifting threshold between the divine and demonic, violating approved social values and customs—"going up the down-current," as a Bengali Tantric once put it to me.

All this is a survival of some of the oldest forms of Tantric rites which date back to the early medieval period, when they were once widespread around India. The word "Tantra" is a reference to ancient texts that deal with yogic practices, magical rites, metaphysics and philosophy, and which straddle the world of Hindu Vaishnavites and Shavites, and cross over into not only Jainism and Mahayana Buddhism, but even Chinese Daoism and some forms of Sufi Islam.

Though Tantrism became well defined only at the end of the first millennium AD, some of its constituent elements, such as its goddess cults, shamanism and sexual yoga, may date back to pre-Aryan and pre-Vedic religious currents, and in many ways are fundamentally opposed to the ideas and structures of the *Vedas*, which emphasise the social and religious hierarchies. Tantrics, in contrast, oppose society's conventions and encourage the individual of whatever background to develop a mystical relationship with the deity within, placing *kama*, desire in every sense of the word, in the service of liberation. While Tantric texts can represent an elevated philosophical tradition, popular Tantric practice is often oral and spontaneous. It aims at ritually gaining access to the energy of the godhead that created and controls the universe, then concentrating and internalising that power in the body of the devotee. This turns the world and the body into channels of salvation, and a means of merging with the Absolute, but also grants tangible magical powers to the devotee, in this life, in the present.

Shaivite Tantrics regard the universe as the product of the divine play of Shakti and Shiva, which are ultimately identical, separate aspects of the same unity, like fire and heat. To access this energy, early Hindu Tantric rituals seem to have encouraged blood sacrifice in cremation grounds as a means of feeding and winning over a series of terrifying and blood-thirsty Tantric deities. By the tenth century there was a change of emphasis towards a type of eroticomystical practice involving congress with the Yoginis, powerful and predatory female Shakti divinities who demanded that they be worshipped and fed with offerings of sexual emissions, as well as with human and animal sacrifice.

Once satisfied, the Yoginis were believed to reveal themselves as ravishing young women by incarnating in female devotees with whom male practitioners sexually interacted. Especially important was the oral ingestion of sexual fluids thought to give the devotee access to the goddess's supernatural powers. In this way Tantric sex was used to awaken latent energies from the base of the body and bring them to the fore, so using the physical body with its blood and semen, desires and energies, as a way of accessing the spiritual, and the divine. The elaborate scenes of group and oral sex displayed on the walls of the temples at Khajuraho may well illustrate such rites. Yet while Tantra has come in the West to be associated almost exclusively with "Tantric sex," the Tantric texts which survive from this period were always more concerned with death and transcendence than the sexualisation of ritual, which was only one part of a much larger whole.

Moreover, the sexual aspect of medieval Indian Tantra is quite different both in aim and practice from the "Tantric sex" marketed in illustrated manuals published in the contemporary West. Early Tantric texts make no reference to pleasure, bliss or ecstasy: the sexual intercourse involved in the rites was not an end itself so much as a means of generating the semen whose consumption lay at the heart of these Tantric fertility rituals—a sort of inverted Tantric version of the offerings made in Vedic fire sacrifices. This original Devi-propitiating Tantric sex stands at an unimaginable distance away from the sort of faddish Tantra cults embraced by Western rock stars, with their celebration of aromatherapy and *coitus reservatus,* a movement well described by the French writer Michel Houllebecq as "a combination of bumping and grinding, fuzzy spirituality and extreme egotism."

These original esoteric medieval Tantric traditions nearly died out in India, sinking from view around the thirteenth century AD, probably partly as a result of the disruption that followed in the wake of the violence of the Islamic invasions, which broke many of the lines of guru-disciple relationships through which Tantric secrets were passed. Tantrics later became a particular target of European missionaries, who made "the obscene ceremonies of the Hindoos" central to their polemics. The nineteenth-century rise of the Hindu reform movements, many of which emanated from Bengal in reaction to British missionaries, nearly finished this process. For the reform movements championed what some scholars have called the "Rama-fication" of Hindu worship in the Ganges plains: the rise of the Vaishnavite *bhakti* cults of Lord Krishna and especially Lord Rama, to the extent that they eclipsed many other more traditional and popular forms of local devotion involving Devi cults and blood sacrifices, which were judged primitive, superstitious and anti-modern by the urban and often Western-educated reformers.

All this conspired to make Tantra a marginal phenomenon almost everywhere except in certain areas of Bengal, Kerala and Assam, as well as in Nepal and Bhutan, where Tantra still flourishes as a mainstream form of religion, in the latter case within a Buddhist rather than Hindu context.

At the root of popular modern Tantric practice lies a deeply subversive and heterodox concept: the idea of reaching God through opposing convention, ignoring social mores and breaking taboos. Whereas caste Hindus believe that purity and good living are safeguarded by avoiding meat and alcohol, by keeping away from unclean places like cremation grounds and avoiding polluting substances such as bodily fluids, Tantrics believe that one path to salvation lies in pushing every boundary and inverting these strictures, so turning what is polluting into instruments of power.

Tarapith, in other words, is a place where the ordinary world is comprehensively turned upside down. Today, the rites that take place in the burning ground involve forbidden substances and practices—alcohol, *ganja* and ritualised sex, sometimes with menstruating women—for Tara's devotees believe that the goddess transmutes all that is forbidden and taboo, and turns these banned acts and forbidden objects into pathways of power. Onto this base of transgressive sacrality has grown a whole body of esoteric practice involving secret knowledge, rituals, mantras and mandalas.

The dark and wooded cremation ground in Tarapith is the perfect backdrop to these practices and beliefs, and attracts scores of the hardest of hardcore Tantric sadhus—wanderers, sorcerers and skull feeders. Many of these have been partially unhinged by their experiences or extreme acts of asceticism, and are now looked upon as holy madmen, living in a mystical anarchy in a great open-air lunatic asylum for the divinely mad. These red-robed sadhus live here with their skulls and their spells, with the half-burned corpses, and the dogs and the jackals, the vultures and the carrion crows, occasionally throwing bones at passing visitors to warn them off.

Here on the boundaries of life and on the cusp of reason, they pray and meditate, daily confronting their fear of death. Caught suddenly by the influence of the goddess, these crazed anchorites roll on the ground in ecstasy, screaming *"Jaya Tara!"* ("Victory to the goddess Tara!"). It is also here, within the bounds of the cremation ground, on nights with no moon—the most inauspicious time in the month according to orthodox Hindus—that they perform their Tantric rites.

Yet, just as Manisha Ma had said, in many ways what is most striking about this place is not any sinister quality, so much as its oddly villagey and almost cosy feel. There is a palpable sense of community among the vulnerable outcastes, lunatics and misfits who have come to live there, and those who might be locked up, chained, sedated, hidden, mocked or shunned elsewhere are here venerated and respected as enlightened lunatics full of crazy wisdom. In turn, they look after one another and appear to tolerate one another's eccentricities. It is a place where even the most damaged and marginal can find intimacy and community, and establish their own centre of gravity.

Later that evening, when Manisha Ma took me to the temple, I got a small glimpse of how Tantra still plays its part in modern Indian politics. Inside the sacred enclosure, a line of pilgrims were queuing to have *darshan* of the image of the goddess, but although it was approaching the time for the evening *aarti,* the place was surprisingly empty for such a famous shrine. Separate from the main crowd, in an enclosure to the east, however, stood a group of burly men wearing homespun *khadi,* and one of these was clutching a goat.

"I am a Bollywood fight director," explained the man holding the goat, "and for many years I was a stunt fighter. Now I am standing for election. That is why I have brought this *bakri* all the way from Bihar, in my own car—to offer it to the goddess."

Milan Ghoshal leaned a little closer, in a confidential manner. "My seven colleagues have come to Ma Tara too," he said, waving his hand at his entourage of tough-looking moustachioed men in short sleeves loitering some distance away. "You see," he explained, "in our state, politics is only for the strong. There are many tough and violent men competing for power in the Bihar Assembly."

This, I knew, was certainly true. Bihar has long been renowned as the most lawless state in India: in recent elections, many of the candidates actually fought their campaign from behind bars, and a large number of Bihar's Legislative Assembly MLAs have criminal records. Milan certainly looked the right man to fight an election in such a place: he had a thin beard and a shaven head, a firm jawline and a broken nose that, together with the deep scar above the left eyebrow, gave him a harsh and brutish expression. Yet for all the broad-shouldered, village wrestler physique, he wore the simple long white homespun kurta of the politician, and around his neck he had strung a *rudraksh* rosary.

"In Bombay," he said, "they call me Milan Thakur—Milan the Boss. I trained in martial arts in Bhutan, and now I am a master. No one can beat me in a fight; not in Bombay and not in Bihar."

"And all this is important in Bihar elections?"

"Of course," he said, putting the goat down. "Bihar is a rough place. I need Ma Tara to fight alongside me. If she accepts my offering, then maybe with her protection, I will win. Ma Tara can help get us power. If not, I have no hope. I am not a rich man, and I cannot spend the money that some of the other candidates will be throwing at the people."

I introduced Manisha Ma, who had just come up from the temple, where she had queued to have *darshan*. When Milan learned that Manisha lived in the cremation ground, he bent forward and made a gesture of touching her feet. "Tantra is much more powerful than conventional religion," he explained. "Without the *shakti* of the Devi and her followers you cannot do anything."

"And you think this is the place to access that power?" I asked Milan.

"There are very few places where *shakti* is still worshipped," he replied. "That is why I drove for eight hours to come here, getting up before dawn. In my part of Bihar, when men seek *shakti* they know they must come to Tarapith. We chose today because tomorrow is an *amavashya*, a night with no moon. On this night and the next, we believe, the goddess is at large, and more open to our prayers."

Milan indicated a platform where a priest was chanting amid a *yantra*—a Tantric symbol made from flowers, coconuts, bamboo, vermilion and coloured sand—as part of the *yagna* ritual of sacrifice. A fire was burning in its centre, and flickering candles framed its corners. As the flames rose higher the priest threw in handfuls of rice from a *thali*, all the time reciting Sanskrit mantras, while two of Milan's colleagues sat silently cross-legged on the far side. Milan sat for a while with Manisha and me, watching the priests chanting, and when the ritual was over, he got up. "Now it is time for the sacrifice," he said, "my *astha bhole*."

The goat, which had been tethered a short distance away, was brought forward, and Milan picked it up and put its head in a two-pronged metal stand shaped like a giant tuning fork. One of the priests then painted a saffron stripe on its head and stepped back. Another man, barefoot in a dhoti, came forward with a long, sharp cleaver, just like the one held by Tara in the prints. With a single swipe he cut off the head, and the priest pulled the body away, where it lay writhing on the ground. There was a strong smell of warm blood, moist earth, decaying flowers and incense. Milan placed a bunch of smoking *agarbatti* incense sticks in the sacrifical pit, and dipping his fingers in the bloody sand, smeared his forehead.

"All auspicious work starts in the name of Ma," said Milan. "Tomorrow, on the night of no moon, I will announce my candidacy. With Ma's aid I and my colleagues are ready to fight this battle. She is the most powerful protector you could want. I tell you: with her power, no one can stand against us."

The following day I returned to the cremation ground to talk to Manisha Ma. What interested me was how different her vision of

Tara was to that of Milan, who clearly saw the goddess as a supernatural channel through which he could gain worldly power. Manisha, however, believed that Tara was a motherly figure who had saved her, looked after her when she was most vulnerable and who above all had brought her love. I wondered what this actually meant, and what kind of life Manisha had lived before moving into the burning ground.

As Tapan Sadhu continued following the test match at the back of the hut ("India are ninety-four without loss!"), and as a roving chai wallah poured clay cups of tea to the growing circle of listening sadhus and *sadhvis*, Manisha settled back on a *durree* surrounded by her skulls, and began to tell me her story.

"I was born in the town of Ariadaha in south-west Bengal," she said. "My father worked for the Public Works Department. His job was to announce how the water would be distributed. He had a drum and a megaphone, and used to tell people when the water supply would be cut off and when it would be turned back on again.

"I had seven sisters and one brother. When I was born, before my father got his PWD job, we were very poor, and often ate only once a day. Some days my mother could only afford manioc, which she would cook with a little salt and give to us to eat. I was close to my sisters and also to my father, who loved me very much. But my brother was the one my mother loved. He was very spoilt: if the slightest thing went wrong for him she would stop eating and go on a fast, and if there was only food for one, then he would get it. One of my sisters died when I was three: we both had a fever and as my father could afford only one piece of fish, he gave it to me. The next day I got well, but my sister's fever increased and she died. My mother still says your sister died because of your father. If he had given her the fish, she would have lived.

"After my father got his job with the PWD, I went to school, but only until class five, when I was eleven. Even before then I was not a good student: the school made me feel confined and I was always running away. My parents scolded me, but it never suited my temperament. I still am not good at reading or writing. After I had passed out of class five, my father decided that we needed more money as he couldn't feed us properly on his small government salary. So when I was thirteen, we moved to Calcutta, and both my mother and he went to work in one of the jute mills in Baguhati. We used to wait impatiently for them to return. My mother would bring flour, and when she got home we all made chapatis. Sometimes I earned a little too, cleaning the dishes and washing the clothes of our neighbours. But I didn't mind. I was very excited to be in Calcutta, which was full of cars and buses and cinemas and all manner of things we rarely saw in Ariadaha. We were staying in a third-floor apartment, and my sisters and I would look out at the Howrah Bridge rising in the distance and all the great sights of the city.

"Two years later, when I was fifteen, I went to work at the mill too, and was put in the finishing department. When the jute came out of the machine, I was part of the team that cut it up and made it into the jute bales which were then sent to America. It was very hard work, and so dusty that everyone who worked there developed breathing problems. Some of the girls got caught in the machine and were badly injured. But I used to pray to the goddess and she always looked after me.

"From my childhood I was very spiritual. Both my parents were religious too, and at home we had a small *puja* to the goddess every day. I was always attracted to the Devi, in her different forms—Ma Kali, Ma Durga, Ma Tara and so on—and I always believed that it was she who saved me from danger. Even as a child I used to love to attend festivals and *melas*, and especially the Durga Puja, which was my favourite week of the year. I loved to see the immersion of the goddess in the river at the end of the ten-day festival. While we were there I would seek out the company of sadhus and ask them questions. One of my earliest memories is of the Durga Puja, which I first visited in my father's arms. It was a pleasure just to look at the fair and all the bangles and bracelets on sale. On that day my father would always save up and buy us all hot *jalebis*.

"When I was sixteen, I was married off. I never met my husband before the ceremony, and I didn't really know what it was all about. My husband's family owned a small shop selling *paan* and cigarettes and groceries. My father had begun to drink by then, and he never had any money, so my maternal uncle gave Rs 3,000 for the marriage. I cried a lot when I had to move to my in-laws' house. I was leaving my father and going to a strange place. It was over a year before I would sleep with my husband, and this made him angry. My mother-in-law also did not like me, and kept saying: 'What are you crying for?'

"It was shortly after I moved into my husband's room that I was possessed by the goddess, and had a fit for the first time. A few months later, when I first became pregnant, and went back to my mother to have the child, I went into a full trance. A friend of my mother observed me in this state and said: 'This is not an illness, this is possession.' Over the next few years it became more and more frequent: I would start shaking or faint, and fall unconscious. The doctors could do nothing. My children became quite used to it: they thought all mothers were like this. But my husband and my mother-in-law were embarrassed and angry. He would beat me and say: 'What is this trance? Why is this happening? The customers do not like it and you will drive them away. We cannot afford this.'

"None of this stopped me. Instead, I became increasingly preoccupied with the goddess and spent more and more of my time in the temple, listening to *kirtans*. This led to more conflict still. My mother-in-law kept asking: 'Why do you go to the temple the whole time? You have children.' But I continued to sneak out whenever I could. I loved to hear the chanting of the names of the goddess, and it always calmed me down and made me happy when I could put garlands around her image.

"One day I was possessed when I was in the temple, and when I came to, I found the pundit of the temple had garlanded me. Not only that, he had washed my feet and put a sandalwood-paste *tilak* on my forehead. I asked why he had done this, but he just replied: 'Ma—don't refuse.' From that point on, people at the temple used to worship me, as they thought I was possessed by the goddess, and they gave me offerings and tried to interpret what I was saying during my fits. This frightened me at first, but slowly I grew more confident. My three daughters were no longer babies and I felt better able to imagine taking my own path. But there was increasing conflict at home, especially when devotees followed me and would knock at the door to ask for blessings. I don't know why, but it seemed that the more angry and violent my husband became, the more often I went into a state of trance. Maybe this also was the doing of the goddess.

"Before long, quite large numbers of devotees would come to see me in this state—five or ten people a day would come to the house, or the shop if I was working there, and of course they disrupted everything. My husband got more and more furious, saying I had turned our store into a temple. Then one afternoon, after he beat me very badly, I heard a call from Ma Tara. It was a sound which came in the breeze, Tara Ma saying, very clearly: 'Come to me. All that you may lose, you will recover. I will take care of your daughters. Your place is now with me.'

"It was not my will. Mother called me, and I had to go. I walked out of the house then and there, taking nothing with me other than the clothes I was wearing. I didn't even have time to say goodbye to my children. It was already over with my husband; we no longer had a relationship. I spent the first night in the temple of the goddess Kali. That was the lowest moment. I didn't sleep at all and felt depressed, as if my whole life had broken apart, and I had failed in everything. In fact the first few weeks were very hard. But I kept telling myself that when the Mother calls, there is nothing you can do. I stayed in the temple for two years, living off offerings, and sleeping in the courtyard.

"Only after much wandering did I finally find my way here to Tarapith. I have now been here twenty years. It was here that Ma Tara fulfilled her promises to me. I have been on many pilgrimages since then, but from the day I arrived here, and after Tapan Sadhu became my protector, Tarapith became my home. I missed my children, of course—the youngest was only four, and none of them were old enough to understand. Often I would weep. But my devotees came to fill the hole in my heart left by the absence of my girls. Now the whole world is full of my children: when I miss my daughters I see my other children, and my heart turns to them. So many people now call me Ma.

"From the day I left my husband, my trances became less frequent, but I feel her presence more than ever now. I will be sitting here in my hut with Tapan and suddenly I feel that she is here—I feel this with tremendous force—even though I cannot see her with my eyes. This is a very ancient site, and many great saints have attained perfection here though *tapasya* [ascetism] and meditation. Those who invoke the energy of the Mother here can access her power, and her imagination. She is present in all the rituals that are performed here.

"One of the reasons I collect skulls is to help visualise her; many saints have seen her using the skulls. The great Bama Khepa—one of the first saints to realise the power of this place—saw her in a circle of fire in the form of a very young girl. Skulls remind us of our mortality, and of the world of illusion that surrounds our daily life. But we also believe that if you awake the skulls through *sadhana* [Tantric practice], and tame their spirits, they will give you more power and help show you the path to reach the goddess and access her power. They help you to invoke her, and call her to you.

"The spirits of the dead often stay with the skull. They are formless and shapeless. No one can enclose them or burn them or drown them. You have to worship them, appease them and feed them regularly. You must offer them perfume, flowers and oil. Not all skulls work, of course—you have to give them time. You can tell by the way the skull behaves with food. You feed them rice, dal, raw meat from sacrifices, even whisky. If the skull moves its face away or recedes, then it is not accepting the food, and the skull's spirit will not help you.

"What you are looking for is a dissatisfied and troubled spirit. If a person has a peaceful death, and all the funeral rites are conducted properly, he will be reincarnated. But unsatisfied spirits, the ones that have died unfortunate deaths when they are young: they are the ones that linger on, and wander. They take a long time to reincarnate and they are the ones we can call through the midnight air. With luck, they are the ones we can work with.

"You can't master spirits. They are wilful and independent. They will come if they want to, and if you please them with special mantras. Some that Tapan taught me are so powerful he said that they can split the tombs open, and make the bodies manifest themselves. You must draw a circle around yourself for protection. Then, when the spirits which you have invoked come, you have to know the mantras which can help you talk with them, and use their *shakti*.

These are rare skills and great secrets. Compared to Tapan and some of the other masters here, I am just a novice.

"Now, however, I am beginning to think that Tantra only really works properly when it is coupled with intense devotion, with *bhakti*. When I was younger and I first came here, I was very obsessed with skulls and the secrets of Tantra. I would do anything to collect new skulls and tend to them—putting vermilion on them, feeding them as well as I could, and bathing them in ghee, yoghurt and honey. I had a whole room filled with them. Once you feed them and they accept the offerings, they are pacified and will help you, protecting you from evil spirits. I found the *shakti* they gave me exhilarating. I found I could sometimes predict the future. Tapan Sadhu even taught me the secret mantras through which you can get the spirits to bring rain in time of drought.

"But now my attention is more directed on Ma Tara herself, and increasingly I believe that the most important thing is to get close to her through devotional love. Skulls are still useful and they can be very powerful, but these days I am concentrating simply on the love and worship of the Mother—although in such a way as not to alienate the skulls. You could say that I am bringing them with me on my journey. Love is the most important thing.

"Tantra on its own can be very dangerous. The skulls may help us to awaken the goddess, but if you make one mistake in the ritual, you can go mad. Some tried to do battle with the goddess, to tame her with magic. Look what happened to them! There are many here who made mistakes in their *sadhana*, and went insane. So what you need is to find a balance between *bhakti* and Tantra. With the two of them together, with both love and sacrifice, I believe you are on the right path, and when she thinks you are worthy she will reveal herself. Until then she sends me dreams, and I know I am daily receiving her compassion.

"Tapan Sadhu taught me all I know about Tantra and love. I met him first in Calcutta, when I was still living in the Kali Mandir. I was passing by, and he was there with his disciples, and he said, 'You want a *paan*?' Over the following years I noticed him when he came to the temple. I was impressed because people said he was very strong and had great powers, but he was a kind and gentle man too.

Somewhere at the back of my mind, I realised that if I wished to follow the Tantric path, I needed someone with whom I could perform *sadhana*. I also realised I needed to find a man who would protect me, because if I went out on the roads on my own I would be vulnerable, and might be attacked.

"Then Tara Ma sent me a dream, in which I saw the face of Tapan Sadhu, and a voice said, 'He is waiting for you now.' I recognised him immediately, so I went to Tarapith, where he lived. For a long while I didn't dare address a word to him, even though I had settled near his hut, under a tree. Even in Calcutta we had barely talked. But before long the people here began to gossip, and said we were having an affair. So eventually I went to him and said, 'Since people are saying these things, why don't we solve the problem by living together? We are not greedy for property: we only need each other.' So he invited me to his hut, and from that day we stayed together.

"In Tarapith, thanks to the Mother, I moved onto a different plane. I collected many disciples, and found that the life here suited me. At the end of the first year, Tapan Sadhu said we should go on a *yatra*, and I agreed to go with him. We travelled in trains across India to Benares, Haridwar and Rishikesh. We had no money for tickets, but the ticket inspectors are a little afraid of the sadhus and they never ask for money.

"From Rishikesh we walked up into the snows to Badrinath and Kedarnath. By the time we got there it was very cold and the winter blizzards were beginning. But it was still wonderful—I felt I was in heaven. Whatever he ate, I ate. We used to practise yoga and *asanas*, and live a life of meditation in the silence of the high Himalayas. For me it was pure joy. Looking back at my old domestic life, it seemed meaningless, without any spiritual substance. I felt free for the first time. It was a total release.

"We stayed up there a whole winter, and then the summer too. In the hot weather, the waters of Ma Ganga were cool and refreshing. But we were too attached to Tara Ma to stay there for longer than that. Ma Ganga is very powerful, but Ma Tara is stronger and more compassionate. The greatest pleasure we have is here, with her. It is here in this place of death, amid the skulls and bones and smoking funeral pyres, that we have found love."

That night was the *amavashya,* the Night of No Moon.

Crowds started to arrive in the cremation ground around mid-afternoon. By sunset, preparations had begun in earnest for the sacrificial rituals that were to be performed after midnight. Piles of kindling were carried on the heads of the Tantrics, and goats led in, some pulled on leads by individual sadhus, others in great herds by villagers looking to sell them. In every hut, lamps were lit.

Many of those who drifted into the burning grounds were sadhus and Baul minstrels, but as the day wore on, a surprising number of those who gathered were ordinary middle-class Bengali families from Bolpur, Shantiniketan and even Calcutta. All, for their different reasons, were determined to access the *shakti* of the goddess on the night when she was at her most powerful. I asked Manisha if it was unusual that so very many goats were being led into the cremation ground for slaughter.

"The mother is very hungry," she replied. "She is constantly needing to be fed, and of course she never moves by herself. To summon her you have to be prepared to feed her entourage of *dakinis* and *yakshis* too. They want their pleasures, their drink and the blood of a goat."

As darkness fell, and the shadows grew longer, Tapan Sadhu began to build a large pit for the sacred *homa* fire immediately in front of the hut. It was the first time I'd had a good look at him. Tapan was a handsome old man in his seventies, with a long grey beard and a surprisingly lean and toned body, the fruit of many years of yoga. He brought kindling and wood from the back of the hut, as well as one of the tridents, the biggest skull and a handful of incense sticks. He placed the trident at the edge of the hearth, and the skull at its base. He then garlanded the skull with marigolds and red hibiscus flowers, hanging his *rudraksh* rosary around it, and carefully placing a *thali* of offerings and a lit candle beside it. As he was busy with his work, a well-dressed Bengali businessman approached and asked Tapan if he could make the sacrifice for him and his family. After some haggling, terms were agreed.

Before long, other fires were beginning to flicker through the trees. Across the cremation ground you could see squatting sadhus silhouetted against the flames. Some were muscular and naked, sitting crossed-legged in meditation amid clouds of incense. Others were building *yantras* of coloured sand under the banyan trees, with candles marking the eight points of the Tara Chakra. A few were passing chillums of *bhang* around circles of fire watchers. Shrouded, dreadlocked and topknotted figures emerged from the dusk, passed into the light of a fire, then disappeared again into the darkness. From somewhere in the dark I could hear the voice of a lone Baul singing a song about the Devi to the strumming of a *dotara* and the rasping twang of a *khomok*:

> *I am sick of living, Ma, sick.*
> *Life and money have run out,*
> *But I go on crying, Tara, Tara!*
> *Hoping. You are the Mother of All,*
> *And our nurse. You carry the Three Worlds,*
> *In Your Belly.*

> *I am not calling you Mother any more,*
> *All you give me is trouble.*
> *Oh my mad, mad heart!*
> *Once I had a home and a family,*
> *Now I am a beggar. What will you think of*
> *Next, my wild-haired Devi?*

> *How many times, Mother, will you tie me to this wheel*
> *Like a blindfolded ox, grinding out oil?*
> *Take the blindfold off, oh my dark Devi,*
> *So I can see*
> *The feet that give comfort.*

At the next fire, one of the sadhus began to blow a conch shell. From other hearths came the noise of wild drumming and ecstatic shouts of *"Jaya Tara! Jaya Guru! Jaya Jaya Ma Tara!"*

> *If you wish to search for Tara,*
> *Come to the pyres of Tarapith.*

The Mother plays here night and day,
Foxes dance with serpents.
With meat and wine and liquor.
It is here that Tara's secrets
Are revealed.

Tapan had now lit his *homa* fire, and soon the flames were shooting up into the darkness. Ironically, it is the Tantrics, who have inverted so much of Hindu ritual, that have remained uniquely faithful to the Vedic fire sacrifices lost almost everywhere else in modern Hinduism; and like the Brahmins they emphasise the need to perform their rituals correctly and exactly.

The businessman, who introduced himself as Mr. Basu, gathered his family around Tapan's fire, as casual, eager and relaxed and as at ease as their British equivalents would be on Guy Fawkes Night.

"We are praying for the improvement of our domestic life," he explained, "and for our business also."

"We want peace in the home," added his wife, "and children doing well at school."

Tapan began to chant mantras, occasionally ringing the bell he kept in his left hand. With his right, every so often he threw a spoonful of ghee on the fire, which made the flames shoot up higher than ever. I took a seat beside Manisha, a little back from the Basu family, and asked her about Tapan's story.

"Tapan Sadhu is a Brahmin, a Chatterjee," she said. "Like me, he was called by the goddess when he was a householder in Calcutta. Like me, he left behind a family."

"Is his wife still alive?" I asked.

"She died recently," said Manisha. "He had been married to her for fifteen years before the call came from Ma." She paused. "He happened to be in Calcutta, so he went to her funeral. But his son would not speak to him."

At this point, Tapan, who had been half-listening as he tended his fire, left the Basus, who had begun to sing some *kirtans*. He came and squatted beside us, at the foot of the trident, next to the skull. I asked him what had happened.

"It gave me great pain," he said, shaking his head. "My son was very angry with me. He said I had never taken any interest in him, and never been in touch."

"Was that true?"

"It was partly true," said Tapan. "After I answered the call of the Mother, I never found a way of connecting back with them." He sighed, and threw a piece of kindling into the fire. "Now my son feels obliged to the people who brought him up, not to me. He says they are the people who supported him. He doesn't want to try to understand my point of view."

"How did you come to hear about your wife's death?" I asked.

"I was in Calcutta with some disciples when a call came from my brother saying, 'Your wife has expired.' I went straight to the crematorium, and as I walked in, there was my son. I recognised him immediately, after nearly twenty years. How could I not recognise my own son? But even as I was heading towards him, I heard my niece's husband commenting, 'Look at him! After all these years he hasn't been here, and now she's dead he reappears.' My son wouldn't even look at me, and his wife's family formed a sort of wall between me and him. Without saying anything, they gave me the feeling I should not approach him."

In the light of the fire, Tapan Sadhu suddenly looked old and vulnerable.

"This was my own kith and kin," he said. "They were preventing me from talking to my son."

Tapan fell silent again, staring into the flames.

"They are not spiritual, and probably don't even believe in God," he said eventually. "They belong to a very different world. My niece is a professor, and her husband does electrocardiograms. My son is now an accountant with Tata. He was very smartly dressed, in a blazer. A good-looking boy. But they all reject the world I live in. I don't think I can ever explain it to him."

"Now he is married," said Manisha, "maybe his wife will change his mind?"

"I don't think so," replied Tapan Sadhu, stroking his beard. "What signs are there? My son is dominated by the people around him. He is not strong enough to think independently."

The Basus were still singing around the fire. Tapan looked to see if they needed him, but they seemed engrossed in their chants.

"So what did you do?" I asked.

"I stayed at the back. After the ceremony was finished I left. I won't ever go back."

"As long as there is life in you," said Manisha, "you should be full of hope."

"This life of renunciation, of *sanyas*, is a life of joy," said Tapan. "But in the life of every sadhu, some pain is there. The longer you live as a sadhu, the more you enjoy the life, and the more you forget your past. Then something happens to remind you, and you weep."

"I have been more lucky," said Manisha. "When my husband was dying he told my daughters that I was in Tarapith. Someone from my village had seen me here, and reported back. So after his death, the girls came to the burning ground looking for me. 'Have you seen a woman whose skin is flecked with white?' they asked. A sadhu pointed out my hut and my daughters came and touched my feet. It had been over twenty years. When I left them they were children. Now they were all middle-aged women, two of them with children of their own.

"It was a very tense moment. We looked at each other for a moment, then we all embraced, and burst into tears. They told me that my husband was now dead, so then and there I broke my bangles. The youngest one, the only one who is unmarried, decided to move to Tarapith, along with my mother. Now they both stay in the town, and we see each other every day. She was here this morning."

Manisha looked at Tapan. "Tapan Sadhu has come to love my daughters and is like a father for them." She paused. "I know it is not exactly like every family, but in this burning ground, in this place of sorrow, we have found new hope."

From behind us there were more cries of *"Jai Tara!"* as sacrificial flames streaked up across the burning ghat. The woody noise of a *bansuri* flute could be heard drifting through the trees from the tarpaulins of an encampment of sadhus. The two elderly Tantrics exchanged a shy glance.

"When I look at her feet," said Tapan Sadhu, "I am happy. What I see in Ma Tara, I see in her."

"He found a live Tara in Tarapith," said Manisha. "Now Tapan Sadhu looks after us. He is as strong as Tara Ma."

"As long as you are in my protection, no one will harm you."

"And by the grace of Ma, I have my daughters back. I thought I had lost them forever."

"Things have worked out for us all."

"I never imagined it would be possible to see them again," said Manisha. "People think that we who live in the burning ground are crazy. But you get here what you cannot find anywhere else: pure human beings."

"When she first came to me," said Tapan Sadhu, "I thought: look at this girl, how vulnerable she is, all on her own. Only later did I begin to realise what a gift she was."

"You were sent a woman who understands your calling."

"Some people here protested when we got together," said Tapan. "But we didn't listen."

"This is the will of Tara," said Manisha. "Everyone must accept it."

"She gives us what we need."

"My only wish now," said Manisha, "is to finish my days in the arms of Tara, and that she takes me in a good way, with all the proper rites."

Mr. Basu had now brought the goat he had earlier tethered to a tree, and was looking expectantly at Tapan.

"Come," said Tapan. "Enough talking. This is the night of Tara. We should be praying, not chatting."

"It is true," said Manisha. "It is late now—the time Ma comes. It is time to get ready for our sacrifice."

The Song of the Blind Minstrel

On the feast of Makar Sakranti, the new moon night on which the sun passes through the winter solstice, from the Tropic of Cancer to the Tropic of Capricorn, a great gathering takes places on the banks of the Ajoy River in West Bengal.

Around the middle of January, several thousand saffron-clad wandering minstrels, or Bauls—the word means simply "mad" or "possessed" in Bengali—begin to gather at Kenduli, in the flat flood-plains near Tagore's old home of Shantiniketan. As they have done on this site for at least 500 years, the Bauls wander the huge camp-site, greeting old friends, smoking *ganja* and exchanging gossip. Then, as the night draws in, they gather around their fires, and begin the singing and dancing that will carry on until dawn.

You approach the festival through green wetlands, past bullocks ploughing the rich mud of the rice paddy. Reed-thatched or tin-topped Bengali cottages are surrounded by clumps of young green bamboo and groves of giant banyans, through which evening clouds of parakeets whirr and screech. As you near the Baul monastery of Tamalatala, which acts as the focus of the festival, the stream of pilgrims slowly thickens along the roadsides. Bengali villagers herding their goats and ducks along the high embankments give way to lines of lean, dark, wiry men with matted hair and straggling beards. Some travel in groups of two or three; others travel alone, carrying hand drums or the Bauls' simple single-stringed instrument, the *ektara*.

Throughout their 500-year history, the Bauls of Bengal have refused to conform to the conventions of caste-conscious Bengali society. Subversive and seductive, wild and abandoned, they have preserved a series of esoteric spiritual teachings on breathing techniques, sex, asceticism, philosophy and mystical devotion. They have also amassed a treasury of beautifully melancholic and often enigmatic teaching songs which help map out their path to inner vision.

For the Bauls believe that God is found not in a stone or bronze idol, or in the heavens, or even in the afterlife, but in the present moment, in the body of the man or woman who seeks the truth; all that is required is that you give up your possessions, take up the life of the road, find a guru and adhere to the path of love. Each man is alone, they believe, and must find his own way. Drawing elements from Sufism, Tantra, Shakta, Sahajiya, Vaishnavism and Buddhism, they revere deities such as Krishna or Kali, and visit temples, mosques and wayside shrines—but only as helpful symbols and signposts along a road to Enlightenment, never as an end in themselves.

Their goal is to discover the divine inner knowledge: the "Unknown Bird," "The Golden Man" or the "Man of the Heart"—*Moner Manush*—an ideal that they believe lives within the body of every man, but may take a lifetime to discover. As such they reject the authority of the Brahmins and the usefulness of religious rituals, while some—though not all—Bauls come close to a form of atheism, denying the existence of any transcendental deity, and seeking instead ultimate truth in this present physical world, in every human body and every human heart. Man is the final measure for the Bauls.

The near-atheism and humanism of these singing philosophers is not in any sense a new departure in Indian thought, and dates back at least to the sceptical and materialistic Charvaka school of the sixth century BC, which rejected the idea of God and professed that no living creature was immortal. Ancient India in fact has a larger atheistic and agnostic literature than any other classical civilisation, and an Indian tradition of ambiguity in the face of eternity can be traced back as far as the *Rig Veda*, which enshrines at its centre the idea of uncertainty about the divine. "Who really knows?" it asks. "Who will here proclaim it? Whence was it produced? Whence is this creation? Perhaps it formed itself, perhaps it did not. The one who looks down on it from the highest heaven, only he knows—or perhaps he does not know." The strange mix of spirituality and scepticism in Baul philosophy is thus rooted in a very ancient strand of Hindu agnostic thought.

In pursuit of this path, the Bauls defy distinctions of caste and religion. Bauls can be from any background, and they straddle the frontiers of Hinduism and Islam. The music of "God's Troubadours" reflects their impulsive restlessness and their love of the open road:

The Mirror of the sky,
reflects my soul.
O Baul of the road,
O Baul, my heart,
What keeps you tied,
to the corner of the room?

As the storm rampages
In your crumbling hut,
the water rises to your bed.
Your tattered quilt
Floats on the flood,
Your shelter is down.

O Baul of the road,
O Baul, my heart,
What keeps you tied,
to the corner of the room?

Travelling from village to village, owning nothing but a multi-coloured patchwork robe known as an *alkhalla*, they sit in tea shops and under roadside banyan trees, in the compartments of trains and at village bus stops, busking their ballads of love and mysticism, divine madness and universal brotherhood, and the goal of *Maha-sukha*, the great bliss of the void, to gatherings of ordinary Bengali farmers and villagers.

They break the rhythm of rural life, inviting intimacies and wooing and consoling their audience with poetry and song, rather than hectoring them with sermons or speeches. They sing of desire and devotion, ecstasy and madness; of life as a river and the body as a boat. They sing of Radha's mad love for the elusive Krishna, of the individual as the crazed Lover, and the Divine as the unattainable Beloved. They remind their listeners of the transitory nature of this life, and encourage them to renounce the divisions and hatreds of the world, so provoking them into facing themselves. Inner knowledge, they teach, is acquired not through power over others, but over the Self.

Once a year, however, the Bauls leave their wanderings and converge on Kenduli for their biggest annual festival. It's the largest gathering of singers and Tantrics in South Asia. To get there I flew to Calcutta and took a train north to Shantiniketan, determined to see this gathering for myself.

But first I had to find Manisha Ma's friend Kanai Das Baul.

Manisha had told me something of Kanai's story when I was with her in the Tarapith cremation ground.

When he was six months old, Kanai caught smallpox and went blind. His parents—day labourers—despaired as to how their son would make a living. Then one day, when Kanai was ten, a passing Baul guru heard the boy singing as he took a bath amid the water hyacinths of the village pond, or *pukur*. In Bengal, the *pukur* is to village life what the green was to medieval England—the centre of rural life—as well as swimming pool, duck pond and communal laundromat. Kanai's voice was high, sad and elegiac, and the Baul guru asked Kanai's parents if they would consider letting him take Kanai as a pupil. "Once your parents have gone," he said, "you will be able to support yourself if you let us teach you to sing."

In due course, many years later, after a terrible family tragedy, Kanai remembered the guru's words and set off to find him. He joined him on the road, learning the songs and becoming in time one of the Bauls' most celebrated singers.

Then, after the death of his guru, Kanai took up residence in the cremation ground of Tarapith, where Manisha, Tapan Sadhu and some of their friends helped arrange a marriage for him, to a young widow who looked after the shoes of visitors.

Kanai, Manisha told me, had arrived at the Kenduli Mela a few days ahead of me, and had already joined up with an itinerant group of other Bauls. They were all staying in a small house off the main bazaar: to get there you had to leave the bathers washing on the banks of the Ajoy and pick your way through the usual mêlée of Indian religious festivals: street children selling balloons and marigold garlands; a contortionist and a holy man begging for alms; a group of argumentative naked Naga sadhus; a hissing snake goddess and her attendants; lines of bullock carts loaded up with clay images of the goddess Durga; beggars and mendicants; a man selling pink candyfloss to a blare of Bollywood strings emerging from a huge pink loudspeaker attached to the flossing machine. All along the main drag of the encampment, rival *akharas,* or monasteries, of the different Baul gurus had been erected, interspersed with tented temples full of brightly lit idols, constellations of clay lamps and camphor flames winking amid the wafts of sandalwood incense filling the warm, dusty Bengali darkness.

By the time I found the house—a simple unfurnished Bengali hut—it was dark and Kanai's Bauls were in full song. They had scattered straw on the ground and were sitting in a circle around the fire, cross-legged on the floor, breaking their singing only to pass a chillum of *ganja* from one to the other.

There were six of them: Kanai himself, a thin, delicate and self-possessed man in his fifties with a straggling grey beard and a pair of small cymbals in his hand. Beside him sat a fabulously handsome old Baul, Kanai's great friend and travelling companion Debdas, singing with a *dugi* drum in one hand and an *ektara* in the other. His hair hung loose, as did his great fan of grey beard, while a string of copper bells was attached to the big toe of his right foot, which he jingled as he sang.

Facing them was another of the most celebrated Baul singers in Bengal, Paban Das Baul, who was flanked by his *khepi*, or Baul partner, Mimlu Sen, and his two younger sisters. Paban was a lithe, handsome and hyperactive figure in his late forties, with full lips, a shock of wiry pepper-and-salt hair, a short goatee and bushy sideburns. He was playing a small, two-stringed *dotara* and dominating the group as much by the sheer manic energy of his performance as by his singing: "Never plunge into the river of lust," he sang with his rich, velvety voice, "for you will not reach the shore."

> *It is a river without banks,*
> *where typhoons rage,*
> *and the current is strong.*

> *Only those who are masters,*
> *of the five* rasas, *the juices of love,*
> *Know the play of the tides.*

> *Their boats do not sink.*
> *Paddled by oars of Love,*
> *They row strongly upstream.*

The three men–Kanai, Debdas and Paban–were old friends, and as the music gathered momentum they passed verses and songs back and forth, so that when one would ask a philosophical question, the other would answer it: a symposium in song. Paban sang a verse of a traditional Bengali folksong about his wish to visit Krishna's home:

> *The peacock cries–*
> *Oh who will show me the way to Vrindavan?*
> *He raises his tail and cries:*
> *Krishna! Krishna!*

Kanai then answered with a verse reminding Paban that the only proper place of pilgrimage for a Baul was the human heart:

> *Oh my deaf ears and blind eyes!*
> *How will I ever rid myself of this urge*
> *to find you, except in my own soul?*
> *If you want to go to Vrindavan,*
> *Look first into your heart . . .*

"Who knows if the gods exist at all?" sang Debdas, supporting Kanai.

> *Can you find them in the heavens?*
> *Or the Himalayas?*
> *On the earth, or in the air?*
> *Nowhere else can God be found,*
> *But in the heart of the seeker of Truth.*

The voices of all three men were perfectly complementary, Paban's resonant and smoky, alternately urgent and sensuous; Debdas's a fine tenor; Kanai's softer, more vulnerable, tender and high-pitched—at times almost a falsetto—with a fine, reed-like clarity. As Paban sang, he twanged a *khomok* hand drum or thundered away at the *dubki*, a sort of small, rustic tambourine. Kanai, in contrast, invariably sang with his sightless blue eyes fixed ecstatically upwards, gazing at the heavens. Paban would occasionally tickle his chin, and tease him: "Don't give me that wicked smile, Kanai . . ."

The songs all drew on the world and images of the Bengali village, and contained parables that anyone could understand: the body, sang Paban, is like a pot of clay; the human soul the water of love. Inner knowledge found with the help of the guru fires the pot and bakes the clay, for an unfired pot cannot contain water. Other songs were sprinkled with readily comprehensible images of boats and nets, rice fields, fish ponds and the village shop:

> *Cut the rice stalks,*
> *O rice-growing brother.*

Cut them in a bunch
Before they begin to smell
Rotten like your body
Without a living heart.

Sell your goods, my store-keeping brother,
While the market is brisk,
When the sun fades
And your customers depart,
Your store is a lonely place . . .

Later, after dinner, Paban and the other Bauls went out to hear a rival Baul singer perform in the Kenduli market place, leaving Kanai on his own, sitting cross-legged on the rug, singing softly. I sat beside him and asked what he was doing.

"This is how I remember the songs," he said. "I am blind, so I cannot read and write the verses. Instead, when I am left alone, I hum a few bars and repeat the songs to myself to help me commit them to memory. It is by repeating them that I remember."

Kanai smiled. "There are some advantages to being blind," he said. "I can learn songs much quicker than other people, and pick up tunes very fast. Debdas says that I see with my ears. When he forgets, I have to remind him, even if it is a song that he originally taught me, or sometimes, even one he composed."

At Kanai's request, I lit a cigarette for him, and we chatted about his childhood, as he filled out the brief picture of his life that Manisha had painted for me.

"I was born in the village of Tetulia," he said, leaning back and puffing contentedly away, "not far from here, near Birbhum. I was born with eyes that could see, but lost my sight when I caught smallpox before my first birthday. Who knows? Maybe I did something wrong in a previous life to be punished like this.

"My father had no land of his own, so used to work during the harvest and the planting season for the local *zamindar*. The landlord gave him a small house, and eventually he got to own it. I had two sisters and a brother, as well as fourteen cousins, and at one point there were as many as twenty-three people sleeping in the house, so we used to take our rest in shifts. All my uncles were casual labourers too, except one who was a silk weaver: every day he used to go to the *zamindar*'s estate house, where the looms were kept. The *zamindar* looked after the village and treated us all as if we were his extended family. He employed everyone in the village, either in his fields or in his silk business. He was a good man, but there was not much money—things were always tight for us.

"I was ten when my brother was killed in an accident involving a heavily laden bullock cart, and eleven when my father passed away too, from an asthma attack. This left me with the responsibility to feed my two sisters. They were growing girls and needed food. At first it wasn't too hard. Once I got used to begging from my own friends, from door to door, I found it wasn't difficult to get enough to fill all our stomachs. We were loved and looked after: I only had to say, 'I am hungry,' and I would be fed. The door of the poor man is always open—it is only the doors of the rich that close as you approach. If the people in the village came to hear that another family was going through a hard time they would always give them rice or a cow dung cake for fuel.

"I used to go out in the morning with my stick and my bowl, taking the name of Hari [Krishna], and would come back by lunch. Whatever I had collected we shared, and ate. People knew the family, and knew what had happened to us. They felt sorry for us, and although they were very poor themselves they would always give something: a rupee, or some rice and vegetables. The problems only began when one of my sisters became eligible for marriage.

"I was fifteen, and beginning to talk to prospective grooms, but it was clear from the beginning that it wasn't going to be easy. Some people in the village thought we were cursed because of all the bad luck we had suffered—first with me going blind, then the two deaths in rapid succession. Others considered my proposal, but demanded dowries I knew I would never be able to pay. I became more and more depressed, and without realising it I must have communicated this to my sister. One day I was at a friend's place drinking tea when

I was told I had to go back home immediately. When I returned, I discovered that my sister had committed suicide. I had no idea she was even near doing such a thing: she must have thought she was too much of a burden on me, and that we could not afford the wedding. Whatever the reason, she hanged herself from the ceiling beam of our one room.

"Coming after the death of my father and brother, this sent me mad with grief: I was shattered, and blamed myself. I stayed at home for weeks and then I decided I couldn't remain in the village any longer; I must make a new life for myself. It was then that I remembered Gyanand Sadhu, the Baul guru who had heard me singing when I was bathing in the *pukur* as a boy. I had loved the way he sang just as much as he liked my voice. I knew that his ashram was near Rampurhat, so I decided to go and see if he would take me on as his disciple, his *chela*.

"My mother and other sister were very angry at my decision. They said, 'Why are you going? Don't you care for us?' I was very sad to leave them in this way, but I had a feeling this was what I needed to do in order for the family to survive. I was always very religious, but it wasn't just that; it seemed a practical decision too. A blind man cannot be a farmer, but he can be a singer.

"Ever since I was a boy I had been picking up holy songs and *bhajans*, and all through my childhood I used to sing the songs of the Bauls, and the *shyama Kali sangeet* of the Tantric sadhus, playing the spokes of my father's bullock cart with a stick, like a drum. Because I had a good voice the sadhus and the Bauls loved me, and all the villagers would gather around when I sang; but it was the songs themselves that led me to the life of a singer. I said to myself, I will treat singing the songs as my form of devotion, my *sadhana*, and put my whole heart into it. That way I can live the life of the heart—and also save money to send to my mother and sister. At that moment, when my fortunes were at their lowest, it was my ability to sing that saved me.

"It was the season of the rains. I caught a bus to Tarapith, and changed buses there, and late that evening I arrived in Mallarpur, near Rampurhat, where Gyanand Sadhu's ashram was located. It was raining very heavily, and as it was late there was no one about to ask for directions. When I got off the bus, the water was already ankle-deep. As I walked on in the direction that the conductor had sent me, straight along the road, the water got deeper until it was up to my thighs. There was no one around to help, and there was nothing to do but carry on, even as the water rose to my waist and the thunder boomed overhead.

"But I persevered, and despite my fears, the road turned out to be the right one. Climbing a small hill, I hit dry land. Soon after that I came to the gate of the ashram. I was drenched, it was the middle of the night, and I expected to be turned away. But instead the *chowkidar* ushered me straight into the presence of Gyananand. The moment he saw me, he said, 'I have been waiting for you. I always knew that boy in the *pukur* would come to me sooner or later.' He welcomed me warmly, gave me food and dry clothes and took me on as his *chela*. I stayed there seven years, wandering in the cold season and staying with Gyananand in his *akhara* during the rains. He provided for my mother and sister, and gave me money to take home to them.

"I joined the Bauls partly because it seemed the only way I could make a livelihood. But my guru soon taught me that there are much more important things than getting by, or making money, or material pleasures. I am still very poor, but thanks to the lessons of my guru, my soul is rich. He taught me to seek inner knowledge and to inspire our people to seek this too. He told me to concentrate on singing and did not encourage me to take the path of a Tantric yogi, though I have picked up a lot of knowledge of this sort from other sadhus and Bauls over the years."

"Is it a good life?" I asked.

"It is the best life," said Kanai without hesitation. "The world is my home. We Bauls can walk anywhere and are welcome anywhere. When you walk you are freed from the worries of ordinary life, from the imprisonment of being rooted in the same place. I cannot complain. Far from it—I am often in a state of bliss."

"But don't you miss your home? Don't you tire of the road?"

"When you first become a Baul, you have to leave your family, and for twelve years you must wander in strange countries where you have no relatives. There is a saying, 'No Baul should live under the same tree for more than three days.' At first you feel alone, disorientated. But people are always pleased to see the Bauls: when the villagers see our coloured robes they shout: 'Look, the madmen are coming! Now we can take the day off and have some fun!'

"Wherever we go, the people stop what they are doing and come and listen to us. They bring fish from the fish ponds, and cook some rice and dal for us, and while they do that we sing and teach them. We try to give back some of the love we receive, to reconcile people and offer them peace and solace. We try to help them with their difficulties, and to show them the path to discover the Man of the Heart."

I asked: "How do you do that?"

"With our songs," said Kanai. "For us Bauls, our songs are a source of both love and knowledge. We tease the rich and the arrogant, and make digs at the hypocrisy of the Brahmins. We sing against caste, and against injustice. We tell the people that God is not in the temple, or in the Himalayas, nor in the skies or the earth or in the air. We teach that Krishna was just a man. What is special about him in essence is in me now. Whatever is in the cosmos is in our bodies; what is not in the body is not in the cosmos. It is all inside—truth lies within. If this is so, then why bother going to the mosque or the temple? So to the Bauls a temple or a shrine has little value: it is just a way for the priests to make money and to mislead people. The body is the true temple, the true mosque, the true church."

"But in what way?"

"We believe that the way to God lies not in rituals but in living a simple life, walking the country on foot and doing what your guru says. The joy of walking on foot along unknown roads brings you closer to God. You learn to recognise that the divine is everywhere—even in the rocks. You learn also that music and dance is a way of discovering the Unknown Bird. You come to understand that God is the purest form of joy—complete joy."

Kanai shook his long grey locks. "There is no jealousy in this life," he said. "No Brahmin or Dalit, no Hindu or Muslim. Wherever I am, that is my home.

"For many years now I have wandered the roads of Bengal,

spending the rains with my guru, and after he died, in the cremation ground at Tarapith. Sometimes when I have tired of walking, I would work the trains between Calcutta and Shantiniketan. That was how I first met Debdas."

"In a train?"

"He was only sixteen," said Kanai, "and had just run away from home. He was from the family of a pundit, and had a childhood in which he needed to ask for nothing. But then he was thrown out for mixing with Muslims and Bauls, and he was innocent of the ways of the world. He had an *ektara*, but at that stage he knew hardly any songs. Though I was blind, and he could see, it was I who taught him how to survive, and the words of the songs of the Bauls. Although we are from very different worlds, the road brought us together, and we have become inseparable friends."

Kanai smiled. "But I shouldn't be telling you his story," he said. "You must ask him yourself."

So saying, without moving, Kanai went back to humming his songs to himself, remembering and repeating the words:

> *You and I are bound together,*
> *In the six-petalled lotus of the heart.*
> *There is honey in this flower, the nectar of the moon,*
> *As sweet as Kama's dart.*

> *Through the garden of emotion,*
> *A raging river flows.*
> *On its banks we're bound together,*
> *In the six-petalled lotus of the heart.*

It was nearly midnight when Debdas rejoined us.

He and Paban came back from their concert in high spirits, and as glasses of Old Monk rum and chillums of *ganja* were passed around the room, the music began again, and it was some time before I was able to get Debdas on his own and ask him about how he came to join up with Kanai. Eventually, when Paban left for another late-night concert at the *akhara* of a friend of his, Debdas settled back and told the story of how he and Kanai had first met. As he talked, Kanai occasionally interrupted, or corrected Debdas's version of events.

"For many years, I have been Kanai's eyes, and he my voice," said Debdas, puffing at a chillum and exhaling a great cloud of strongly scented *ganja* smoke. "He taught me everything: how to reject the outer garb of religion and to dive deep into the ocean of the heart. He is a friend, a teacher, a brother, a guru. He is my memory. He is everything to me."

"And Debdas is my eyes, my helper, my student, my co-traveller and my friend," said Kanai, tapping his heart.

"We have travelled the road together for many years now," said Debdas.

"Pushkar, Varanasi, Pondicherry . . ."

"Allahabad, Hardwar, Gangotri . . ."

"Always holding each other's hands. Over the years we have become very close"—he held up two fingers—"like this. *Chelo*, Kanai!"

"We are connected at the navel," said Kanai, gesturing towards his belly button. "When Sri Chaitanya Mahaprabhu, the Madman of Madmen, went to Keshava Bharati, who had initiated him as a *sanyasi*, he said to his friend, 'Give me the world.' Keshava Bharati asked, 'What worlds can I give you?' Chaitanya replied, 'The very same that I gave to you.' We are like that, Debdas and I . . ."

"At times, I am Kanai's guru," said Debdas. "And at times, Kanai is my guru. He reminds me even of my own songs."

I asked Debdas to tell me about his childhood, and how he first came to meet his friend, and taking another puff of his chillum, he began his story.

"I was born in a village about fifteen miles from that of Kanai, not very far from Tarapith," he said, exhaling another great cloud of

smoke, and passing the chillum to Kanai's waiting fingers, and helping his friend lift it to his mouth. "But we were from very different backgrounds. My father was a *purohit*, the Brahmin of the village Kali temple. My father and I always had very different values. He was obsessed with his idols and his round of *pujas*. I was also pious, but I never embraced that sort of ritualistic religion. I didn't know what was in, or not in, the piece of stone in the sanctuary of my father's temple: how could I? How can anyone? For me, from the time I was very young, the company I kept was always more important to me than idols or rituals, status or material comforts.

"My best friend was a little Muslim boy, Anwar. His father made *beedi* cigarettes at the other end of the village. My father would smoke the *beedis*, but before he lit them he would always touch them against cow dung to purify them. He would pressure me not to mix so widely, and if I drank water in a Muslim house, he would make me have a bath before he let me inside our home. There was a house of some Bairagi sadhus in the village who sang wonderful Baul songs, and Krishna *bhajans*, and my father didn't like me going there either. I even shared cigarettes with the [untouchable] Doms who ran the village cremation ground. Even when I was very young, my mind was full of doubts about all these boundaries and restrictions my father thought were so important.

"It was the songs of the Bauls that lured me towards their path. In our locality lived the great singer Sudhir Das Baul. One day, the schoolmaster invited him to come and sing to us on the feast of Saraswati Puja. I was thirteen or fourteen, and then and there I lost my heart to his music! He had such a voice, and such spirit: he could take a *rasa* to its very essence."

"Oh, he was marvellous!" interjected Kanai, leaning forward, sightless eyes gazing upwards, with folded hands. "What a voice!"

"It was after hearing him," said Debdas, "that I made up my mind to become a Baul and sing the songs of Krishna. After some time, I went and visited him at his home, and told him I wanted to learn music. So Sudhir said, 'If you want to become a Baul you must attend the great festival at Kenduli.' He called it 'the great festival of the Enlightened.' He told me the date—it's always at the middle or towards the end of January—and promised to take me along.

"I knew that my family would never allow it, so when the day came, I climbed the walls of the house and slipped out without telling anyone where I was going. I had agreed to meet Sudhir at the station in time to catch the 4 a.m. train to Shantiniketan. From the station there we walked on foot to the *mela*.

"The *mela* was beyond my dreams: you can see for yourself what it is like. The atmosphere was wonderful—the music-making, the dancing, the rapture, the *matajis* putting hair oil on the *babajis*, the intoxication of the madmen, the joy, the freedom . . . I drank in the pure life of those Bauls, and understood for the first time the real pleasure of living. It made me yearn to roam through the world and escape from my village life."

"And you never told your parents where you were?" Kanai giggled.

"Wait," said Debdas, smiling. "We'll come to that.

"For four days I walked the lanes of the festival, happier than I had ever been, meeting the Bauls and learning their songs. On the fourth day, as everyone began to pack up, I asked Sudhir Das, 'What do I do now?' I hadn't left my parents a note—nothing. He advised me to go back home quietly, and he took me back on the train, holding my hand to give me courage. We parted at the station, and I headed home. But I was frightened of what my father would say, so I doubled back and went to the home of my Muslim friend, Anwar, and ate there.

"By now it was dusk, and it was only after dark that I finally headed back home. Nobody said a word as I walked in. In silence I washed at the pump, but just as I was entering the house, my father stopped me and asked me to sit in the courtyard. My mother understood what was about to happen, and called me to join her in the kitchen, but just then my elder brother, who was the village police chief, blocked my way. He shouted at me that I had dishonoured the family, and that I was a good-for-nothing who only mixed with Muslims and vagrants. He said that he would teach me a lesson that I would never forget.

"He had his *lathi* with him, and he began beating me with it. My father joined in, using his wooden slippers. For nearly an hour they both beat me—it seemed like much longer, at that age things hurt more—until eventually the neighbours had to come and separate us. Then they kicked me out of the courtyard into the street. I sat there shuddering with tears, hurting both inside and out. There were welts all over my back, my shorts were torn and my shirt was covered in blood."

"Your father really gave it to you," said Kanai, shaking his head.

"For a while I just lay there, and then eventually I got up and went to the train station. I washed in the pump on the platform. I knew I would get into trouble, but I never thought it would be so bad. I now had to think what to do. I didn't have a rupee in my pocket, my clothes were torn, it was November and there was a chill in the air. So I thought very deep and hard. As I was thinking a train puffed in, heading for Howrah, and I jumped on, without any particular plan, and eventually got off at Burdwan Junction. I sat for a long time on the platform in the dark. I knew I wanted to become a Baul, but how to get there? How could I feed myself?

"As I was sitting there another train came in, the Toofan Express, coming from Vrindavan, the home of Lord Krishna. It was now 11:30 p.m. As I sat there in the half-light of the platform, a small group of Bauls and sadhus got off the train, carrying musical instruments, and they settled down close to where I was sitting. One was a very old man—he must have been at least ninety. He saw me sitting there with blood on my clothes, and a black eye coming up, so he walked over, and said, 'You've run away from home, haven't you?' He asked me to bring him some water, which I did. He then said, 'You must be hungry.' So he gave me a chapati from his tiffin, and shared his dal with me, and as we ate, I told him the whole story.

"He listened very carefully, and then told me I should catch the Toofan Express back to Vrindavan, and that if I went there, Lord Krishna would help me. At 2 a.m., the Express hooted that it was about to leave. He helped me on, and gave me a blanket, and handed me his most precious possession, his *ektara*. 'Don't worry,' he said. 'Just play the *ektara*, and sing the name of Krishna, and you'll be looked after.'

"So with that *ektara* in my hand, and still wearing my torn vest and shorts, I got on, and we headed off, away from Bengal. I didn't eat again for four days—I didn't know how to beg, couldn't speak Hindi, couldn't play the *ektara*. I only knew the two songs I had learned at Kenduli, and of those I only knew a couple of verses. But when I reached Vrindavan, I heard there was food available to poor pilgrims at the Govind Mandir: they were giving out rice pudding as *lungar* [alms]. So I ate bowl after bowl, until I was no longer hungry. Then I went down to the banks of the Yamuna River and said a prayer, asking for the strength to become a Baul and never to give up and go back home and submit to my father. With that prayer on my lips, I threw my sacred thread into the river.

"For me, that ended forever my identity as a Brahmin. That very day I changed my name. I had been Dev Kumar Bhattacharyya—any Bengali knows that that is a Brahmin name, with all the privileges that go with it. But a Baul has to name himself as a *Das*—a slave of the Lord—so I became simply Debdas Baul. The Brahmins had rejected me, so I rejected them, just as I rejected their whole horrible idea of caste and the divisions it creates. I wanted freedom from that whole system.

"Then I took the blanket the old Baul had given me, and cut it into an *alkhalla*. In that attire, with the *ektara*, I found that people would always give me a little change if I sang a Krishna *bhajan*. I was only fourteen, and knew nothing of the world. At first, I was sure I had made a mistake. But I was too proud to go back, and slowly I learned how to survive.

"I stayed in a room in a temple and would wander from shrine to shrine, from *akhara* to *akhara*, making friends with the other sadhus, and trying to learn the words of the songs they were singing. With money that pilgrims had given me, I bought a notebook, and I would jot down all the words of the songs I heard the Bauls and the sadhus singing on the ghats at Vrindavan. My mind was totally focused on becoming a Baul; for me at that stage, God was the song I was singing. I just wanted to find out what was in those songs, and how to decode their hidden meanings.

"After two years, I went back home, and tried to make peace with my family. As I entered, my mother was sitting there right in front of me, in the middle of the courtyard. She kept sitting there, looking at me as if I was a ghost. I greeted her, and from inside came the voice of my father asking, 'Who is there?' My mother said, 'It is Debu.' So my father came out and looked at me, amazed, without speaking. Then his face clouded over. 'You've become a Baul,' he said, firmly but not unkindly. 'Now you must live with them. There is no place for a Baul in my house.' Then my brother came back, and started threatening me with dire consequences if I didn't leave. My mother and sister were crying, and I was crying inside, but I was too scared to cling to them, or even say goodbye. The whole scene lasted less than an hour, maybe less than that. I've never seen them again.

"Just as I had two years earlier, I walked the road to the railway station, and again I boarded the first train that came in. I was miserable—it was one of the lowest points in my life. The train pulled out, and I sat gazing out of the window, feeling as if I might as well just throw myself out of the train into the river. But then something remarkable happened. After a few minutes, I heard some singing further down the train. It was Paban, and his brother and his father, and with them, in a different carriage, was Sudhir Das, the Baul who had taken me to Kenduli, and with him was Kanai.

"I had known Paban's family since I was a boy, as they lived in the next village, and they were very surprised to see me living like a Baul and wearing the *alkhalla*. But they embraced me, and looked after me, and Kanai began to teach me songs. We began to sing together on the trains and to sleep on the platforms of stations. We were perpetually on the move—from train to train, festival to festival. I was very happy, partly because I was back in Bengal—the Bengalis understand our ways and love our songs—and partly because I really liked the freedom of this life. But mainly I was happy because Kanai and the others recognised me as another Baul, and made me their friend and companion. I forgot the pain of being rejected by my family and immersed myself in the family of the Bauls, and the kinship of their songs. Kanai and I were together from this time.

"There was only one time when I left him for an extended period. This was when I became obsessed with trying to live without food, like the saints and yogis in the old stories. These saints controlled all their desires and so never ate: they lived on air alone. I wanted to find out if it was still possible to do this. So I went off on my own, and found a *bel*–a wood apple tree–in a forest near a pond: we believe these trees are very auspicious. I sat there in a loincloth and meditated for two years, eating less and less until I stopped eating altogether, taking a vow that no food was to pass my lips until I reached my goal, and achieved Enlightenment. I don't know how I lived. I had matted dreadlocks down to my knees, and sat there not eating, not smoking, and drinking nothing but water. I focused inwards, conserving my energies. I sat there like that through two monsoons and two cold winters."

"I used to visit him," said Kanai. "The villagers knew where he was, and would lead me to him through the forest. They called him *'Bel-talar Babaji'*–the sadhu who sits under a wood apple tree. He was very thin and very weak. He hardly moved or talked–only very short sentences. I was very anxious that he wouldn't survive, and it pained me that he wouldn't eat. I brought him food, but he refused to eat it. He was very determined."

"I don't know what I attained with this penance," said Debdas, "but I know my mind was at peace as never before. My hair was matted, but the knots of my heart were untied. After a certain point, I stopped feeling hunger. I was at the end of desire, beyond the senses. It was then that I started hallucinating. I was no longer living inside my body–I was somewhere outside of myself, in a state of ecstasy and rapture. I have never felt anything like it, before or since.

"Then one cold starry night, around the time of Makar Sakranti, I felt suddenly lost, as if my mind had finally detached itself from my body–like a bird flying high. It was Kanai who brought me back."

"What do you mean?"

"I was unaware of it, but there had been a terrible storm. Kanai had a premonition that I was in trouble, and came over from Tarapith to see if I was all right. He arrived early in the morning with a group of villagers, and found me up to my neck in a pool of mud, fast asleep. They all thought I was dead–and I suppose I almost was. Kanai brought me back to his house in Tarapith, and nursed me back to health."

"The blind man saved the man who could see," said Kanai,

chuckling to himself. "Sometimes the mad and sightless can understand things better, and more clearly, than the sane and the sighted."

"The blind are never deceived by appearances," said Debdas.

"Maybe," said Kanai, "it is only those of us who have no eyes that can see through the lure of *maya,* and glimpse reality for what it is."

For five days I followed Kanai and Debdas around the Kenduli *mela,* as Debdas held Kanai's hand and guided him.

All over the huge campsite, at all hours of the day and night, you could see groups of musicians breaking into song. Sometimes this was part of a formal concert: the Bengal State Government had put up a small stage in honour of Kenduli's celebrated court poet Joydeb, the twelfth-century author of the great Sanskrit poem on the loves of Krishna, the *Gita Govinda,* and each night different Baul groups competed to sing the poem. Usually, however, the music was spontaneous. Groups of Bauls began singing around a campfire and were soon joined by old friends not seen since the last festival.

The Bauls were always happy to talk about their lives and songs and beliefs, but were not prepared to discuss in public the esoteric sexual practices which each guru teaches to his pupils when he considers they are ready. These folk Tantric practices of the Bauls, or *sadhana,* are closely guarded secrets, but embrace control of breathing and orgasm in elaborately ritualised sexual rites. Sometimes this involves sex with menstruating women, which in their songs they call "the full moon at the new moon." Occasionally this is combined with the ingestion of a drink compounded of semen, blood and bodily fluids—so making a firm Tantric statement about flouting established norms and taboos.

Kanai talked briefly to me about the Bauls' sexual yoga, "drinking nectar from the moon," explaining it as a way of awakening and controlling the latent erotic energies from the base of your body and bringing them to the fore. His words were explained to me by another new arrival at the festival: the Delhi-based writer on religion

Bhaskar Bhattacharyya, who had once lived for an extended period with Kanai in Tarapith, and who had researched the customs of the Bauls as deeply as anyone.

The Bauls, explained Bhaskar, seek to channel the mysteries of sexuality and the sexual urge—the most powerful emotional force in the human body—as a way of reaching and revealing the divinity of the inner self. "They use it as a sort of booster rocket," he explained. "Just as a rocket uses huge amounts of energy to blast out of the field of gravity, so the Bauls use their Tantric sexual yoga as a powerhouse to drive the mind out of the gravity of everyday life, to make sex not so much enjoyable as something approaching a divine experience. Yet the sex is useless if it is not performed with love, and even then sex is just the beginning of a long journey. It's how you learn to use it, how you learn to control it, that is the real art."

For the Bauls, these sexual exotica are part of a much wider set of yogic practices which aim to make the sacred physiology of the body supple and coordinated with itself, using the mastery of breathing, meditation, posture and exercises as a way of charging and taming energies and drives, and perfecting the body in order to transform it. "For the Bauls, the body is the chariot that can take you up into the sky, towards the sun," as Bhaskar put it.

For this reason, marriage is very important for the Bauls, and to be a fully initiated Baul you have to have a partner with whom you can perform Tantric *sadhana*. Debdas had in fact been married twice. His first wife was Radha Rani, the daughter of his guru, Sudhir Das, the Baul who had first taken him to Kenduli. Aged eighteen, he was staying in Sudhir Das's *akhara* when he caught a fever.

"I was almost unconscious and Radha Rani tended me," Debdas told me. "She was a beauty and a wonderful singer. The trap was laid: it was like a football match with only one goalpost. Whatever happened, happened. I was so ill that I was hardly aware of what was going on."

"Ha!" said Kanai from across the room.

"I was snared," said Debdas. "Completely in love."

"He was like an intoxicated elephant," said Kanai.

"Ah—she was wonderful," continued Debdas. "I wanted to team up with her and travel Bengal with her, singing. But in the end we were only together two years. Our love soured. Things built up, and one day the bomb burst. I just walked out. By then we had a six-month-old baby. In life, happiness and sorrow go hand in hand. Sorrow is part of life. We have to find the happiness that lies beside it."

I asked how he had met his current wife.

"Several years later I joined the *akhara* of Ramananda Das Goswami," said Debdas. "After a while I asked him to give me both musical and spiritual direction, and to teach me Tantric *sadhana*. I wanted to learn how to close the mouth of the snake and boil the milk of bliss [to make love without ejaculating]. My guru replied, 'You are asking for water, do you have a container?' He meant did I have a woman. I replied that I was single. So he said, 'There is a girl with us, Hari Dasi, why don't you marry her and I will teach you both?' I agreed, and Hari Dasi and I have been together ever since. She has enriched me in many ways, and been my route to our secret practices. I can't tell you about our *sadhana* together—this can only be shared with initiated Bauls who have taken *diksha*—but I can tell you it transformed my life."

Kanai came to marriage later than Debdas, and it was Manisha Ma who brought him together with his wife. When Debdas was at the *akhara* of Ramananda Das Goswami, Kanai spent the monsoon breaks in the cremation ground of Tarapith.

"My friends in the burning ground got together and decided it was about time I was married," said Kanai. "Arati, who became my *khepi*, had been married before, but her husband had fallen from a tree and had been totally disabled. He used to come to the cremation ground in a little cart and take care of the shoes at the entrance. After he died, Arati took over his job, and would sit by the entrance with her young son, all alone in the world. Manisha Ma said to her that she was very young, and needed a protector: why didn't she tie up with Kanai? All the sadhus thought it was a good idea, so my mother came and met her, and liked her. She wanted me looked after and settled before she died, so she said to Arati, 'Look after my son—he may be blind, but he's a good boy.'

"According to the Hindu *shastras* you marry only once, and Arati had already been married. So the *purohit* did what is usual in such cases: he married me to a banana tree, and then I put *sindhoor* on Arati's forehead.

"I was completely innocent when I was married. How could I know how to make the frog dance before the serpent? I can't see! For this reason, my guru Gyananand had advised me to concentrate on singing, and not try to get involved in Tantric *sadhana*. So in these matters Arati was my guru.

"Nothing happened the first night. My education took place a week later in the new home the sadhus had helped me rent. She was a good teacher, and we now have four children. I owe this happiness to Manisha and the other sadhus of Tarapith: without them I would never have reached this plain of life. I tell you—there is such a lot of love in that place."

On the last day of the Kenduli festival, I went for a walk with Kanai through the Baul encampment. The festival-goers were beginning to strike their tents and head off back on the road. Everywhere canvas awnings were being folded up and loaded on to bullock carts.

Only two old people seemed to be sitting still. Near the Kenduli cremation ground, I came across a Baul couple who were old friends of Kanai. Both were sitting cross-legged on the projecting ledge of a small roadside temple. Subhol Kapa and his wife, Lalita, were old but were still singing Baul songs to anyone who cared to stop and listen to them. They hailed Kanai, and he introduced us.

"I am eighty-three," said Subhol, "and Lalita is seventy. Our age prevents us walking the roads like we used to. But we can still dance and sing, and listen to the other Bauls. Lalita is a good singer—much better than I. These days I am so sick, but when I sing or listen to Lalita it makes me forget my illness."

"It's true," said Lalita. "When I sing I forget everything else. Often I don't sing for anyone, just for myself, for my soul. I could not live without this life. I need to dance and to sing. I feel ecstatic when I sing."

"It is enough for me too," said Kanai. "I need nothing else."

"Song helps you transcend the material life," said Subhol. "It takes you to a different spiritual level."

"When a Baul sings he gets so carried away he starts dancing," said Kanai. "The happiness and joy that comes with the music helps you find God inside yourself."

"The songs of the Bauls are my companions in my old age," said Subhol. "We sing together, or with other Bauls like Debdas, Paban and Kanai if they come here. But when I am alone I take up my *dubki,* and sing to myself to keep myself company."

"Did you both used to wander the roads together?" I asked.

"We used to be ordinary householders," said Lalita. "Only after I had finished rearing my four sons did we become Bauls together—some twenty-five or thirty years back."

"Even before then we used to sing," said Subhol, "but after we became Bauls we were welcomed everywhere, with love and warmth and respect. It has made our life complete."

"For eighteen years we walked the roads of this country," said Lalita, "until we were too old to walk any more. This temple was my guru's ashram. Now we cannot wander, we live here following the Baul way, protecting our bodies and keeping our hearts alive."

"But I thought Bauls didn't believe in temples?"

"This temple is just to attract people," explained Subhol.

"For us Bauls it is just a building," said Kanai. "It has nothing to do with God."

"But people come here and tell us about their problems," said Subhol, "and then we can give them solutions."

"God resides in everything," said Lalita, looking out over the river.

"You have to learn to recognise God everywhere," said Kanai. "We have a song about this. You would like to hear it?"

"Very much," I said.

The old people went inside a room to one side of the shrine and returned a few minutes later, with Lalita carrying a harmonium and Subhol an *ektara.* Lalita squatted in front of the harmonium and Subhol plucked a few notes on the *ektara,* then began to sing, while Kanai provided a high, reedy descant.

My soul cries out,
Caught in the snare of beauty,
Of the formless one.

As I cry by myself,
Night and day,
Beauty amassed before my eyes,
Surpasses moons and suns.

If I look at the clouds in the sky,
I see his beauty afloat.
And I see him walk on the stars,
Blazing within my heart.

Before long, despite his age and fragility, Subhol was rocking backwards and forwards, hopping from one leg to another, transported by the music he was singing. Kanai and Lalita sat cross-legged, swaying to the music, lost in its beauty. When he had finished, the three settled together on the ledge of the temple, looking out in silence over the river. It was getting late now, and the sun was setting over the Ajoy—the time Bengalis call *godhuli bela,* cow dust time.

"When I hear this music," said Lalita after a few minutes, breaking the silence, "I don't care if I die tomorrow. It makes everything in life seem sweet."

"It's true," said Subhol. "Thanks to this music, we live out our old age in great peace."

"It makes us so happy," said Kanai, "that we don't remember what sadness is."

GLOSSARY

Aarti Ceremonial waving of a lamp in front of an effigy of a god as an offering of light during a *puja*.

Agarbatti Incense sticks.

Ahimsa Non-violence, from the Sanskrit for "do no harm."

Akhara A community or monastery of holy men (lit. "wrestling arena").

Alkhalla The coloured patchwork robe worn by the Bauls of Bengal.

Amavashya A night with no moon.

Aparigraha A Jain term meaning to limit possessions to what is necessary or important. A Jain monk does not have any possessions except a brush, a water pot and a robe.

Appam A hopper or South Indian rice pancake.

Artha The creation of wealth.

Arthav Explanatory declamatory recitation sung in front of a phad as part of the epic performance.

Ashram A place of religious retreat; hermitage.

Asthabhole Blood sacrifice.

Atta Flour.

Avatar An incarnation.

Azazeel Satan.

Ba Tibetan yurt. A round tent made of skins.

Babaji A respectful name for a sadhu.

Bairagi A Vaishnavite ascetic.

Bakri A goat.

Bansuri Wooden flute.

Barat A procession bringing the groom to a wedding.

Barelvi Sunni Muslims in South Asia who reject the more puritanical reformed Islam of the Wahhabis, Salafis and Deobandis and who embrace the popular Islam of the Sufi cult of saints. The name derives from Maulana Raza Khan of Bareilly, who espoused a liberal form of Sufi Islam.

Baul	A wandering Bengali minstrel, ascetic and holy man.
Beedi	A thin hand-rolled Indian cigarette wrapped in a leaf.
Bel	Wood apple tree (in Bengali).
Bhajan	A Hindu devotional song.
Bhakti	Devotion, or the practice of focussing worship upon a much loved deity.
Bhang	Marijuana.
Bhomiyas	Rajasthani warrior martyr-heroes who die attempting to rescue stolen cattle and are sometimes later deified.
Bhopa	A shaman, bard and singer of epics.
Bi-shar	Outside Sharia law.
Cenda	A large goat hide drum used in Keralan for ritual performances.
Chakra	A sacred wheel or disc.
Charpoy	A rope-strung bed on which the population of rural India spend much of their lives (lit. "four feet").
Charvaka	A system of Indian philosophy within Hinduism which rejected a transcendental deity and assumed various forms of philosophical scepticism and religious indifference while embracing the search for wealth and pleasure in this life.
Chaturmasa	The four-month monsoon break, when Buddhist, Hindu and Jain ascetics cease their wanderings and gather in one place.
Chela	A disciple or pupil.
Chelo	Let's go!
Chowkidar	A guard or gatekeeper.
Chuba	An ankle-length Tibetan coat.
Chu-zhi Gang-drung	Lit. "Four Rivers, Six Ranges"–The Tibetan Resistance.
Crore	Ten million (or 100 lakh).
Dacoit	An outlaw; a member of a robber gang.
Dakini	A Tantric deity, or attendant on a deity, embodying energy. Lit. (from the Sanskrit) "sky dancer."
Dal	A lentil dish; eaten with rice or chapatis, it is an Indian staple.
Dalits	Lit. "the oppressed." Below the base of the caste pyramid, formerly known as "untouchables."
Damaru	Small, double-sided drum shaped like an hour glass and associated with Shiva as Nataraja. It symbolises the primaeval sound of the manifesting universe.
Danda	A club.
Dargah	A Sufi shrine, usually built over the grave of a saint.

Darshan   A sighting, a glimpse, or view, especially of an idol of a deity in a temple, or of a holy or eminent personage.

Dastan   An oral epic, story or history in North India and Central Asia, told by *dastan-go* performers.

Deccan   The plateau covering most of central and southern India, framed on the north by the Vindhyas, and bounded on either side by the Eastern and Western Ghats.

Deobandis   Sunni Muslims influenced by the reformed and somewhat puritanical form of Islam propagated by the madrasa at Deoband, north of Delhi. In Pakistan, many Deobandis have embraced an extreme form of Deobandism influenced by Saudi Wahhabi Islam.

Devadasi   Lit. "Slave girls of the Gods" temple dancers, prostitutes and courtesans who were given to the great Hindu temples, usually in infancy, by their parents.

Devi   The great goddess. Synonymous with Shakti, the female aspect of the divine.

Dhammal   An ecstatic Sufi dance to the sound of drums.

Dhanda   Lit. "work," but as used by the devadasis, prostitution or sex work.

Dharma   Duty, religion, virtue.

Dharamsala Pilgrim's rest house.

Dholak   A long tubular wooden north Indian drum.

Dhoti   The traditional loin-wrap of Hindu males.

Digambara   The "Sky-Clad" or naked Jains—one of the two great sects of the Jain faith.

Diksha   A ritual of initiation.

Doms   Untouchable funeral attendants who man the pyres in cremation grounds.

Dosham   Marital misfortune.

Dotara   A small, two-stringed instrument resembling a guitar or lute and popular among the Bauls.

Dravidian   A speaker of the South Indian Dravidian family of languages, often contrasted with the North Indian Indo-Aryan language group.

Dremong   Brown Tibetan mountain bears.

Dri   Female yak.

Dubki   Small rustic tambourine-like drum used by the Bauls of Bengal.

Dugi   Small Bengali hand drum.

Durree   A rug or carpet.

Ektara   A single-stringed instrument, popular among the Bauls.

Fakir   Lit. "poor." Sufi holy man, dervish or wandering Muslim ascetic.

Fana	Total immersion in the absolute.
Firangi	A foreigner.
Gagra-choli	A long skirt and blouse popular in northern India, especially rural Rajasthan.
Gali	Abuse.
Gandharva	A spirit being or lower male deity, often a musician. The male equivalent of the apsaras.
Ganja	Marijuana.
Gharwalli	Landlady.
Ghat	Steps leading to a bathing place or river.
Ghee	Clarified butter.
Gindi	A rustic form of hockey played with sticks and balls.
Gompa	A Buddhist monastery.
Gopura	A Ceremonial South Indian temple gateway, usually pyramidal in shape.
Gowkari	"To graze": the phrase used by Jains for the search for food by Jain monks and nuns.
Gujar	North Indian cattle-herding caste, once largely nomadic.
Gulab jamun	A sweet, syrupy rosewater-scented pudding.
Gundas	Thugs.
Gungroo	Dancer's ankle-bells.
Haveli	A courtyard house or traditional mansion.
Henna	A tropical shrub whose leaves are used as a red dye. Much in demand in the North-West Frontier for dyeing the beards of Pathan tribesmen.
Homa	A sacrificial fire or the practice of making offerings in a consecrated fire.
Hunkara	The audience response during a performance of an epic.
'Ishq	Love.
Jadoo	Magic.
Jaggery	Unrefined sugar.
Jalebis	Sweets made of fried sugar-syrup.
Jamun	A fruit tree.
Jinas	"The liberators." Also known as *Tirthankaras,* or Ford-Makers, Jains believe these heroic ascetics have shown the way to Nirvana, making a spiritual ford through the rivers of suffering, and across the oceans of existence and rebirth, to create a crossing place between *samsara*—the illusory physical world—and liberation.
Jivan	Life, spirit.
Jyot	A lamp.

Kalimah   The Islamic Credo (lit. "the phrase"). Affirmation of the *Kalimah* is the first of the five pillars of Islam. Belief in the meaning of the *Kalimah* is the primary distinguising feature of a Muslim. The phrase means in English "There is no God but Allah, Muhammad is His Messenger."

Kama   Sexual desire.

Kar Sevak   An RSS volunteer/activist.

Kathakali   A Keralan dance drama.

Kavu   A small, usually rural Hindu shrine in Kerala.

Khadi   A home-spun cotton cloth, once associated with followers of Mahatma Gandhi, now the garb of politicians.

Khejri   A desert tree, revered by the bishnoi.

Khepi   A female Baul, the partner of a male Baul.

Khomok   The tension drum of the Bauls of Bengal. It has a skin head pierced by a string, which passes through the wooden drum-shaped body to attach to a small brass handle. The *khomok* is played by placing the drum body under the arm and plucking the string while pulling on the brass handle, which applies tension to the string and drum head. Variations of tension on the string produce a twanging sound.

Kikkar   A desert tree whose fruit is used in Rajasthan as goat food.

Kirtan   Lit. "singing the praises of God," usually in a devotional gathering.

Kucha   Informal, rough.

Kufr   Infidelity, disbelief.

Kumari   Sanskrit for "virgin." Today the word often refers to the tradition of worshipping pre-pubescent girls as manifestations of the divine female energy or Devi in South Asian countries.

Kumkum   A red powder (vermilion) emblematic of the sexual power of goddesses, given to women at temples and during festivals.

Kurta-dhoti   A long shirt and cotton loin-cloth waist-wrap.

Ladoo   A milky sweet.

Lathi   A bamboo staff, normally used by police and *chowkidars*.

Lingam   The phallic symbol associated with Lord Shiva in his role as Divine Creator.

Lota   A small copper water pot used for ablutions.

Lungar   A free kitchen or distribution of food alms at a temple or during the religious festival.

Lungi   A sarong-style loin-wrap; simplification of the *dhoti*.

Mahasiddhas   Immortal perfected beings in Nath theology.

Mahasukha   The great bliss of the void.

Mahayagna   Great sacrifice.

Mahayana   Lit. "Great Vehicle." One of the two principal branches of Buddhism.

Malang	A wandering fakir, dervish or *qalander*.
Mandala	A circle or circular diagram; symbolic depiction of, and instruction about, the way to Enlightenment.
Mataji	A white-clad Digambara nun (lit. "respected mother").
Math	A monastery.
Maulana	A title for a respected religious leader–lit. "Our Lord."
Maya	Illusion.
Mazar	Lit. (in Arabic) "tomb or mausoleum," but usually in practice the tomb of a saint, and hence a Sufi shrine.
Mehndi	The application of henna patterns on the hands, usually at an Indian wedding.
Mela	A gathering, meeting, festival or fair.
Mihrab	A prayer niche indicating the direction of Mecca.
Minar	A small minarette on a Muslim shrine or mosque.
Moksha	Enlightenment or spiritual liberation.
Momos	Steamed Tibetan snacks, usually containing lamb or chicken.
Mudra	Symbolic or ritual gestures in Hinduism, Buddhism and Indian dance.
Muni	A Jain monk or nun.
Murid	A disciple.
Murti	An image or statue.
Muttu	A devadasi's necklace or red and white coral beads.
Naan	Bread cooked in a tandoor.
Nadeswaram	Giant oboe-like instrument used in Tamil temple rituals.
Naga sadhus	A sect of naked holy men.
Namaaz	Muslim prayers, traditionally offered five times a day.
Namaskar	Hindu words of greeting (lit. "I bow to thee").
Nath yogis	A sect of ash-smeared Shaivite mystics who invented hatha yoga in the twelfth century, and who claimed that their exercises and breathing techniques gave them great supernatural powers.
Navras	The nine essences of classical Hindu aesthetics.
Nirvana	Enlightenment, state of spiritual revelation.
Oran	A protected sacred grove, dedicated to a deity in Rajasthan.
Paan	An Indian delicacy and digestive. It consists of a folded leaf containing (among other ingredients) betel nut, a mild stimulant.
Padmasana	The lotus position.
Paramatma	The Supreme soul, or absolute *atman* in Hindu Vedantic philosophy.
Parathas	Fried chapattis.

Parikrama	A pilgrimage circuit.
Pashto	The language of the Pashtun people of the North-West Frontier of Pakistan and southern Afghanistan.
Pedha	Milky sweetmeats.
Phad	A long narrative textile-painting, which serves both as an illustration of the highlights of *The Epic of Pabuji* and a portable temple of Pabuji the god.
Pir	A Muslim holy man or Sufi saint.
Prasad	The portion of consecrated offering—usually food or small white sweets—returned to the worshipper at a Hindu temple.
Puja	A religious devotions ("lit. adoration").
Pukka	Good, proper, correct.
Pukur	A village pond in Bengal.
Pundit	Brahmin (lit. "a learned man").
Purohit	A Brahmin priest.
Qalander	A Sufi mendicant or holy fool.
Qawwali	Rousing poems and hymns sung at Sufi shrines.
Rakhi	A thread tied around the wrist, usually by brothers and sisters as a symbol of sisterly or fraternal love and protection, especially on the festival of *raksha bandhan*.
Rangoli	Decoration using coloured sand, paint or salt, usually on floors outside houses.
Rani	Queen.
Rasa	Lit. juice, flavour or essence: an essential concept in Hindu aesthetics, denoting an essential mental state, and the dominant emotional theme of a work of art. Hence *navras:* the nine essences.
Rasgulla	A sweet.
Rath	A chariot, esp. in Hindu temple festivals.
Ravanhatta	A Rajasthani zither or spike fiddle with eighteen strings and no frets.
Rinpoche	An honorific used for senior monks in Tibetan Buddhism. It means literally "precious one."
Rishi	A poet-sage and scribe-ascetic through whom the ancient Hindu scriptures and Vedic hymns flowed.
Roti	Bread.
Rudraksh	A large evergreen broad-leaved tree whose hard, dried seed is traditionally used for prayer beads or rosaries in Hinduism, often on strings of 108 beads.
Sadhana	A spiritual, ritual or Tantric practice or discipline.
Sadhu	A Hindu holy man.
Sahajiya	A spontaneous or natural form of Indian spirituality. *Vaishnava-Sahajiya* was a Tantric Hindu cult that became popular in

seventeenth-century Bengal. The *Vaishnava-Sahajiya* sought religious experience through the five senses, which included sexual love.

Sajjada nasheens	Hereditary guardians of Sufi shrines, usually descended from the founding saint.
Salwar-kameez	A long tunic and matching loose trousers favoured mainly by girls in North India and by both sexes in Pakistan and Afghanistan.
Sallekhana	The final renunciation for a Jain: the gradual, voluntary, intentional and ritualised giving up of all food and sustenance, until the monk or nun finally dies of starvation. Jains do not regard *sallekhana* as suicide so much as the ultimate form of detachment. Around 240 Jains embrace *sallekhana* each year.
Samadhi	Detachment from the body, through fasting or concentrated prayer. For Jains the word has a more specific meaning of gathering to pray around a monk or nun who is undergoing *sallekhana*–the deliberate and permanent separation of the soul from the body. The word is also used for a mausoleum or place of cremation.
Samsara	The illusory physical world and its cycle of rebirths. The word is derived from the Sanskrit for "to flow together," to go or pass through states, to wander.
Sangha	A community or association, usually used today in the context of a Buddhist or Jain monastic community.
Sannyas	A life of renunciation, a state of homelessness.
Sanyasi	A Hindu wanderer or ascetic.
Sati	The old Hindu practice of widow burning, now illegal (lit. "a good woman").
Saz	A lute-like stringed instrument popular in the Middle East and Afghanistan.
Shaheed	A Muslim martyr.
Shakta	The denomination of Hinduism that concentrates on the worship of Shakti, or the Devi: the female principle of the Divine Mother.
Shakti	The personification of the creative power and energy of the divine feminine.
Shamiana	An Indian marquee, or the screen formed around the perimeter of a tented area.
Shastra	An ancient Hindu and Buddhist treatise or text; the word in Sanskrit means "rules."
Shirk	Heresy, polytheism or idolatry.
Siddi	The Afro-Indians who settled on the coast of Sindh and Gujarat and usually engaged in fishing and coastal trading and sailing.
Sindhoor	A red powder (vermilion) which is traditionally applied at the beginning of or completely along the parting-line of a woman's hair. Similar to *kumkum*.
Sloka	A stanza in a Sanskrit poem.

Svetambara	One of the two great sects of the Jain faith. The Sventambaran Jain monks do not go naked like the "Sky Clad" Digambara Jains.
Tablighi Jamaat	A missionary group of the Islamic reform movement, with theological beliefs similar to the Deobandis and Wahhabis, and with a particular emphasis on textual and ritual rectitude and orthodoxy.
Talib	A student—hence Taliban, the student army that emerged from the madrasas.
Tanti	An amulet of knotted chord (in Rajasthan).
Tantra	An esoteric form of Hinduism and Buddhism aiming at gaining access to the energy of the Godhead, then concentrating and internalising that power in the body of the devotee. In Hindu Tantra Shakti is usually the main deity worshipped, and the universe is regarded as the result of the divine play of Shakti and Shiva. Tantrics defy convention and reverse most of the strictures and taboos of orthodox religiosity.
Tapasya	Ascetic penance, self-testing and deprivation; voluntary austerity.
Ta'wiz	A Sufi charm or amulet, usually containing verses from the Quran.
Thakur	A gentleman landowner or squire.
Thali	A tray or large plate.
Thangka	A Buddhist painted or embroidered prayer banner, usually hung in a monastery or a family altar, and occasionally carried by monks in ceremonial processions.
Thevaram	Lit. "Garland of God"—a multi-volume collection of Tamil devotional Shaivite hymns and poetry.
Theyyam	The possession dance of northern Kerala. A *theyyam* performer is called a *theyyamkkaran*.
Thottam	Ritualistic songs appropriate for the *theyyam* dance of northern Kerala.
Thukpa	Tibetan noodle soup.
Tilak	The sacred mark on the centre of a Hindu forehead.
Tirthankara	Lit. "Ford-maker." The Jains believe these heroic ascetic figures, also known as *Jinas* or "liberators," have shown the way to Nirvana, making a spiritual ford through the rivers of suffering, and across the wild oceans of existence and rebirth, so as to create a crossing place between *samsara*—the illusory physical world—and liberation.
Toddy	Keralan and Goan firewater, brewed from fermented coconut juice.
Upanishads	The collection of Hindu scriptures, dating from 1000 BC to the medieval period, which form the core teachings of Vedanta.
'Urs	Annual festival held in Sufi shrines to commemorate the death of a saint.
Vaishnavite	A follower of the Hindu god Vishnu or his associated avatars, principally Rama or Krishna.
Vajra	A short metal weapon symbolising a thunderbolt and representing spiritual power in Buddhist art.

Vedanta   A group of ancient Hindu philosophical traditions concerned with the self-realisation by which one can understand the ultimate nature of reality.

Vibhuti   The white ash powder smeared on the body of Shiva; and hence also his devotees among the sadhus.

Vimana   The pyramid-shaped tower of Tamil temples.

Wahhabi   A member of the reformed and puritanical form of Islam, first propagated by Ibn Abd al-Wahhab in Medina in the eighteenth century, which aimed to strip Islam of all non-Muslim accretions, most notably idolatry and the cult of saints. Wahhabism is now the state religion in Saudi Arabia. Saudi oil wealth has been used to propagate its missionary activity, through which Wahhabism has developed considerable influence in the Islamic world through the funding of newspapers, television stations, printing presses, madrasas and mosques.

Yakshi   Female Hindu fertility nymphs, often associated with sacred trees and pools. In Kerala they are believed to be malevolent and to have the appetites and proclivities associated with vampires in Europe.

Yantra   A symbol or geometric figure, in paint or coloured sand. They are used in various mystical traditions in Hinduism and Buddhism to balance the mind or focus it on spiritual concepts. Tantrics believe that the act of wearing, depicting, enacting or concentrating on a *yantra* is held to have spiritual, astrological or magical benefits.

Yatra   A pilgrimage.

Yatri   Traveller or pilgrim.

Zamindar   Landholder.

BIBLIOGRAPHY

1. THE NUN'S TALE

Colette Caillat and Ravi Kumar, *The Jain Cosmology*, New York, 1981

Michael Carrithers and Caroline Humphrey, *The Assembly of Listeners: Jains in Society*, Cambridge, 1991

Ananda Coomaraswamy, *Jaina Art*, New Delhi, 1994

John E. Cort, *Jains in the World: Religious Values and Ideology in India*, Oxford, 2001

——, "The Rite of Veneration of Jina Images," in Donald S. Lopez, Jr. (ed.), *Religions of India in Practice*, Princeton, 1995

——, *Singing the Glory of Asceticism: Devotion of Asceticism in Jainism, Journal of the American Academy of Religion*, December 2002, Vol. 70, No. 4

Paul Dundas, *The Jains*, London, 1992

Phyllis Granoff, *The Clever Adultress and Other Stories: A Treasury of Jain Literature*, Ontario, 1990

——, *The Forest of Thieves and the Magic Garden: An Anthology of Medieval Jain Stories*, New Delhi, 1998

Hemacandra (trans. R.C.C. Fynes), *The Lives of the Jain Elders*, New Delhi, 1998

Padmanabh S. Jaini, *Gender and Salvation: Jaina Debates on the Spiritual Liberation of Women*, New Delhi, 1991

——, *The Jaina Path of Purification*, Berkeley, 1979

James Laidlaw, *Riches and Renunciation: Religion, Economy and Society Among the Jains*, Oxford 1995

Pratapaditya Pal, *The Peaceful Liberators: Jain Art from India*, Los Angeles, 1994

Aidan Rankin, *The Jain Path*, Winchester, 2006

Jina Ratna (trans. R.C.C. Fynes), *The Epitome of Queen Lilavati*, New York, 2005

U.P. Shah and M.A. Dhaky, *Aspects of Jaina Art and Architecture*, Ahmedabad, 1975

2. THE DANCER OF KANNUR

T.V. Chandran, *Ritual as Ideology: Text and Context in Theyyam*, New Delhi, 2006

J.R. Freeman, "Purity and Violence: Sacred Power in the Theyyam Worship of Malabar," unpublished PhD dissertation, University of Pennsylvania, 1991

Mayuri Koga, "The Politics of Ritual and Art in Kerala: Controversies Concerning the Staging of Theyyam," *Journal of the Japanese Association of South Asian Studies*, 15 2003

K.K.N. Kurup, *The Cult of Theyyam and Hero Worship in Kerala*, Calicut, 2000

Dilip M. Menon, "The Moral Community of the Teyyattam: Popular Culture in Late Colonial Malabar," *Studies in History*, 1993, 9:187

Frederick M. Smith, *The Self Possessed: Deity and Spirit Possession in South Asian Literature and Civilisation*, New York, 2006

3. THE DAUGHTERS OF YELLAMMA

Daud Ali, *Courtly Culture and Political Life in Early Medieval India*, Cambridge, 2004
——, "War, Servitude and the Imperial Household: A Study of Palace Women in the Chola Period," in Indrani Chatterjee and Richard M. Eaton, *Slavery and South Asian History*, Indiana, 2006
Kali Prasad Goswami, *Devadasi*, New Delhi, 2000
R.K. Gupta, *Changing Status of Devadasis in India*, New Delhi, 2007
Kay K. Jordan, *From Sacred Servant to Profane Prostitute: A History of the Changing Legal Status of the Devadasis*, New Delhi, 2003
Saskia C. Kersenboom, *Nityasumangali: Devadasi Tradition in South India*, New Delhi, 1987
John O'Neil, Treena Orchard, R.C. Swarankar, James F. Blanchard, Kaveri Gurav and Stephen Moses, "Dhanda, Dharma and Disease: Traditional Sex Work and HIV/AIDS in Rural India," in *Social Science and Medicine* 59, 2004
——, "Understanding the Social and Cultural Contexts of Female Sex Workers in Karnataka, India: Implications for the Prevention of HIV Infection," in *The Journal of Infectious Diseases*, 2005; 191 (suppl. 1): S.139–46
Treena Rae Orchard, "Girl, Woman, Lover, Mother: Towards a New Understanding of Child Prostitution Among Young Devadasis in Rural Karnataka, India," in *Social Science and Medicine* 64, 2007
Leslie C. Orr, *Donors, Devotees, and Daughters*, New York, 2000
Shashi Panjrath and O.P. Ralhan, *Devadasi System in India*, Faridabad, 2000
A.K. Ramanujan, Velcheru Narayana Rao and David Shulman, *When God Is a Customer: Telegu Courtesan Songs by Ksetrayya and Others*, California, 1994

4. THE SINGER OF EPICS

Rustom Bharucha, *Rajasthan: An Oral History—Conversations with Komal Kothari*, New Delhi, 2003
Vidya Dehejia, "India's Visual Narratives: The Dominance of Space Over Time," in Giles Tillotson (ed.), *Paradigms of Indian Architecture: Space and Time in Representation and Design*, London, 1998
Graham Dwyer, *The Divine and the Demonic: Supernatural Affliction and Its Treatment in North India*, London, 2003
Alf Hiltebeitel, *Rethinking India's Oral and Classical Epics*, Chicago, 1999
O.P. Joshi, *Painted Folklore & Folklore Painters of India*, New Delhi, 1976
Sudhir Kakar, *Shamans, Mystics and Doctors: A Psychological Inquiry into India and Its Healing Traditions*, Oxford, 1982
Albert B. Lord, *The Singer of Tales*, Harvard, 2000
Victor H. Mair, *Painting and Performance: Chinese Picture Recitation and Its Indian Genesis*, Hawaii, 1988
Aditya Malik with Hukmaram Bhopa and Motaram Gujar (eds.), *Sri Devnarayan Katha: An Oral Narrative of Mewar*, New Delhi, 2003
Joseph Charles Miller, "The Twenty-four Brothers of Lord Devnarayan: The Story and

Performance of a Folk Epic of Rajasthan, India," unpublished PhD dissertation, University of Pennsylvania, 1994

Daniel Neuman and Shubha Chaudhuri with Komal Kothari, *Bard, Ballad and Boundaries: An Ethnographic Atlas of Music Traditions in West Rajasthan*, Calcutta, 2006

Kavita Singh, "The God Who Looks Away: Phad Paintings of Rajasthan," in Harsha V. Dehejia, *Gods Beyond Temples*, New Delhi, 2006

——, "To Show, To see, To Tell, To Know: Patuas, Bhopas and Their Audiences," in Jyotindra Jain, *Insights into the Narrative Tradition in Indian Art*, Bombay, 1998

John D. Smith, *The Epic of Pabuji—A Study, Transcription and Translation*, Cambridge, 1991

——, *The Epic of Pabuji*, New Delhi, 2005

Jeffrey G. Snodgrass, *Casting Kings: Bards and Modernity*, Oxford, 2006

Ernst Van de Wetering, "Fighting a Tiger: Stability and Flexibility in the Style of Pabuji Pars," *South Asian Studies* 8, 1992

5. THE RED FAIRY

Alice Albinia, *Empires of the Indus: The Story of a River*, London, 2008

D.H. Bhutani, *The Melody and Philosophy of Shah Latif*, New Delhi, 1991

Motilal Jotwani, *Sufis of Sindh*, New Delhi, 1986

Amena Khamisani (trans.), *The Risalo of Shah Abdul Latif Bhitai*, Bhitshah, 2003

Shah Abdul Latif (trans. Anju Makhija and Hari Dilgir), *Seeking the Beloved*, New Delhi, 2005

Peter Mayne, *Saints of Sindh*, London, 1956

Roland and Sabrina Michaud, *Derviches du Hind et du Sind*, Paris, 1991

Annemarie Schimmel, *Pain and Grace: A Study of Two Mystical Writers of Eighteenth Century Muslim India*, Leiden, 1976

6. THE MONK'S TALE

John F. Avedon, *In Exile from the Land of Snows*, New York, 1986

Noel Barber, *From the Land of Lost Content: The Dalai Lama's Flight from Tibet*, London, 1969

John Ross Carter and Mahinda Palihawadana (trans. and ed.), *The Dhammapada: The Sayings of the Buddha*, Oxford, 1987

Mary Craig, *Tears of Blood: A Cry for Tibet*, New York, 1999

HH Dalai Lama, *My Land, My People: Memoirs*, New Delhi 1977

Kunga Samten Dewatshang, *Flight at the Cuckoo's Behest: The Life and Times of a Tibetan Freedom Fighter*, New Delhi, 1977

Mikel Dunham, *Buddha's Warriors: The Story of the CIA-Backed Tibetan Freedom Fighters, the Chinese Invasion, and the Ultimate Fall of Tibet*, London, 2004

Melvyn C. Goldstein, *A History of Modern Tibet*, Vol. 1, 1913–1951, *The Demise of a Lamaist State*, Berkeley, 1989

Palden Gyatso, *Fire Under Snow: Testimony of a Tibetan Prisoner*, London, 1997

Heinrich Harrer, *Seven Years in Tibet*, London, 1952

Pico Iyer, *The Open Road: The Global Journey of the Fourteenth Dalai Lama*, New York, 2008

Donald S. Lopez (ed.), *Buddhist Scriptures*, London, 2004

Ani Pachen with Adelaide Donnelley, *Sorrow Mountain: The Journey of a Tibetan Warrior Nun*, New York, 2002

Tsering Shakya, *The Dragon in the Land of Snows: A History of Modern Tibet Since 1947*, New York, 1999

Keutsang Trulku Jampel Yeshe, *Memoirs of Keutsang Lama: Life in Tibet After the Chinese "Liberation,"* New Delhi, 2001

7. THE MAKER OF IDOLS

Crispin Branfoot, *Gods on the Move: Architecture and Ritual in the South Indian Temple*, London, 2007

Richard H. Davis, *Lives of Indian Images*, Princeton, 1977

Vidya Dehejia, *Art of the Imperial Cholas*, New York, 1990

——, *Chola: Sacred Bronzes of Southern India*, London, 2006

——, "Patron, Artist and Temple," in *Royal Patrons and Great Temple Art*, Bombay, 1998

——, *Slaves of the Lord: The Path of the Tamil Saints*, Delhi, 1998

——, *The Sensuous and the Sacred: Chola Bronzes from South India*, Washington, 2002

Diana L. Eck, *Darsan: Seeing the Divine Image in India*, Columbia, 1998

——, "India's *Tirthas*: 'Crossings' in Sacred Geography," *History of Religions* 20, No. 4, 1981

C.J. Fuller, *The Camphor Flame: Popular Hinduism and Society in India*, Princeton, 1992

——, *Servants of the Goddess: The Priests of a South Indian Temple*, Cambridge, 1984

John Guy, *Indian Temple Sculpture*, London, 2007

James Heitzman, *Gifts of Power: Lordship in an Early Indian State*, Oxford, 1977

Thomas E. Levy, *Masters of Fire: Hereditary Bronze Casters of South India*, Bochum, 2008

James McConnachie, *The Book of Love: In Search of the Kama Sutra*, London, 2007

A.K. Ramanujan, *The Interior Landscape: Love Poems from a Classical Tamil Anthology*, Ontario, 1975

David Dean Shulman, *Tamil Temple Myths: Sacrifice and Divine Marriage in the South Indian Saiva Tradition*, Princeton, 1980

Michael Wood, *The Smile of Murugan: A South Indian Journey*, London, 1995

8. THE LADY TWILIGHT

Agehananda Bharati, *The Tantric Tradition*, London, 1965

N.N. Bhattacharyya, *The Indian Mother Goddess*, Delhi, 1999

Douglas Renfrew Brooks, *The Secret of the Three Cities: An Introduction to Hindu Shakta Tantrism*, Chicago, 1990

June McDaniel, *Making Virtuous Daughters and Wives: An Introduction to Women's Brata Rituals in Bengali Folk Religion*, New York, 2003

——, *Offering Flowers, Feeding Skulls: Popular Goddess Worship in West Bengal*, Oxford, 2004

Vidya Dehejia, *Devi: The Great Goddess*, Washington, 1999

——, *Yogini Cult and Temples: A Tantric Tradition*, New Delhi, 1986

Edward C. Dimock Jr., *The Place of the Hidden Moon: Erotic Mysticism in the Vaisnava-sahajiya Cult in Bengal*, Chicago, 1966

Sanjukta Gupta, Dirk Jan Hoens and Teun Goudriann, *Hindu Tantrism*, Leiden, 1979

Madhu Khanna, *Yantra: The Tantric Symbol of Cosmic Unity*, London, 1981

David Kinsley, *Hindu Goddesses—Visions of the Divine Feminine in the Hindu Religious Tradition*, Berkeley, 1998

——, *Tantric Visions of the Divine Feminine: The Ten Mahavidyas*, New Delhi, 1998
Ajit Mookerjee and Madhu Khanna, *The Tantric Way: Art, Science, Ritual*, London, 1977
Debashis Mukherjee, *Tarapith*, Calcutta, 2000
Philip Rawson, *Art of Tantra*, London, 1973
Ramprasad Sen (trans. Leonard Nathan and Clinton Seely), *Grace and Mercy in Her Wild Hair*, Arizona, 1999
D.C. Sirkar, *The Sakta Pithas*, Delhi, 1973
David Gordon White, *Kiss of the Yogini: "Tantric Sex" in Its South Asian Contexts*, Chicago, 2003
——, *Tantra in Practice*, Princeton, 2000

9. THE SONG OF THE BLIND MINSTREL

Pranab Bandyopadhyay, *Bauls of Bengal*, Calcutta, 1989
Bhaskar Bhattacharyya, *The Path of the Mystic Lover: Baul Songs of Passion and Ecstasy*, Rochester, 1993
Deben Bhattacharyya, *The Mirror of the Sky: Songs of the Bauls of Bengal*, New York, 1969
Charles H. Capwell, "The Esoteric Belief of the Bauls of Bengal," *Journal of Asian Studies*, Vol. XXXIII, No. 2, February 1974
Rajeshwari Datta, "The Religious Aspect of the Baul Songs of Bengal," *Journal of Asian Studies*, Vol. XXXVII, No. 3, May 1978
June McDaniel, *The Madness of the Saints*, Chicago, 1989
Jeanne Openshaw, *Seeking Bauls of Bengal*, Cambridge, 2004
R.M. Sarkar, *Bauls of Bengal: In Quest of a Man of the Heart*, New Delhi, 1990
Mimlu Sen, *Baulsphere: My Travels with the Wandering Bards of Bengal*, New Delhi, 2009

INDEX

THE LAST MUGHAL
The Fall of a Dynasty: Delhi, 1857

In this evocative study of the fall of the Mughal Empire and the beginning of the Raj, award-winning historian William Dalrymple uses previously undiscovered sources to investigate a pivotal moment in history. The last Mughal emperor, Zafar, came to the throne when the political power of the Mughals was already in steep decline. Nonetheless, Zafar—a mystic, poet, and calligrapher of great accomplishment—created a court of unparalleled brilliance, and gave rise to perhaps the greatest literary renaissance in modern Indian history. All the while, the British were progressively taking over the emperor's power. When, in May 1857, Zafar was declared the leader of an uprising against the British, he was powerless to resist though he strongly suspected that the action was doomed. Four months later, the British took Delhi, the capital, with catastrophic results. With an unsurpassed understanding of British and Indian history, Dalrymple crafts a provocative, revelatory account of one of the bloodiest upheavals in history.

History/India/978-1-4000-7833-2

INDIA UNBOUND
The Social and Economic Revolution from Independence to the Global Information Age
by Gurcharan Das

India today is a vibrant free-market democracy on its way to over-coming decades of widespread poverty. The nation's rise is one of the great international stories of the late twentieth century, and in this vividly written book the acclaimed columnist Gurcharan Das offers a sweeping economic history of India from independence to the new millennium. Impassioned, erudite, and eminently readable, *India Unbound* is a must for anyone interested in the global economy and its future.

Business/International Affairs/978-0-385-72074-8

IN SPITE OF THE GODS
The Rise of Modern India
by Edward Luce

India remains a mystery to many Americans, even as it is poised to become the world's third largest economy within a generation, out-stripping Japan. *In Spite of the Gods* is an enlightening study of the forces shaping India as it tries to balance the traditions of the past with a modernizing present. Deeply informed by scholarship and history, leavened by humor and rich in anecdote, it shows that India has huge opportunities as well as tremendous challenges that make the future "hers to lose."

Current Affairs/978-1-4000-7977-3

KARMA COLA
Marketing the Mystic East
by Gita Mehta

Sometime in the 1960s, the West adopted India as its newest spiritual resort. The next anyone knew, the Beatles were squatting at the feet of the Maharishi Mahesh Yogi. No one has observed the West's invasion of India more astutely than Gita Mehta. In *Karma Cola* the acclaimed novelist trains an unblinking journalistic eye on jaded sadhus and beatific acid burnouts, the Bhagwan and Allen Ginsberg, guilt-tripping English girls and a guru who teaches guillible tourists how to view their previous incarnations. Brilliantly irreverent, Mehta's book is the definitive epitaph for the era of spiritual tourism and all its casualties—both Eastern and Western.

Travel/Cultural Studies/978-0-679-75433-6

A NEW WORLD
by Amit Chaudhuri

A year after his divorce, Jayojit Chatterjee, an economics professor in the American Midwest, travels to his native Calcutta with his young son, Bonny, to spend the summer holidays with his parents. Together, the unlikely foursome struggles to pass the protracted days of summer, each in his or her own way mourning Jayojit's failed marriage. And as Jayojit walks the streets of Calcutta, he finds himself not only caught between clashing memories of India and America, but also between different versions of his life, revisiting lost opportunity, realized potential, and lingering desire.

Fiction/Literature/978-0-375-72480-0

MAXIMUM CITY
Bombay Lost and Found
by Suketu Mehta

A native of Bombay, Suketu Mehta gives us an insider's view of this stunning metropolis. He approaches the city from unexpected angles, taking us into the criminal underworld of rival Muslim and Hindu gangs, following the life of a bar dancer raised amid poverty and abuse, opening the door into the inner sanctums of Bollywood, and delving into the stories of countless villagers who come in search of a better life. Candid, funny, and heartrending, *Maximum City* is a revelation of an ancient and ever-changing world.

Travel/978-0-375-70340-9

KA
Stories of the Mind and Gods of India
by Roberto Calasso

With the same narrative fecundity he brought to his acclaimed retelling of the Greek myths, Roberto Calasso plunges Western readers into the mind of ancient India. He begins with a mystery: Why is the most important god in the Rg Veda, the oldest of India's sacred texts, known by a secret name—"Ka," or Who? What ensues is not an explanation, but an unveiling. A tour de force of scholarship and seduction, *Ka* is irresistible.

Fiction/Literature/978-0-679-77547-8

VINTAGE AND ANCHOR BOOKS
Available at your local bookstore, or visit www.randomhouse.com